A GOD IN THE MOON

A GOD IN THE MOON

Your Guide to the World
of the Trinity Matrix

Roger A Turner

To order additional copies of this book, contact:
Xlibris
1-800-455-039
www.Xlibris.com.au
Orders@Xlibris.com.au
787778

CONTENTS

Dedication

From the Greek Dei + dicare.

This book is dedicated to all the true seekers, free thinkers, explorers and those of us who want to know. To the people who enjoy uncovering mysteries with the common goal of expanding the view of this universe and our reality.

True seekers will find the secrets deep,
The rest will falter and fall asleep.

"Three is the mystery, come from the great one,
Hear, and light on thee will dawn.
In the primeval dwell three unities,
Other than these none can exist."

Thoth.

INTRODUCTION

Matrix: 1. a substance, situation or environment in which something has its origin, takes form or is enclosed. (From Late Latin: womb, from 'mater' mother)

In the popular movie 'The Matrix' humans are kept captive in a world of illusion. The captor-force is a purely physical/mechanical parasitic mind feeding on the electrical energy produced by human life. This story is not far from the truth. The difference is that the captor-force is already built into our bodies. This force, feeds on the negative emotional energy of humans stimulated by fear, drama and pain and creates our reality according to its needs.

Since the beginning of human history, stories have been told to pass down the memories and experiences of ancestors long gone into the past. Ambitious for control, the captor-force has manipulated these stories, myths and legends to create an illusion that hides the truth about the state of humankind. Maintaining this illusion keeps us in a passive state of domestic toil, in a state of subservience and easily managed by the empires of power that control this world. But within these stories lies a basic truth about our past and the origin of the universe passed down within the stories developed around the Trinities of many religions.

The concepts in this book may seem unusual but most have been written about before, it is the connections of The Trinity Matrix forming our world that I hope you will see. This book is meant to be a guide to prompt you to take a look at the alternative view to what you have accepted as the truth presented to you by schools, churches, books, TV, the World Wide Web or whatever source you were educated by. Through education we can change the world even if we are just changing our view of it.

This book was written to help break through the illusion and to be used as a reference for further research, which can open up a much wider view of the reality around us. My intention is not to say what is and expect you to believe it, but to prompt you in to taking a look and find connections for yourself.

"The acquisition of a new truth is like the acquisition of a new sense, which renders a man capable of perceiving and recognising a large number of phenomena that are invisible and hidden from another, as they were from him originally." From *'Chemise Briefe'*, by Justus von Liebig 1803-1873.

I am still researching. Changes to this book will develop in time and hopefully future editions will become increasingly accurate. One thing I have realised from my research is that even the best researchers make some noticeable mistakes including referring to previous works that seem to have no evidence to back up their claims. I sometimes fear that I may unknowingly be guilty of this same sin. I try not to include material that is in my mind questionable until enough evidence becomes apparent to warrant its inclusion in this book and material is removed when evidence of falsity is obvious. It is taking a lot of time to sort out what is truth and what is not. Take the time to check references when doubts arise. Working on this project has been an eye opener, my preconceptions and beliefs have changed and I no longer believe what I am told without questioning as a sceptic. I have found that there is so much misinformation placed in public view for either political or religious reasons or just attention-seeking sensationalism. Even some authorities in the scientific fields have their own agendas or agendas that other forces pay them to promote. My perspective of the world has changed and in turn it has changed me. The understanding of the make-up of this universe has helped me understand myself and others and why this world seemed so crazy. This knowledge has given me stability and increased my sense of purpose in sharing this knowledge with other people. I hope that this book also helps you to understand why the world is the way it is. Recognising and accepting the problem is the first step in solving it.

Please Note: To piece together the threads and clues presented in this book it is essential to read through this book at least three times. This book is like the skeleton of a body and designed to be used in conjunction with dictionaries, encyclopaedias, libraries and the Internet to add the flesh. Reference sources are mentioned throughout the book to assist in searching. Please research the words that you find unfamiliar. If you come to a dead end don't worry, be patient and the answer will come when you least expect it. Sometimes the best way to find a needle in a haystack is just to give up for a while and sit down on the hay. Its location will sometimes become painfully obvious.

This is a journey of discovery that started with an imagined prehistory, a possibility of harmony.

HARMONY

When the people of ancient times looked upwards to the sky, they saw two great celestial bodies appearing to be exactly equal in size, the Sun and the Moon and many points of light. Like us, they probably stood and stared at the beauty and wonder of the vast expanse of mystery above them.

The Sun followed them during the day, giving warmth and light and consistent companionship even though it receded each year as the cold of winter came. At night the Moon opened and closed like an eye over the month thirteen times a year. Humans realised that the Moon had a close connection with the tides, the bleeding cycles of women, the fertility of the soil and the growth of plants. Looking down they saw and felt the Earth and the surrounding abundant life that nourished, sheltered and healed them. In their small bands without the rules and expectations of imperial societies they were probably in their natural state of being childlike with strong family bonds and affection for the parents who nurtured and taught them the ways of survival. As the young ones grew older, the Earth would eventually take back their parents and leave them with memories and a sense of longing for their loved elders. Life was a cycle of change, but some things stayed constant and reliable and were always there for them. Like immortal parents, the Earth, the Sun and the Moon stayed with them, giving all the food, shelter, medicine and materials that they needed to keep their species alive.

This natural trinity of the Sun, Moon and Earth was like the three-legged stool that remained upright and stable as long as all three legs remained equal. Each of these three had their own role to play in supporting life with their own characteristics and influences. Early people recognised the power specific to each one of this trinity.

This balanced trinity gave humans life, and humans knew that the trinity would take back what it gave to continue its natural cycles. This would have been the understanding of the exchange and it would have been respected, as life was respected. However things changed for humans; wisdom came only to be conquered by the knowledge and illusion of the Moon.

LOSS OF INNOCENCE

The loss of innocence to the illusion may have started with the anthropo-morphism of the Earth and its forces of nature. The wind, the seas, lightning and thunder, earthquakes and floods were seen to be the expressions of a supernatural humanlike deity.

The discovery of the figurine 'Venus of Willendorf' from around 27,000 BC and the earlier 'Venus of Hohle Fels' from around 37,000 BC show that ancient Europeans may have been worshipping an Earth Mother fertility goddess as their main focus of culture. This culture continued from the Palaeolithic period to the Neolithic period and sometime into the Bronze Age. The predominance of female figurines can be seen with the finding of 'The Venus Figurines' indicating a mother goddess religion that spread across Europe to the Steppes of Russia. European peoples at this time were developing an agricultural way of life that was generally peaceful with little evidence of warfare, only occasional violence, but still recognising the trinity of the Sun, Moon and Earth. On places of healing energy where ley lines crossed, these people worked together to construct the megalithic monuments of massive stones that line up with each other across Europe and maybe across the world. One of the most famous of these is Stonehenge on the Salisbury Plains, an area also well known for the appearance of 'Crop Circles'.

Today many of these sacred healing sites are beneath chapels, churches and cathedrals like the one at Glastonbury in the U.K. How did these people accurately line up stones sometimes hundreds of miles apart? Is there evidence of an ancient advanced global civilization that created the megalithic temples of old? What science of navigation did their Druid priests develop or learn?

Sumerian, Phoenician, Egyptian and earlier merchantmen plied the coastal routes around Europe as far north as Finland, not only trading spices, resins, oils and clothe from the Near East but also technology and religious ideas. Mediterranean Aryan colonists, merchants and immigrants brought with them not only their knowledge, but also the idea of the Patriarchal Godhead Trinity. The patriarchal religions had long been established in the civilizations of the Far East. Civi-lisation means the organization of peoples into a group living in a city (the greek word 'civi' means city).

The predynastic Egyptian civilisations sprang up more than 13,000 years ago under the leadership of the Netjeru and the Shemsu-Hor. (See Aegyptus.)

The Meso-potamian based civilisation of the Sumerians had started up more than 10,000 years ago worshipping a pan-thera of Dragon gods and goddesses headed by Anu a male patriarch. The Sumerians and succeeding peoples of Mesopotamia like the Accadians, Chaldeans and Babylonians followed a male dominated trinity that was to become the basis of many of the religions we know of today.

Around 1000 BC, Europe was subjected to invasions from Indo-European nomadic horse-mounted tribes from the area we call Iran and the Black Sea. These Aryan warriors spread their empire Westward across Europe, South as far as Egypt and North Africa and Eastward as far as China. The cannabis-using Kurgan/ Scyth/ Saka/ Sacksens became one of the most influential nomadic cultures of the ancient world making a cultural impact on other nations. (See Celtic Culture, Saxons.)

It seems that these militant tribes worshipped the aggression and physical power of the patriarchal father figure and the wealth of the imperial society. The symbol of the Scoloti, Royal Scythians and the later Sarmatians was the Dragon Afrasiab.

According to Hellenic legend, Hercules mated with a beautiful Dragon Queen who bore two sons. Hercules left his bow and told her that one boy will be strong enough to draw the bow. This boy killed his brother with his first shot and became the father of the Scythians.

Around the same time, agricultural societies of absolute matriarchal dominance appeared in the Mediterranean area worshipping humanlike goddesses. These societies probably developed as a counter to the patriarchal dominance. They became heavily influenced by moon worship that was accompanied by the story of the subdued serpent as in the pre-Hellenic Pelasgian culture, which inhabited the coastal areas of the country we know as Greece.

Those who abandoned the treaty with the Natural Trinity took up the political-militant way of life and the balanced stool of the Natural Trinity started tipping.

The suppression of the Earth and Sun worship cultures followed.

MAN AND GOD

Early civilizations claimed that their cultural teachers such as the Annunaki, the Annedoti, Viracochans, Kachinas, Neteru and the giant Nephilim came from the sky or the sea. Some of these gods had superhuman knowledge and powers and were said to have bred with humans. Many ancient documents show that these non-human or half-human gods possessed either supernatural abilities much like our modern superheroes or that they had knowledge and technology that was far superior to the humans who were awed by them. There are ancient texts telling of gods from other worlds that were able to do miraculous things, which are still in advance of what we can achieve in our modern societies.

The old tribes had strong beliefs in the immortality of the soul; when a great king or chief died, his soul was revered and called upon to help with the problems of the tribe. Some rulers were 'deified' while they were still living, either in recognition of their outstanding achievements of military service to their country and other brave deeds or by right of their inheritance. Through 'apotheosis' they became Living Gods or Demigods in many ancient cultures.

It was a common practice in some Indo-European societies to ritually sacrifice an elected sacred king after a term of seven years. The king's head would be buried at a city gate to make sure that as a 'Lar' (ghost or spirit) he would protect the city. Some city state cultures allowed the king to choose a proxy (Inter-rex) for his ritual death and this honoured person, usually a young man was crowned for a day and at sunrise the next day was killed. His blood was sprinkled on the fields to symbolically fertilise them for next season's crops. At sunset the real king/rex would be resurrected from his tomb where he was hiding. (See the Festival of Sacaea.)

In early Egyptian culture a sacred king who personified the god Osiris, was ritually killed after a thirty-year reign and his flesh was cooked and ceremonially eaten in the Sed Festival. (See 'Researches in Sinai' by F. Petrie, p. 185.) Apparently the ritual of consumption of the blood and flesh of sacrificed sacred kings was quite common in ancient societies, sometimes after a seven-year reign.

The royal dynasty system still relied on a human: it could be questioned and did not allow for an ongoing power base to be passed down to the next generation with consistency. A king, chief or queen had weaknesses and a mortality that could be seen, so the best figurehead would be an invisible immortal of total authority.

A god that cannot be questioned is almost invincible unless those who believe in it die out. The select few who are trained in the rituals necessary to communicate with the god maintain a set of rules with the support of the people. The people are told they cannot survive without the god and that what the god says is infallible; whoever questions this is to be punished for the sin of heresy. Control is thus maintained through the fear of non-survival, e.g. *"you will be killed and you will go straight to hell"*. Under this type of imperial religious system the priest or priestess class became the primary power; the royalty or ruling class became secondary puppet representatives and the people below are trained to an aggressive military, political and commercial system of empire.

Empire

An Empire is an aggressive group of peoples directed by a hierarchal institution formed to maintain a way of living and control of a spreading culture that is dominated by an elite group. Empires grow by aggressive takeovers, expanding to obtain resources and to negate competition.

The collective groups that establish empires seem to start with a family group, they become strong either through physical strength or technical advantage. A strong 'thug'or 'smart' family became powerful and wealthy by using their advantages over other tribes that were neither stronger nor smarter. Competition for resources from neighboring tribes would have to be negated. Competing groups built stockades or fortified villages that eventually grew into cities within protective walls and from there the successful groups expanded their territories as City States.

'Sargon the Great, Priest of Anu, the Great Ensi of Enlil' is attributed with the establishment of the first true centrally ruled empire of Accad/Agade around 2,300 BC. His armies conquered Mesopotamia and parts of modern day Iran, Asia Minor and Syria. He was known as a ruthless dictator showing no mercy to his enemies, completely leveling the cities of those who opposed him.

Empires have risen and fallen many times throughout man's history and it is within these institutions that civilization and technology has developed in many beneficial ways but usually with a separation of classes with the elite founding families holding and controlling the wealth and power with the others being little more than servants/serfs and slaves. Maintaining an empire in this world requires a persistent and oppressive struggle to control the members of the collective and constantly guard against threats real or imagined.

Many City States and countries built their empires invading other countries utilising the brute force of their military might to gain land and other resources. Some empires gradually invaded other territories by the way of protecting their merchants. Merchant traders and missionary organisations travelled to find new resources to sell to new markets, if they and their interests are threatened they ask for help from their Mother Empire (e.g. The Opium Wars). An armed force is sent to protect their fellow countrymen and if the threat escalates more troops are sent. The increased troops require acceptable housing, food and facilities so the presence of the invading force became more permanent and entrenched as happened with the expanding Roman Empire. Politicians see that hostile leaders are eliminated and friendly puppet administrators are placed in positions of power so the resources that the empire needs are secured (e.g. The Oil Wars). Roman, Greek, Persian, British, US, capitalist, socialist it doesn't matter, all empires start more or less the same way.

One of the techniques for building an empire is subversive division of groups of people. The aim of the game is to gain control over two allied groups by turning them against each other or a supposed enemy then stepping-in offering protection and armaments to the first group in exchange for payment of assets such as land, gold, metals, slaves, oil or other valuable resources. Once accepted as an ally, the imperial power takes over the group by installing a subservient leader, thus securing the empire's material interests. Once a strong hold has been established in the first group, the empire will use the people of the first group to attack its old ally, the second group. Another technique was the infiltration of the two groups to subvert their alliance in the hope that they would turn against each other in combat, with one group eventually asking the empirical force for assistance. This technique was known to the Romans as *"divide and conquer"*, and today it is still used in 'Psy-Ops'.

Another sneaky technique is to gather the people or allies against a supposed enemy either by creating a real or imagined threat (e.g. Weapons of Mass Destruction). Another is to move your allies by presenting a moral or religious threat. The story of the war against Troy is a typical example even though it maybe fictitious. The Greeks needed an excuse to unite and mobilise their people and allies against Troy. Troy was an extremely rich city that controlled one of the major trade routes and the Greek King Aga-mem-non wanted it. Men-elaus (brother to the King) was deeply insulted and dishonoured when his wife Helen ran off with Paris a Trojan prince (was she playing a part in executing the plan?). This was the moral/idealistic excuse the Greeks were waiting for. Was a massively expensive ten-year war fought for an ally's honour or for the treasures in one of the richest cities on the Aegean?

The old formula for empire building is Order Out of Chaos; make the chaos, provide the solution, create the new order. (See Hegelian Dialectic Triad.)

Setting two groups against each other still goes on in our societies to keep people mesmerised by the emotional highs of competition and eventual victory. Even in politics there are usually only two major parties to choose from at election time with smaller parties around the fringe. This competition between giants becomes a major, expensive and dramatic spectacle, a circus, funded by vested interests. But, the end result is all the same, promises are forgotten and the same agendas are followed, the same power mongers are still in power with a different face. It's just like a fake wrestling match. It would be different if the competing factions had to sign a valid contract before their employment. A three strikes system would be a good start, 'three broken promises and you're OUT!' but we keep on tolerating lies.

"If voting changed things, they would never let us do it." Mark Twain.

The principles of rulers and emperors were later refined and documented in the Middle Ages by the politician Niccolo Machiavelli (1469-1527) who wrote *'Il Principe'*, outlining the principles of leadership in the hope of prompting a 'restorer' to re-establish the Italian/Roman Empire. (See 'machiavellian'.)

To maintain a position of superior power one must maintain an illusion that all others are inferior and subservient to one-self. It is important to create a maze of illusion so that all others are fooled into believing that they are inferior and unworthy of being equal individuals. The system of heir-archy is still present in our societies and is based on the control systems of military institutes. The influence of military hierarchy can still be seen but was stronger in the time of our grandparents who were seen to be more convential, strict and stuffy.

Other than religion, 'class systems' have always been used by rulers to control their empires. Two well-known examples of these hierarchies are the Western Trinity or Three-Class System and the Hindu Caste System that was created by invading Aryans to keep native Indians subservient.

The Three Class System of Western society having an 'upper class' of wealth, a 'middle class' of administration and a 'lower' or 'working class' is an illusion created to keep the empire orderly and the plebeian masses controllable. Above this class system is another hier-archy of ruling families who compete for power using the classes below them much like chess pieces. The game of Chess is an ages old model of imperial hierarchy, take a look on the chess board and see who stands closest to the rulers.

Maintaining an empire is tricky and most empires collapsed under their own greed, using up resources that were hard to replace. Imperial civilizations are programmed by the most basic of instincts, the most prominent being the urge to dominate to prevent being dominated. The instinct to dominate becomes an obsession beyond reason and is expressed as an aggressive accumulation of resources. The problem is that this drive is not rationalised and citizens of the empire become emotionally locked in to the process of status progression and resource accumulation, even when this process is proved to be detrimental to the whole empire. This obsessive behaviour is still manifesting in our modern world driven by corporate empires.

If the status-hungry ruling families are not taking the lead in curbing the demand for material wealth in concern for their own survival then the civilisation will eventually collapse under the strain of trying to hold it all together.

Most empires collapsed through fatigue, broken communication lines, poor leadership, insanity, abuse of power, degradation of agricultural land

and forests, division of wealth classes and attack from the neighbours they robbed and subjugated. As an empire dies, it goes through the death throes of initiating last minute and ill-planned desperate measures. The Romans sent troops forward to grab more resources without sufficient support and pay as the political, financial and moral situation back home gradually deteriorated. The politicians fiddled around and sought to keep their positions with 'bread and circus' to appease the masses. The government fell into debt as corrupt officials and the elite families emptied the states coffers for extravagances and family treasuries. Towards the end, unity, order and control crumbled, enemies attacked, the empire and loyalties were divided. They could not pay their armies that began fighting each other and looting the cities. Thousands died in the internal civil and religious wars. Be wary when the empire stops paying its troops and public servants.

Very few collapsed empires made a comeback as the Roman Empire did, exchanging fallible Gods for an unseen, unquestionable feared God that was gaining popularity using the teachings of the miraculous and popular Christ to encourage people to passively submit to a system of control. Old 'pagan' rites and traditions were incorporated into the new belief to make the transition more acceptable to old allies and the Trinity Godhead was resurrected. This was a smart move as it ensured the continuation of the ruling family's power base and kept them in favour with the people who felt that the old gods had abandoned them. The later Romans who also worshipped a Sun God (Sol Invictus) did not see that they were literally taken over, their religion hijacked by the priests of the Moon God hiding behind the light of the Son.

After annihilating opposition, the Holy Roman Empire became the ultimate empire ruling over all the kingdoms of Europe and the Near East headed by men chosen as God's direct representatives; they became the ultimate ruling elite. Pope Zachary used the forged 'Donation of Constantine' to establish the Catholic Church's position of divine superiority over the royal families of Europe and maintain the idea that kings ruled only by the grace of God as the Trinity of The Father, The Son and The Holy Ghost. Even in modern times, factions of the Catholic Church were dominating and manipulating the political powers of Europe. (See 'Behind The Dictators' by Dr L.A Lehman, 1942.) Even today, all Rhodes still lead to Rome.

Many empires collapsed because of sudden environmental catastrophes such as the great drought that the Mayans experienced and the 'Mini Ice Age' (1250-1850 AD) that brought about wide scale famine due to failed food crops. Lesser known is that the Mini Ice Age was preceded by the 'Medieval Warming Period' (approximately 950-1250 AD) that allowed Viking agricultural settlements to flourish for 300 years even as far north as Greenland. Will our current 'Global Warming' period turn into an ice age as well? According to successful weather forecasters such as Kevin Long and Piers Corbyn there's a very good chance that it will. This trend towards global cooling is verified in *'Solar Cycles 24 & 25 and Predicted Climate Response'* by David Archibald published in *'Energy and Environment'* Vol 17, No 1, 2006 (Multi Science Publishing Co, Ltd).

As time goes on more and more evidence is arising to support the view that the world is heading towards a dry-weather cooling event that follows soon after a peak in warming.

"The research (on Ocean Cycles) has been carried out by noted climate scientists, including Professor Mojib Latif. He is a leading member of the UN's Intergovernmental Panel on Climate Change. He and his colleagues predicted the cooling trend in a 2008 paper, and warned of it again at an IPCC conference in Geneva in September". (Daily Mail online 11th January 2010.)

(See Maunder Minimum, record low temps and severe Northern hemisphere winters 2013, 2014, 2015, 2017, Climate4you.com.)

According to researchers, the collapse of the Classic Mayan civilisation could have been brought about by their ruling class's desire for greatness. Especially in the Copan Valley region the working populations of the Mayan city-states were fed with food grown on soil fertilised by plant-matter from shallow lakes. These wetland areas were maintained from water catchments in forests upstream. The forests were gradually cut down to supply wood for burning lime to make plaster used to build the bigger and better monuments demanded by the ruling families. During this time (250 AD to 900 AD), the climate was warming and from 850 AD drought in their fragile lands became more frequent. The lakes dried up after the forests were gone and eroded acid soils from the cleared hills covered the fertile valley soils. In effect they helped to bring about their own demise by feeding their craving for power and status.

Gradual and catastrophic climate changes have brought down civilisations as the whole network of imperial economics depends on consistent growth. Besides solar fluctuations, volcanoes and comet events, man has been responsible for the decline of empires. The clearing of forests to make way for agricultural practices can bring a dryer environment or desertification and, if combined with adverse natural changes, could lead to the collapse of regional food production and the breakdown of the supporting system that the populace relies on.

Our current civilisation depends on a global network of industrial food production, which has become more independent of natural forces but, has created a situation of non-regulated forest clearing and over-harvesting of natural resources, which in itself contributes to change in the weather on a global scale.

Our industrial method of food production also depends on a limited source of energy in the form of fossil oil and will come to an abrupt end if resources are not channelled into providing economical energy alternatives. (See 'Collapse, How Societies Choose to Fail or Survive' by Jared Diamond, Penguin books, 2005.)

Learn to grow your own food; this skill is more valuable than money. *"We're only truly secure when we can look out our kitchen window and see our food growing and our friends working nearby".* Bill Mollison, founder of Permaculture.

We have reached a level of sophistication that has never been seen before in our history and we have the capability of overcoming most threats to our survival. This capability could be our undoing as our population increases we are using up our valuable resources exponentially. Naturally, disease or natural catastrophic events would have culled the populations and kept the numbers at sustainable levels. Our civilisation is geared to increase growth at the expense of the Earth and our overall quality of life.

Empires not only conquered by brute force, but also with the ever-present institutions of religion. Religions were more effective in pacifying the conquered populations and setting the empires rules of conduct than any army could enforce. Many invading forces took with them their priests who felt it was their duty to save the souls of 'naïve savages'. During the Middle Ages it was common for Catholic bishops to lead armies into battle.

The empires of the world were held together by the religious beliefs that gave their actions of conquest a moral justification. Those empires that banned theological religion still had their own religion in the form of ideologies that they considered superior and much more beneficial for all people. Conquering a nation to save their people from the axis of evils eases the conscience more than the truth of looting and pillaging a nation's resources for greedy leaders of industry. The word 'religion' comes from the Latin word 're-ligere' (ligament), which means to 're-bind' (as in bind people together) around one central controlling organisation. (See Fascism, Fasces, Collectivism, Corporatism, corporal.)

An imperial system is government by the oligarchy, for the parasitic oligarchy, feeding on the people. Today's Democracy is supposed to be *"government by the people for the people"* as Cleisthenes the father of democracy intended it. This has never been the case, 'the plebs' become factory and cannon fodder for the hidden ruling families. Even under a Peoples Republic, Mao and Stalin's policies caused millions of the people to die for standing up for their basic rights. Capitalist or Socialist it does not matter, the 'plutonic' rule, and the 'plebeians' pay a heavy price for not recognising their servile situation.

THE HIDDEN PATTERN

If the truth is kept hidden, power over the masses can be maintained and freewill diminished.

Religious stories or myths have developed over time to explain the creation of the world and to create some semblance of order and reason for human behavior. Not only do the stories give a basic matrix on which to hang the ideas of morality or the rules of society but they also form the trunk that grows many different viewpoints. Each branch in itself leads to the trunk that takes the mind of men deeper into the dark maze of the roots and mythological complexity that stops them seeing the simplicity of a hidden pattern.

Many books have been written to explain the hidden secrets of our society's religious and mystic institutions. These institutions are as different as the many trees within a forest each bearing their own fruit, smells and flavors. It is a complex maze of confusion, but like the trees they have their roots within the same soil. You can climb to the top of a tree only to see that there are just more trees. You can get out of the forest and walk along its edges and you will see that each tree is actually a recognisable but hidden pattern of similar design.

Most religions seem to be modelled on a basic pattern, a trinity of characters, which could have represented the trinity of our Sun, Earth and Moon. Many so-called experts have vehemently denied that the basis of religions were astrological, however there is more than enough evidence to show that the influence of the Sun, planets, Moon and stars were paramount. Taking into account that the patterns found in microcosms reflect those found in macrocosms, this basic model could represent the genetics of creation and its three forces, as follows...

The SUN is the giver of energy. It is consistently giving forth, no matter what surface is presented. It is mainly gaseous and supposedly not very dense except for an iron core. The sun created our solar system and is the source of the Moon and the Earth.

The MOON is the reflector of light. It has a light and dark-side and is a cold, dense mass, a stone with no sustaining atmosphere. It affects the tides and fertility of the Earth and appears like an opening and closing eye during each lunar cycle.

The EARTH is prolific with life. It is warm, moist, gentle, tempestuous, passive, violent and nurturing. Its waters swell in tides to the Moon. The Earth receives the energy of the Sun and with the influence of the Moon nurtures life. It also has light in day and dark in night

This is a natural trinity. Without it life as we know it could not exist. Each part has its function and neither one nor the other is evil or good, they are just necessary.

"There is nothing either good or bad, but thinking makes it so" from the play 'Hamlet' by the playwright and philosopher William Shakespeare.

Through the Trinity runs the essential duality: male and female, hot and cold, night and day, light and dark. To keep the balance of duality both polarities are essential; the illusion hides this fact to create division, pitting one against the other with the power of words.

SUN   EARTH   MOON

The Words

Words are the most powerful tool of mankind not only for communication but also for mass manipulation. Looking at the definitions of words, symbols and names associated with the Sun, Moon and Earth that have been used throughout Indo-European history makes less obvious connections visible.

Over thousands of years, words and their meanings that were used to maintain myths, legends and cultural beliefs became mixed and redefined to suit the religious and political environment of each era. It is hard to say that each culture had a set belief, as war, invasion and religious change kept them constantly evolving.

Definitions, spelling and names changed from culture-to-culture and century-to-century, but the connections as concepts and sounds are still there. Definitions still vary considerably, as do the stories and myths, so I used averages to get an idea of the basic concepts if the definitions were too inconsistent.

Looking beyond the generalisations found in history books and info sites on the internet gets difficult when you are trying to work out what is true. If you read, for example that the colonial Phoenicians worshipped Ammon, you will have to ask what reference does that come from, what time period, what country, what culture was this colony influenced by, who were they allied to and was the ruler at the time from another culture or married to a spouse from another culture that worshipped Ammon, how many other colonies worshipped Ammon? As you can see it gets complicated.

The religious and politically motivated conversion to Latin changed many definitions of the words passed on from the ancient Greeks and other ancient cultures. I believe that this served to hide the precise language that the Ancients used to define the spiritual and physical reality of this world.

The Collins English Dictionary was used as the main reference for this project. Even though the matching of definitions and originations seems to have been done in a haphazard way it was still one of the best dictionaries I could find. Online dictionaries were used to find more detail about words, definitions and their origins.

The definitions in dictionaries are changing all the time as the experts tell us that our language is evolving. Without solid, standard meanings to words anyone can hide the truth of what they mean, this is a dangerous situation. You may sign a document that means one thing to you, but can legally be interpreted to mean something else. Criminals would get away with murder, rape and theft and call it 'war'. Imagine if the history books or the system of weights and measures were constantly evolving, records would be in chaos. Ever played Chinese Whispers?

Words are the tools we use to connect with and understand other people. Keeping words crystal clear would allow us to understand the communications from people of any era or language more clearly. If you read a text in English such as the *'Authorised Version Bible'* (King James Version) from 1611, make sure you use a dictionary from the 1600s to fully understand its meaning.

It seems that many changes to the Latin language were made around the time of the Reformation, so it is important to check the dates that the words were first used. It is also important to note the date or century when a definition was first used for a word, as the word could have been invented or modified according to the politics of that era.

I had to look for the Ancient Greek definitions to try to make sense of the later Latin and more modern words. I also found that many European words originating from Ancient Greek or earlier languages seem to have had their meanings changed when Late Latin evolved. For example, 'legere' is defined as Latin for 'to read', and later 'to pick' (harvest) or 'to choose', you choose! Another example is the Late Latin word 'luxus', means either displace as in luxate or extravagance as in luxury, which are two totally different things. Lux means light. Beware the deceptions and vagaries of Latin!

Many Greek words and myths originated in Egypt (Kemet), as they were once close partners in commerce and culture. Ancient Hebrew contributed much to both of these cultures and vice-versa. The city of Alexandria was home to Jews, Greeks and Egyptians; together they created one of the worlds most celebrated schools of learning.

Our words are made up from the 26 letters in the alphabet that had its origins in very ancient times primarily based on the Roman letters that were based on the Greek alpha-bet and the Hebrew Aleph-beth, which was based on Phoenician script. The Phoenicians developed their own form of writing possibly from the ancient Luso-Iberico Script of Atlantis/Tartessos? (See *Atlantis and the Silver City* by Peter Daughtrey, Pegasus Books.)

Hidden knowledge can be found in some words, one is the Greek word theo as in theology, going back to the Egyptian word for gods, theoi/thi-ta, which means 'those who watch, arrange, organise or plan'. Theo is associated with the words teth and theta, when connected can lead you to a theory. (See theatre/theo-atrium, a place to watch events.)

The sounds Ti, Te and Ta seem to be the root sounds to designate 'life', gods, divine beings or spirits in many cultures around the world (eg, P'tah, Tane, Tammuz, Tali, Tehu, Teol, Tibir, Tiki, Tiamat, Tiu, Shang Ti, etc.). In later languages like Sanskrit or Greek and Latin, Ti, Te and Ta became, Di, De and Da (eg, diva, deus, dyaus, dyu, dai and daemon meaning a god, divine being, spirit).

Most of the world's languages seem to have similar sounds (root words) for general concepts and meanings, which could mean that most originated from a common Mother Tongue or Proto-World language from a long forgotten global culture. There are about 45 languages worldwide, having connecting 'root words' that may be evidence of a global 'First Tongue'.

In the 'New World' the South American Mayans knew the word 'babel-than' as 'to speak in confusion', which is much the same as the English 'babble' from Assyrian 'Bab,ilu' (Gate of God). In the Nahuatl language of the Aztecs 'teo-calli' means 'house of God', in ancient Greek 'theo-u-kalia' is 'Gods house'. (See Nostratic language family.)

"The Basque forms a suitable stepping-stone from which to enter the peculiar linguistic domain of the New World, since there is no other dialect of the Old World which so much resembles in structure the American languages." From *'The Life and Growth of Language, An Outline of Linguistic Science'* by Professor W. D. Whitney, p. 258. Bibliolife, 2009. ISBN 10: 1103710974.

The language of the Basque people of Spain may be closely related to the languages of the Americas since a migration of peoples from the area we call Spain may have taken place 12,000 years ago. Flint work of this era from the Americas shows a great similarity to flint tools found in Spain.

The ancient Hindu teachers taught that everything has a state of being that corresponds to a sound. The sound for the universe is the well-known OM. Indian Sanskrit letters have their own special sounds and a combination of these sounds make-up the word that fits the thing it is a label for. Musical notes were matched to the Earth as 'sar', the Sun as 'pa' and the Moon as 'ma'. In Sanskrit everything has a specific resonance that matches a sound. In Hebrew tradition, everything was created from a word that god uttered, everything had its own word given to it by God. (See cymatics.)

Many of the words that we use in modern languages are composites of words and the way we have been taught to pronounce these words hides the original meaning, for example the word malevolent is made up of two words, male (ill) and volent (will), meaning a wish to harm. It can be a surprise to find out that the word 'male' can mean ill, harm, evil or bad, but it does not mean that the male gender is bad and that fe-male is good, both words contain the word 'male'. The Biblical Adam and Eve were both declared guilty for finding out what the serpent knew and both were punished for their illegitimate actions. (See malus, mal, malicious, volent, volunteer.)

The English word 'man' originating from 'mannaz' in Proto Germanic (or manu in ancient Sanskrit) was commonly accepted as meaning the human race or any member of it and basically means 'to think' or 'capable of thinking' (having a mind, men-tal). In the Mayan language, the word 'men' means to believe, to create, this is what we do with our minds. (See Manus, Mannus in Hindu mythology and Homme, Homo, Hombre.)

Please remember to go beyond Latin and look at the Ancient Greek definitions or earlier for greater clarity of concepts.

I have broken a lot of words into their component parts to demonstrate that they were originally derived from more than one word. It will make it easier for you to find them on the Internet if you join them back together.

Remember, the average words and sounds are the keys to look for. Words are just pointers to the truth, words change and sometimes their meanings change but, sometimes understanding the way the word is used opens the truth the word conveys.

"Meaning is attained by much learning, and much learning is attained by becoming conversant with meaning and not with words; therefore, let seekers for truth reverently approach those who are wise and avoid the sticklers for particular words." From *'The Bhuddist Bible, The Lankavatara Sutra'*, chapter 6, page 102.

You will be seeing many numbers amongst the following words. Numbers have their own meaning and are used in many ancient and modern esoteric codes. These codes are often used to convey hidden/occulted meanings or messages and used by secret societies to change frequencies of energy in their practices of magic. To avoid the Moon's illusion, believe only in what you observe to be consistent and question the rest, including what you read in this book.

In the following chapters I present a deluge of information relevant to the three parts of The Trinity Matrix.

THE SUN

(Sen-tient energy, life, yellow, truth, soul, spirit, unity, birth)

The Sun as we now know is the centre of our solar system; it is the source of our solar system and the source of energy for most life forms on Earth. It is mainly a gaseous star with a dense core and is 333,000 times the size of Earth. The Sun's diameter is 864,000 miles (864 = *432* x 2, 8+6+4 = 18, 1+8 = 9).

In many ancient religions the Sun was a symbol of the creator and healer that Ra-dia-tes life-energy the force or spirit that animates all living things. In Astrology it is symbolised as a circle with a central dot, which represents life-energy, unity/oneness, truth and the centre of the universe.

The words circle, circus, circe could come from the Anglo-Saxon word for a small church or temple as most early places of worship were of a circular design and was probably influenced by the Greek word Kurkos = ring = assembly/union. Churchus, church, Kurche, Kirche (German for church) is supposed to originate from the Late Greek word Kurikon (Lords House), Kurios = master/power)

Originally the Sun was represented almost worldwide as a circle with a cross consisting of horizontal and vertical beams or a golden disc. The Astrological sign associated with the Sun is Leo, the lion (Ari) and is the sign of kings, under which the Messiah (the 'Lion of Judah') was to be born.

The Sun is symbolically connected to a cross (see krucus, quincunx, crux, crocus, cruci-fix, cruci-s, cruci-ble a container for melting gold, or for purifying substances). The container for spirit is the soul. The cross was used for thousands of years before Christ as a symbol for the Sun, one of the earliest examples being 'Mabona the Lord of Light'.

In Greek the first letter of Christ is a cross, X as in Xmas. The first cross symbol for Christ looked like an X with a P in the centre, the Labarum originally known as the Chi-Rho. Chi the cross X is the first letter of Christ in Greek. Rho is P or R in Greek derived from the Semetic 'resh' could also refer to the Red Cross, Cross Rose, Rosi-crucis. In ancient astrology the X also represents the crossing of the Zodiac circle and the Celestial Equator. (See Chiron the wounded healer/teacher in Greek mythology, Ky'rois and Ophiuchus.)

In the ancient Phoenician alpha-bet, which predated the Hebrew alphabet the circled cross, represented the letter 'teth/tet' or in Greek 'theta' (a spirit being). (See Celtic cross.)

Many names have been given to the beneficial gods and goddesses of the Sun, Son, Sunu, Surya, Shamash, Sama, Savitar, Senne, Sol, Soliel, Sal, Sul, Horus, Helios, Inti, Bha, Bah'al, Ba'al, Be, Ben, Grannos, Grian, Dayanisi, Apollo, Aton, Aten, Mithra, Merodach, Ra, Raa, Rama, Rana, Ray, Raymi, Rayam, Re, Resh, Ot, Utu, Vishnu etc.

'Ben' or 'Bar' in Hebrew means 'son' as in Ben-ja-min (son/seed of Ja'min); and 'Baha u Ilah' in Arabic means 'Glory (Baha) of God' (Ilah). (See Ba'al, Ben-ben stone, Bennu bird.)

The Sun has also been called a luci-fer (bearer of light, star of the morning), as was Venus (morning star, day star, evening star). In the New Testament, Revelations. 22:16, John quotes Jesus as saying *"...I am the root and the offspring of David, and the bright and morning star"*. (See morning/mor-waning, luteum.)

The Egyptian religious stories are based on the worship of the Sun as Re/Ra 'the Good' and 'the Light' and his representative on Earth, the hawk-headed God Horus/Heru. Horus's right eye was associated with the Sun and his left eye with the Moon.

Near the Egyptian Pyramids stands the mysterious lion bodied Great Sphinx, traditionally believed to be the image of the solar deity Temu-Heraa-khu-ti. The clairvoyant Edgar Cayce told that the Great Sphinx had been built around 10,500 BC and water erosion marks on the Sphinx, coupled with astronomical and astrological knowledge tend to verify his estimation. The head of the Sphinx is sculptured to resemble the head of a pharaoh, but seems to have originally been a lion's head, which faces the sunrise and is consistent with Sun worship. The Zodiac sign of Leo the lion is the sign of the Sun.

For the ancient Egyptians the Sun had its three phases as the dawn Khepera/Kepri the crawling dung beetle, noon Ra/Re Heracte the two legged hawk and sunset as Tmu/Atum the old man with a stick. (See The Riddle of The Sphinx, Tuthmosis IV and Autumn.)

In some parts of early Egypt the Sun was also worshipped as the two-headed entity Hor-Set: Hor (Horus) the life giving aspect of the rising Sun, and Set the destructive scorching 'Sun of the deserts', who also represented the dying or set-ting Sun. In later Egyptian mythology Set became the black left eye of Horus, a dweller of the netherworld (Amen-ti) whose entrance was guarded by the great snake Atmu. Set murdered Osiris the god of death and judgement, the father of Horus. In later versions of the story Horus fought with and overcame Set, imprisoning him underground. Set escaped until Horus caught up with him and eventually killed him. (See 'Signs In The Sky' by Adrian Gilbert, Three Rivers Press, 2000).

In many modern texts Osiris is referred to as a solar deity, but the average that I have found is that Osiris was an ancient hero who was remembered as a deity of different things at different times including god of the moon, king of the underworld Duat and judge of the dead. In the 'Dankmoe' (iv. 5), it is said: -- "Oh, Osiris-Lunus! That renews to thee thy renewal." (See Ossuary.)

Baal: Since the time that the Hebrew god Yahweh was promoted by Moses as the one and only god and accumulated all the characteristics of the competing gods, a massive campaign had been waged against the worship of 'the baals' (rival gods). The name Yahweh is actually not a name but a title (the living God/God who lives) that was given to God by himself when the Isrealites left Egypt. Before this time he was also given the titles of Jah, Adon, El Elyon, El Yah, El Shaddai or just El which means Lord. As El, he had a consort Asherah/Elath and they bore a son named Baal. Yahweh's other titles connect him with the ancient Sumerian God Enlil who had the same Saturnine temperament. Even though Baal was the 'Son of God' of the Israelites, he and his followers were persecuted. Traditionally, Baal's consort is also Asherah, so I would imagine El (Yahweh) had a good reason to be jealous.

The temples dedicated to Asherah and the baals were aggressively destroyed; the followers of Yahweh killed the priests and worshippers. (See Jehu 2, Kings 10, Old Testament.)

Baal has come to be known as the evil one, the Beel-ze-bub 'Lord of the Flies', Satan, a demon and the Devil under the influence of the Hebrew Yahweh, but has this always been the reality linked to Baal? The Canaanites and Phoenicians knew Baal as a Sun-god who defeated the other son of El named Mot who was the demon god of the underworld, a similar story to Jesus defeating Satan or Horus defeating Set.

Why was the campaign against the worshipers of Baal so violent and aggressive?

Was Baal so much of a threat to Yahweh's power?

Baal is the quick way of saying or spelling Ba'al, which gives a clue to his identity almost immediately. The first sound is ba and is a separate word to al, which means lord; ba is the ancient Egyptian word for spirit/soul. In Egyptian mythology 'Ba' is the soul represented as a human with a bird's head. Ba is related in essence to the Egyptian word khu, which is like a persons immortal spirit body or double that exists in the other world. (See Ka.)

The mythical mountain of Ba-khu, at the point of sunrise in the East, was connected with the Sun and was opposed by the mythical mountain of Manu (Moon) at the point of sunset in the West. Together these two mountains were said to hold up the sky. As you can see, the word 'ba' has connections with the soul and the Sun.

In Assyria and Babylon the Sun god Shamash was also known as Babber.

The Canaanite Baal most likely originated from the Babylonian Bel, a son of Ea/Enki and his consort Dumkina. The Aryan word Bhal is similar and means 'to shine', which could also be a reference to the Sun or even the Moon. Bel/Belos another Shemetic deity, the god of the city of Nippur and 'god of the Earth', could also be related to Baal. (See *Legends of the Gods: The Egyptian Texts* by E.A. Wallace Budge, 1912.)

In the cuneiform tablets of Ras Shamrah (Circa 1400 BCE) the Father of the gods was El; his wife was Asherat-of-the-sea (Asherah). After El, the greatest god was Baal, son of El and Asherah. In Lebanon, Baal was equated with Jupiter from the influence of the Roman occupation.

Please note; there appears to be some confusion about Bel being a sun god. Some texts have referred to Bel as being an alternative spelling of Ba'al but some references show that Bel could have been a god of the Earth or 'Lord of the lands' and 'Lord of the underworld' associated more with the god En-lil or Mul-lil in Assyrian and Babylonian religions around 1200 B.C. Bel was known as Merodach or Marduk and was also known as IL-LIL in the earlier Accadian culture. Bel could be from the Hebrew name Belial as mentioned in the Dead Sea Scrolls; he is described as a *"watcher"*, *"a king of evil"*, *"with a visage like a viper"*. The name Bel/Merodach replaced the archetype Enlil in the trinity of Anu, Ea and Bel.

The Celtic god Belenos/Belinus was 'the shining one' and was identified with Granno a sun-god of healing, light and corn ('corn' means any cereal/ grain plant such as wheat, barley or oats). Belinus was also the god of healing-springs and health. The word Bel as used in Celtic Europe may not have originated with the name Ba'al and is probably a shortening of the name Belenos. The Celtic peoples were well known for human sacrificial rites to many gods including their Samradh fertility festival of Beltane/ Cyntefyn. The Roman Emperor Julius Caesar made extensive records of the Celtic cultures of Europe and reported the rites of the peoples he and his army conquered.

(See Beli, Bela, Belisima, Belisimo, Bellona, Bella, grand, granum, granary, Mayday, Ceres.)

In Cormac's Glossary and other texts 'belo-te(p)niâ', from 'belo-s' meaning 'clear' and 'shining', was the root of the names 'Belenos' and 'Belisama', and 'te(p)nos' meaning 'fire'. This word would mean something like 'bright fire', and may not be connected with the Semitic deity Baal. Note the 'te' used in the word for fire, as fire is commonly associated with spirits or the presence of a god in most cultures. (See Tejo.)

According to historians Morris Jastrow, Max Miller and W. H. Roscher, Ba'al was a Babylonian Sun God.

It is possible that the word Ba'al originally came from the Ancient Egyptian language since the Egyptian culture had a great educational influence over the Mediterranean region.

The second part of Ba'al is al, which in the Middle East languages means lord, mighty, powerful, and noble, etc. This word is found as Al, El and Il and is a title of reverence as Lord. In more modern languages Al, El and Il is still used as a masculine title of honor, similar to the English Master, Lord or Sir. Al, el and il also mean masculine 'the' and, just by adding 'o' on the end of this word, you get theo, which takes us back to the words of the Gods. (See theos, theology, theurgy, theta, theory, etc.)

Over hundreds of years of use, the word Ba'al became just a word meaning Lord to many of the ancient peoples as the original meaning became forgotten.

The Phoenicians placed the word Baal in front of some of the names of their Deities as in Baal Hadad meaning Lord Hadad and was also used as a proxy. The name Hadad for instance was not to be spoken by people, so they just said Baal/Lord (see A-dad/Dadu god of storms, thunder). The Canaanites and the Hebrews picked up this practice from the Phoenicians. Baals were suddenly everywhere and even Yahweh was given the title Baal Yahweh or Baali. The name Be-aliah (more accurately be'al-yâ) means 'Yahweh is Baal' or 'Yahweh is Lord' (1 Chronicles 12:6 Tanakh). Yahweh (god who lives) was again a title for the God of Israel that was also known by 72 titles.

"At first the name Baal was used by the Jews for their God without discrimination, but as the struggle between the two religions developed, the name Baal was given up in Judaism as a thing of shame, and even names like Jerubbaal were changed to Jerub-besheth: Hebrew bosheth means 'shame'." From *'Zondervan's Pictorial Bible Dictionary',* 1976.

This could explain why the fearsome Canaanite god Molech/Molok/Melek/Mal'akh was called 'Baal' as in the Baal Hammon (Lord H-ammon) of the Carthigians and confused with the Sun god. Mol-ech was also given the title of Yaveh Melek, which is the same as Yahweh Mel-ek or Yahweh the King. Baal and Moloch were not the same god, they were opposites, Sun and Moon, ben-e-volent and mal-e-volent.

The Assyrian (Babylonian) bēl suggests lordship over men in all North-Semitic languages. In later Hebrew and Arabic, 'ba'al' used in the personal sense means husband, possessor or owner.

Rites of Ba'al and Accompaniments:

"Apart from the offerings of fruits from the earth and the firstlings of cattle, much is not known with regard to the rites of the popular Ba'al-Worship. Self-torture and mutilation characteristic of the Phoenician type were probably absent from the simpler and freer usages of the primitive local observances. It is also doubtful whether the sacrifice of children, proper to the service of Molech, was ever a feature of inland Canaanitic Ba'al-Worship. The shrines were little more than altars with the symbol of the Ashtoreth planted beside it—the sacred tree-stem or pole named from an old Canaanite goddess, Ashera, with whom Ashtoreth was identified. Nearby, sacred pillars were also often reared." From *'Ba'al and Ba'al Worship'* by Morris Jastrow Jr., I. Frederic McCurdy and Duncan B. McDonald.

In many ancient temple shrines a stone pillar (masculine, strength, severity) was placed to one side, a wooden pillar (feminine, mercy, establishment) was on the opposite side and an altar holding a fire was in the centre. Could it be that this arrangement originally represented the trinity of Moon, Earth and Sun?

The Sun also represented the combination of the male and female attributes as a neutral whole being. (See sollus, holistic, holos, holy, halo, hallowed, Helio, hello.)

The Sun has been associated with the cycle of birth, death and resurrection. The Sun loses its power, wanes in winter and is reborn in spring, which was celebrated at the fertility festival of Eoster with painted eggs and h-Ot cross buns bearing the solar cross. (See Easter, Ester, Ishtar, Ostara, Oestrogen, Eos.)

The Red Solar Cross, a red cross on a white background is the flag of England, the emblem of St George who according to legend rescued the Virgin from the Dragon. The same Red Cross was worn by the Knights Hospitalers and is now the symbol for First Aid medical care and Hospitals. The Knights of St John were also protectors of pilgrims to the Holy Lands; they wore black tunics with a white cross, the forerunners of the St John's Ambulance Brigade. (See Rosi Crucis, Knights Templar.)

Emperor Constantine claimed he received a vision of a cross superimposed on the Sun in 312 AD and had a red cross (Chi-ro) painted on each of his soldiers' shields to ensure victory in battle. Constantine was a follower of the popular Roman sun cult that worshipped the Sun as Sol Invictus (see The Invincible Son, Mithras), of which the main celebration day was the 25th of December. Constantine's mother Princess Elaine of Britain (St. Helen) who went in search of the original cross of Christ, was apparently responsible for Constantine's eventual deathbed conversion to Christianity and baptism by the Arian Bishop Eusebius of Nicodemus. Although Constantine was a 'Pagan' he declared himself to be the one true saviour and representative of God. Constantine promoted the Nicene Creed that led to bloody conflict between Athanasian and Arian Christians.

"Probably more Christians were slaughtered by Christians in these two years (342-3) than by all the persecutions of Christians by pagans in the history of Rome". Will Durant.

The followers of Yahweh abandoned the teachings of Jesus; *"Love thy neighbor as thyself"*, (Mathew 19:19 New Testament) and his apostles: *"If we love one another, God dwelleth in us, and His love is perfected in us"*. (First Epistle of John 4:12 New Testament, KJV)

Crucifixion on a cross in Roman times was for the crime of sedition against the state. Pontius Pilate washed his hands of responsibility for the death of Jesus, so Jesus may not have been convicted of sedition and was most probably not hung on a cross. The two thieves that were crucified with him should not have been there either. It was the priests who condemned him for rebellion and the traditional Jewish punishment for a rebellious son was to be beaten or stoned and hung on a tree or wooden post until dead. (See Talmud; Tract Sanhedrin, chapter 6.)

In the New Testament Jesus was mocked by the Roman soldiers who dressed him in a robe of royal colour and formed a crown made of thorns. After mockingly crowning Jesus as 'the king of the Jews' they handed him over to the Priests.

In Biblical Hebrew tradition it was written, *"a rebellious son should be killed by stoning and hanging in a tree"*, Deuteronomy 21: 22. In Acts of the Disciples 5:30 it says, *"The God of our fathers raised up Jesus whom ye slew and hanged on a tree"*.

The symbol of the cross keeps a connection with the worship of Sol Invictus (Mithras) and the traditional festival of the Winter Solstice and all its Sun-Gods. In most parts of the old pagan world winter solstice rituals were performed as part of a twelve day Yule-tide festival to celebrate the Sun's return/rebirth.

(See Yulanna, Yulannu, Jule, Jol, jolly, joy, pagus.)

The cross as we know it is apparently a variation of the Tau or 'T' symbol being the initial of the once popular god Tammuz. Another popular cross from more ancient times is the well-known Egyptian Ankh. The Ankh is a tall cross with a loop on top that represents life and the soul.

The Greek word used in biblical texts that is commonly translated as 'cross' is 'stauros', which really means an upright post or stake used for torture or execution. The Earliest texts of the New Testament were written in Greek as it was the universal academic language of the time.

The Greek writer Homer used the word stauros as meaning an ordinary pole or stake, or a single piece of timber. This is the meaning and use of the word in the Greek classics and was usually a stake set in the ground upon which an execution was carried out either by hanging, nailing or impaling. (See *Iliad* xxiv.453, *Odyssey* xiv.11, *Thucydides* iv.90. *Xenophon, Anabasis* v.2.21.)

The word Christ comes from the Latin Christus from the Greek word Khristos meaning king, coming from the Hindi root word Kris meaning anointed (see Lord Krishna, whose death was also associated with a tree). The word crest comes from the old French word creste, which comes from the Latin crista, which means highest.

The colour for the Sun has usually been yellow or orange, yellow being the peaceful and compassionate spiritual colour. People are still said to be yellow if they refuse to fight thus the association with cowardice.

The Sun has an active (red) energy as its core is apparently composed of iron (red, fertility). Adding red to yellow makes ora-nge.

In the symbology of Freemasonry the Black Sun is present, but as the 'total solar eclipse' where the moon blocks out the light of the sun and takes its corona/crown.

When the Creator manifests its presence as a benign, benevolent human teacher of unity, acceptance, unconditional kindness and healing, it is called the Son of God, the Great Prophet, the Messenger, Messiah, the anointed one, the Teacher, the Healer, Helper etc. (See Asclepious, Messeh, Mashiach, MusHus, solace, solemn, solder, soldier, solid, solidus, salve, salvation, salt, sulter, sultry, summa, summer, etc.)

Sulphur/sulfur/sulfer/sol-fer, the 'carrier of the Sun' is the mineral that makes oxygen available to the body. It also carries amino acids that are essential for the building of proteins and the connective tissues of the body.

In Latin, the word 'sons' means guilt (gylt, Old English), which in archaic use was a sin or crime. A sin (sun-tea, Old High German) is an offence or transgression against God's will. In most religious and mythological stories concerning a trinity of the Father, Mother and Son it is the son who teaches humans a different way of doing things. He opposes the will of the Father for the benefit of humans and is subsequently declared guilty then sacrificed to appease the angry Father God.

Sacrifice was not just the lot of the Biblical son Jesus; many of his followers were sacrificed in some way, as were many 'Sons of God' from other cultures, such as: Alcestos, Apollonius of Tyana, Atys, Bali, Benjamin the Egyptian, Buddha Sakia, Crite, Devatat, Hersus, Ioa, Indra, Ixion, Krishna, Mithra, Mani, Orpheus, Prometheus, Quetzalcoatl, Quirinus and Wittoba. (See *'They Lied To Us In Sunday School'* by Ian Ross Vayro, Joshua Books 2006.)

Aurum is also known as gold. It is the metal attributed to the Sun. Across the world in many cultures Aurum was the sacred metal of the Sun gods. The Great Pyr-amid of Giza symbolised the Sun: it was perfect and complete when its sides were covered with reflective white limestone and the now missing gold apex crowned its peak. Aurum does not corrode and was considered incorruptible and perfect. Ancient alchemists prepared the monoatomic gold known as 'ormes' the food of the soul. Ormes was consumed by the pharaohs to enhance the power of their souls and rejuvenate their bodies. (See aura, auroras, ora, orah, orange, gold, gol, gul, gulr, gula, gulth, gult, gilt, gelt a tribute or payment, gelding, sol-idus, sal-ary.)

Gold is the highest award given in sports achievements as the 'gold medal', part of the trinity of gold, silver and bronze.

The Golden Age in classical mythology was said to be the first and best age of mankind when existence was happy, prosperous, and in-nocent (not harmful). The colours yellow, gold and orange are associated with spiritual and physical healing, and in Asia symbolises holiness. Members of Indo-Asian religions use orange or saffron-coloured robes extensively.

The Sun has also been symbolised across the world from ancient times in Indo-European tradition as a clockwise or counterclockwise Swastika.

Until the Second World War the swastika was widely known as an Aryan symbol of good fortune, ongoing creation and positive power even in Europe. It was not just a sun symbol as it was used for many reasons including a symbol of the moon. It is also the Hindu symbol of the 'pramantha'. The Swastika was used widely in India, Asia, Native America and North and Central Europe. Unfortunately it became a dreaded sign as the Nazi Svastika. The Nazi Svastika is black on a white disc on a red background, the significance of which will become apparent later in the book. In India the clockwise turning swastika represents the male god and the counterclockwise swastika is for the goddess. The left-handed or counterclockwise Sauwastika is also said to be the symbol of Kali the shakti of the destroyer Shiva. (See *An Illustrated Encyclopaedia of Traditional Symbols* by J.C. Cooper, Thames and Hudson Ltd., London 1990 and the 47th proposition of Euclid, Seal of Sumeria.)

The Sun has also been represented as a wheel in association with the chariot/car-riage that carries the Sun god across the heavens (see Phaethon, phaeton). In the 'Edda' texts, the Sun is *"the beautiful, the shining wheel"*, and similar expressions occur in the Hindu Vedas.

The Sun wheel of Ba'al/Shamash/Helios had 4 rays, Ishtar (Venus/Earth) had a star wheel with 8 rays and the 16 ray wheel which is also common. The Sun wheel is also present in the Celtic Cross. 8 is the symbol of the cycle of death and rebirth and is represented by the traditional 8 sides of the baptismal font. 8 is the number for reincarnation and the 8 sided design is used as a portal to other dimensions. Wooden carriage wheels were traditionally made with 16 spokes. The glass dome that brings the light into the Vatican Basilica also has 16 spokes. 16 is the number for spiritual enlightenment.

The Sun wheel is present in St Peter's Square at the Vatican, which happens to be an elliptic circle containing two circles or wheels; the central wheel has 4 rays and the outer wheel has 8 rays. Dominating the wheel, at the hub stands an uninscribed stone obelisk that is thought to have stood at the Temple of Amen-Ra in Egypt before its transport from either Heliopolis/City of the Sun (originally Anu) or Alexandria to be erected at the Circus Caligula, later renamed Circus Nero in Rome.

St Peter's 'Square' is built near the site of the old Roman Circus Nero a chariot racing circuit where St Peter and hundreds of fellow Christians were said to be martyred. (See 'Peter the Rock', petra = rock, petros = stone, Greek.)

Above the 'Tomb of Julii' in the grottoes beneath St Peter's Basilica at the Vatican is a 3rd century mosaic of Christ represented as the solar charioteer Sol/Helios, complete with horses and a four spoked solar wheel connecting Christ with the worship of Sol Invictus/Helios.

It is interesting that a stone phallus has been placed at the centre of the Sun wheel at the Vatican. The word for stone (stion = pebble, Greek) in Breton is 'men'. The word 'stones' in Britain was a common word for testes, hence 'to stone' means to castrate or e-mas-culate. A huge stone formed in the shape of the male phallus is a very strong mas-culine symbol of fertility and domination.

The arrangement at Saint Peter's Square could represent the dominance of the stone/moon/mass over the Sun and the lower placement of Earth/Venus/Ishtar. (See mil/mass, mill-stone, masson, mason/monas/stone, stone-mason, Free-mason, dol-men, men-hir, men =stone/mass and hir =long/tall or higher/superior, hier-archy.)

If it was the erotica-obsessed Caligula who brought the trophy obelisk monument to Rome and originally erected it at the Circus Caligula, it was probably in honour of the god Sol Invictus/Helios the solar charioteer, or was it in honour of Cupid/Eros, whose common worship effigy was an erect stone pillar? (See Ero-tica.)

Pope Sixtus V commissioned Domenico Fontana to move the obelisk to its current position in 1585. The move of 250 metres took 5 months, but the whole exercise including preparations could have taken 12 months or more. It begs the question of how did the Romans move these massive objects over hundreds of kilometres? The Vatican Obelisk was the only one of its kind to survive the ruination of Rome in a vertical position. Was it saved as a standing witness to the many Christians martyred in the Caligula Circus or was this one special in some way? (See 'Digitus Solis', Finger of the Sun.)

Thirteen stone obelisks, one for each of the original lunar months of the year were transported to Rome from Egypt during the rule of the Roman Empire. Some of these obelisks weighed more than 300 tons and stood more than 80 feet tall. It took huge human resources and great expense to move these monuments across the Mediterranean Sea, why? Was the power of the Moon God moved to Rome under the influence of Amen as the power of the Egyptian Empire died?

Obelisks were used as sundials, clocks or chrono-meters for calculating not only daily times but also calendrical divisions, solstices and equinoxes. Obelisks and towers apparently had the properties of energy collectors and were often placed in pairs at the en-trance to temples.

Irish monasteries erected tall stone Round Towers to increase the fertility of their gardens, and they apparently worked well as energy collectors for meditation. (See 'The Mysterious Round Towers of Ireland: Low Energy Radio in Nature'; The Explorer's Journal; Summer, 1993.)

Was Amen-Ra a sun god, as it is often believed? Some Egyptian gods can't make up their minds about what they represent. Since the Egyptian culture lasted so long, rulers seeking political solutions to conflicts between different city-states that preferred different gods diffused the original identities of the gods. My research shows that Amon/Amun/Amen 'The Hidden One' was originally a local Moon/lunar deity of Waset, which was later renamed after the Greek city Thebes. Amon of Thebes became known as Amen of Heliopolis after the Princes of Thebes had taken control of the country during the 12th dynasty. Among other titles, the god Amen was called the 'Only One', but the addition of the words 'who hast no second' showed that the Egyptians had affirmed the existence of a god who had no like or equal. It is certain that when the Egyptians declared that their god was 'One' and that he had no second, they may not have had the same ideas as the Jews and Islamists when they proclaimed their God to be 'One alone' as Egyptians continued to worship a pantheon of many gods. In the 18th dynasty Amen assumed all the attributes of Ra of Heliopolis, becoming Amen-Ra.

Amen was elevated by the growing power and wealth of the Theban rulers to take over Ra's position as 'Father Amen, Supreme God of Egypt', and hijacked the Egyptian Sun throne.

The jealous Moon hid the light of the Sun, taking upon itself the crowning glory of the Sun's corona and falsely declared his reign as the giver of life, a Solar Eclipse.

Amen appears to be connected to the root word 'men' (to abide, to be permanent) and was originally one of a pantheon of 9 gods and took the place of Monsu/Montu.

Amen/Amun/Amon/Ammon/Imen/Amin who is also associated with Menthu and Min of Chemmis, is sometimes depicted as a ram or a goose and also known as Zeus/Deus/Dyaus ('Father of the Gods'), depicted with a ram's head or horns, a powerful symbol of male fertility. (See Baphomet, Idi Amin.)

If it is true that the Vatican obelisk was originally dedicated to Amen Ra then the obelisk in the centre of St Peter's Piazza could represent the domineering Moon force that eclipses the face of the Sun, stands over the Earth Mother and still receives a salutation of recognition after the utterance of prayer: *"for ever and ever, Amen"*. The Hebrew word AMHN pronounced 'aman' is possibly from 'ah, mein' or *'so be it'* in Arabic. Aman may have been introduced into the Hebrew language after their 400-year sojourn in Egypt, but the spelling and pronunciation has reverted back to 'Amen' a salute to the moon god that they were so familiar with.

In the papyrus written for Nesi Khensu during the 21st dynasty, it is written about Amen: *"The God Nu (Amen's creator), the prince who advances at his hour to vivify that which comes forth upon his potters wheel, the disk of the Moon God who opens a way both in heaven and upon Earth for the beautiful form."*

What is the beautiful form? Is it the Sun-child, male or female, that heals with unconditional love? (See the Hindu SaumyavapuH.)

Assyrian solar cross.
(From *'The Mammoth Dictionary of Symbols'* 1996 by Nadia Julien.)

THE MOON

(Mass, fertility, silver, intelligence, knowledge, mind, division, deception, stone, death.)

A female figure in the Mater religions, Lunar symbolises the opposite of the Sun, a nocturnal reflector of the Sun's power.

The moon is an enigma in itself, its origin has been much debated and so many 'coincidences' have brought many people to the conclusion that the Moon was designed and placed in its orbit to promote life. The fact that the moon appears to be exactly the same size as the Sun is just the start. The 'Big Whack' theory is used to explain the oirigin of the Moon as a body formed from debris sent in to Earths's orbit by a collision with another planet when the Earth was very young. Even though rocks collected from the Moon were found to be very similar to Earth's the rocks from the Moon were found to have virtually no heavy metals. The mass of the Moon is very light for it's size. According to NASA seismic readings from the 13th Moon Mission, the Moon could be hollow as it "rang like a bell" after an expired section of the rocket was dumped onto the Moon's surface. The Moon is 1/400th the diameter of the sun and orbits Earth at 1/400th the distance of the earth to the Sun and is 27.3% the size of the Earth. Without the Moon the Earth would not have a stable rotational angle of 22.5 degrees that maintains a habitable surface temperature range. The formation of Earth's continents may not have happened without the Moon's gravitational pull. Oceanic tides that promoted the evolvement of life would not have happened without the Moon being exactly where it is. The Moon is a very important part of the trinity that allowed us our existence.

Originally, there were thirteen months (monaths, moons, lunations) in a year, each having 28 days. The moon has a speed of orbit of 27.3 days, the lunar Synodic Cycle (new-moon to new-moon cycle) is 29.53 days and is dark for 3 days, which leaves 26 days of the visible moon.

Our current calendar of 52 weeks (supposedly being a solar calendar) has 26 fortnights. (See Gregorian calendar, Julian calendar, Mayan calendar.) The number 26 (13+13) is very important in ancient Mayan culture and appears in the Hebrew Quabalah Gematria as 'God's number'.

In Hebrew, Yahweh/YHWH/ adds up to 26 in the Gematria, and there are 26 letters in the English alphabet. The value of GOD in the LUX code and the NOX code is 26. The Holy Word of Tantric Buddhism OM, the Lost Word of the Master Masons MABN or ABMN, also add up to 26.

The YHWH 26 equals the Squaring of the Circle, as the Herme-ticists discovered in pi (ϖ) equalling 22 sevenths (22/7), which when added to the 4 corners of the square or cross gives the number 26 as in the circle cross Å.

The number 26 is also related to the Cube of Measurable Space, made up of 6 faces, 8 corners, and 12 edges, adding up to the Number 26. The 6x 360-degree squares of the cube equal 2160. A circle is measured as 360 degrees (See Pious.)

The number of the cube is 26, an ancient symbol for the body of man, and the 3rd dimension. Salt crystallizes as cubes and we are said to be the 'salt of the earth'. There is a 26-degree angled hallway leading to the Queen's Chamber in the Great Pyramid, when it was first opened its walls were encrusted with up to half an inch of salt.

A black cube is one of the symbols of Saturn.

The average period of human gestation is 260 days. The expected lifespan of humans is about 72 years, which is 26064 days. The period of Precession of the Equinoxes or Great Year is very close to 26,000 years as recorded in the Mayan long count calendar. The Great Year has 12 Great Months of 2160 years. One degree of the Precession of the Equinoxes equals 72 years and adding half (36 years) equals 108.

The Magic Square of Benjamin Franklin who was a Freemason of the 33rd Rite is 8x8 = 64 and adding up these numbers (8+8+6+4) gives 26, which is the magic number of the Mayans and Alchemy.

The number 26 is also the number of the proportion of the Golden Rectangle, which was utilized by Classical and Renaissance artists as a symbol of physical perfection. This rectangle is measured as 5 x 8 units, and 5+8+5+8 = 26, 2+6 = 8 divided by 5 = 1.6 the Golden Ratio.

The moon is 3.33 times denser than water and 2160 is the moon's diameter in miles (*432* x 5 = 2160, 216 = 6x6x6, 2+1+6 = 9 and 4+3+2 = 9), its radius is exactly 1080 miles (1+0+8+0 = 9).

The ancient Sumerian measurement of mass was the 'mana', which was measured as 10800 barley seeds. The 'double mana' was of course 21600 barley seeds.

The cycle of the solar/lunar eclipse is 18 years (1+8 = 9). 18 = 6x3 or 6+6+6.

260 times 1.6 (phi f) = 416.

666 divided by 416 = 1.6?

1080 divided by 666 = 1.6...

Coincidence? Is there a code here left by the architect of The Trinity Matrix? Go figure!

(See *The Harmonic Origins of The World: Sacred Number at The Source of Creation*' by Richard Heath, Inner tradtions, 2018, ISBN 9781620556122.)

The Imperial measurements of miles, yards, feet and inches is based on very ancient duodecimal (12) and sexagesimal (6) systems. The measure of the yard and the metre can be found in many ancient megalithic sites.

1 mile divided by 1 kilometre equals 1.6, the Golden Ratio.

(See the *'De Architectura'* by Marcus Vitruvius Pollio, the Vitruvian man, the Fibonacci sequence, Phi, Thelema 26, Megalithic yard, Golden Mean.)

The Moon is said to have two faces, the light side and the dark side just as the human min-d is said to have two aspects, the conscious mind (Ego) and the sub/unconscious mind (Id) and is synonymous of duality and division just as our brains are divided, rightside-leftside.

The human brain has a trinity of levels:

1. Spinal/brain stem/reptilian;
2. Limbic system/mammalian; and
3. Cerebral cortex/neo-mammalian.

These levels are covered by the 3 protective meninges (membranes), pia mater, arachnoid and dura mater.

The Moon orbits the Earth in a near perfect circular orbit without rotating in relation to the Earth's axis; this is why we see only one side of the Moon from Earth. The side we see is visible to us when it is illuminated by the Sun, when the Moon is dark the so-called 'dark side' is illuminated as this side is facing the Sun. The dark side is not dark all the time: it is dark in the sense that it is 'hidden' from the view of us on Earth. Humans first saw the dark side of the Moon after the Soviet spacecraft 'Luna 3' photographed it in 1959.

One of the characteristics that differentiate the properties of the Moon with the Earth is that it is unchanging and dead. The Moon has a permanent stoniness about it, which is far different than the Earth's volatility and energy in changing its surface through weather and geological upheavals.

This is also a difference between patriarchal and matriarchal social systems of imperial and tribal systems. Tribal society was more matri-centric; there was a constant flow and acceptance of change, and not so much emphasis on permanency. Stories were passed down from generation to generation verbally; through songs and stories that changed slightly each time they were told. In many matricentric tribal cultures the names of those who die were not repeated or said out loud in case the spirits of the deceased were disturbed. Tombs were not considered important since the body and soul were supposedly given back to the Earth.

Under the patriarchal imperialistic systems, written records became more important and there was an emphasis on retaining the memory of those deceased. The Kings of old built massive structures to ensure their permanency in history. It was the male-dominated imperialistic system that developed institutionalisation and built the personal monuments that still stand today under the influence of Amen 'the permanent one' and many other deities. The word 'monument' comes from the Latin word mon-u-mentum, which seems to be a combination of the two words moon/mon and mental. (See mind, re-mind, monere, mem-ory.)

"The association between the mind and the moon is very ancient and also lies at the source of Indo-Aryan myth. In the Hymn of Man, the primordial Adam is sacrificed to become the diversity of the world. Although the sun is his eye, it is the moon who is his mind." (O'Flaherty. 29)

The LIGHT-SIDE of the Moon (a luci-fer; luci = light/lux + fer = carrier/bearer) could be representing the conscious part of the mind of man. The light-side of the Moon is influenced by the source of the soul the Sun. It is the surface of the moon we see reflecting the energy of the Sun transmuted to the energy of knowledge, intelligence, cleverness and sophistication. The word 'sophisticated' comes from Sophos/Sophia was the spirit/goddess of wisdom and brought gifts of civilisation and science. Sophia is regarded by Gnostics as the mother of Yahweh/Yaldabaoth. Thoth/Te-hu-ti also brought civilisation and science to humans; civilisation brought material gain. (See lux-ury, lucky, lu-min-ous, Il/Il-lu-min-ati.)

The Moon could be called a Luci-fer (light carrier). Lucifer was a description that was also given to the morning star (Venus) that heralds the rising Sun. It was only since the Mediaeval 'Reformation' that Lucifer was used as a name for the Biblical Satan even though the essence of Lucifer was about enlightenment, not darkness. There is no mention of a 'Lucifer' in the Bible. (See Luciferians, Luciferian Doctrine.)

The moon appears to give light, but this is just an il-lus-ion, a trick, a deception, as the light originally comes from the Sun, which was also referred to as a luci-fer.

Loki 'the trickster/illusionist/deceiver', the wicked son of Odin from ancient Norse mythology, caused the death of the invincible Bal-dor by tricking his blind brother into throwing a twig of Mistletoe. Mistletoe was used to cast spells and also has the reputation of making a woman open to sexual exploitation, a favourite decoration for the bawdy festival of Saturnalia.

The DARK-SIDE of the Moon (the face of the Hidden One, Darth, Olcars) could be a representation of the subconscious part of our minds as it is also hidden from view. The Dark-side is the side we do not see, not meaning it is always dark as it rotates towards the Sun every lunar cycle, it's just that it always faces away from our view and is always hidden.

When the face of the Moon we see is in darkness (in shadow) it was said in mythologies that the moon had died and was making its journey through the domain of Pluto's underworld/Hades or Satan's Hell. The new moon was the Moon resurrected after its 3 days of death.

The Dark-Side is the fault, error, lie, flaw (men-dus) and the dia-bolos, which we personify as the Devil or Diablo in Spanish. Dia = from the other side, + bolos = ray of light/lump/throw in Latin. (See De-vil, vil-lain, vile, village, Satan, alshaytana, Iblis, Ialdabaoth, Samael, Diavolo, diabolical, Mendacium, mendacity.)

Satan is associated with the dark-side of occult (hidden/covered) worship and is usually described as half-man half-goat or wearing a red skin-suit and carrying a trident, but has this always been true or was it invented by the Church? Is Satan a real being or like a 'Yidam' constructed by mass agreement? (See University of Propaganda Fide, Sacra congregatio de propaganda fide.)

A satan (adversary, opponent; a 'sawtawn' in Hebrew) was originally something of a hindrance or someone with an opposing view, an adversary, an argu-ment or just an opposite, like the other end of a piece of string. To the Hebrews the Roman Empire was a satan, to the Jewish priesthood Christ was a satan, the Jews and Romans were satan to early Christians. Anything or anyone could be called a satan if an opposition is made.

The idea that d'evil one was an individual being has been around in the teachings of dualistic theologies long before the Catholic description of an evil being called Satan. Ancient philosophers not only anthropo-morphised the elements of nature, they also personified concepts and qualities and made them sacred, even the Catholic Church is still referred to as the 'Great Mother'. Mot, Set, Iblis, Hubayu, Humbaba, Angra, Ahriman etc were all personifications of the evil or destructive side of godly or human nature. Mas-te-ma is the dark/evil side of Yahweh (God) as mentioned in the 'Book of Jubilees' as is Azaz-el ('Strength of God') in Leviticus 16:7-10, Tanakh.

It was Augustine who really set to and gave us the modern concept of Satan as a person and his history according to Augustine's interpretation of the 'Book of Revelations'. (Compare the prophecies of the Sybiline Oracles.)

The concept of a real Satan was utilised to justify acts of extreme violence and terrorism.

"The Middle ages saw the continued harnessing of the personal Satan, cosmic combat myth in order to demonise people – Jews and Moslems were demonised as in league with Satan; anti Semetism, crusades and wars against Moslems etc. were all justified with the idea that they were all of 'Satan' – and so any abuse of them was somehow justified. It was claimed that Satan killed Jesus, yet the Jews killed Jesus, therefore, Jews = Satan and should be destroyed." From *'The Real Devil, a Biblical Exploration'* by Duncan Heaster: page 56. www.carelinks. net. (See Holocaust.)

The image of Satan that we know today with his cloven hooves, horns and trident was written in the seventh century AD by Pope Gregory 1 and was modelled on the traditional pagan 'horned' forest fawn god Pan, a Satyr half human, half goat. (See HaShatan, Shaitan, sated, Silvanus, Set, Seth, Cern, Cernunnos, Chimera.)

"Pan was a composite creature, the upper part—with the exception of his horns—being human, and the lower part in the form of a goat. (…)The pipes of Pan signify the natural harmony of the spheres, and the god himself is a symbol of Saturn because this planet is enthroned in Capricorn, whose emblem is a goat". From the *'Secret Teachings of All Ages'* by Manly P. Hall.

The symbols associated with Satan are the head of the Goat (Baphomet), the trident and the inverted Pentagram. The correct pentagram is made up of the mathematics of the Golden Ratio, the Divine Proportion of the Hermetic arts.

According to Herodotus the fourth century BC Greek historian:

"Mendes was the name of the originally Egyptian Pan (the 'God of Shepherds') and was used by them as a word for the goat".

The god 'Men' (Men Askaelos, Mensis) was a god worshipped in Anatolia as the saviour of poor, ill, defenceless people and as a god who gives health and favour by the mystic power of his symbol, the crescent moon. The cult of 'Men' originated in Mesopotamia circa 4000 BC. The worship of Men mixed with several other cults spread from Western Anatolia to the Greek Islands and from there to Italy and other countries of Europe. This god is usually shown with a men-iscus (horned moon, crescent) on his shoulders.

Moses descending from Mt Sinai with a 'shining face' was depicted as being 'horned' in translated scripts since the word for 'shining' in the ancient texts was the word 'qeren' that also meant 'horned'. Moon gods are usually described as 'horned' and 'shining'. During the 'Age of Taurus' gods were associated with the 'bull of heaven' whose shining horns were represented by the meniscus.

Artists depicted Moses as horned in mediaeval art works; one example is Michelangelo's statue of Moses, 1513 AD. Bibles from this era show Exodus High Priests wearing a meniscus on their headdress.

Supernatural beings of good and bad influence have been a part of human mythology since as long as religious ideas have been recorded. We in the Western world know them as 'demons'.

The word 'demon' meaning 'evil spirit' in Latin was not used until somewhere around the 14th century. Previously it was the Greek word 'daimon/daemon', which just means a 'spirit' or 'deity' usually as a guardian or guiding spirit that accompanied and advised a person during a lifetime. The daemon was also known as 'Genii' that provides a person with wisdom, cleverness and inspiration as 'genius'. It wasn't until the time of the horrific 588 year-long period of cruel Inquisitions (1232 to 1820) that it was demonised by the Catholic Church in the name of God, along with the thousands who were tortured and killed for questioning the church's dogma. (See demon, deimon, daemon, demiurge, deity, deva, diva, divine, devious, Jin, Apep/Apopis, Ad Abolendam.)

Interestingly the word daimon is made up from the word dai/dei from deus (deity/god, in Greek), so why does the mon come into it? (See mon-ster.)

The Dark Side of the Moon can be associated with the lower or base instincts of the mind and the symbols of power and desires, money, monarchs, lucre, lust, fool-ishness seem to be strongest at the full moon ('*Fools follow their folli under a full moon*'). The Dark Side is also associated with hate, jealousy, anger, fear, the knowledge of warfare, mor-da (murder), lunacy, forces that accumulate density and darkness and pull life down into mass and matter. (See mor-bid, Animus, Anima, Loopy, Lupi, Lupus, 'Lupercalia' festival of fertility, which was later renamed 'St Valentines Day'.)

Some of the many words beginning with mor, mo, mi, man, men, mel, mir, lun, lum, luc, lo and li are also associated with shining, reflection, mass, liquidity, cleverness, trickery, deception, di-vision, mentality, mania, madness of the mind, darkness and death. The Sumerian word 'lul' and the Quechuan 'ilu ilu' means 'a lie'. (See Loki, the trickster.)

The Roman god of death was known as Mors. (See mortuary, mort, mor, mordēre/murder, Mot.)

The references to 'dark' or 'black' have been historically used for anything seen as evil, sinful or men-acing to authoritarian beliefs, doctrine or power, not just because of the colour of a persons skin. (See Negro, nigra, nigger, Niger, Nigeria, necro, nigro, nekroun Moore/Maure, Mauretania, Moors, Morocco, Morion and Moroni.)

The visible colours of the moon are black (dark moon = mor-mon) and white (full moon, albi-mon/ albumen). These colours have in time taken over from purple (the colour of the Goddess and ancient royalty) as the symbolic colours of imperial authority. Go to the hub of a modern western city and you will notice the predominance of black or dark uniforms worn by politicians, government officials, religious clergy, clerks, lawyers, bankers, merchants, business executives, police, detectives and other people emulating the appearance of power. And what is the colour of official government vehicles?

White uniforms are also worn by some religious clergy and by the other priestly profession, doctors. The Chinese colour of death happens to be white. The colours of the ceremonial dress-uniforms of modern western military officers are black (or dark blue) and white, with a red stripe. The next generation battle-dress of combat soldiers could be black. Modern police are recognised by the chequer squares on their uniforms and cars. Many old churches and cathedrals have floor tiles of chequered black and white squares such as Westminster Abbey and the cathedral of Notre Dame. The same black and white tiles in chequer pattern are seen at Masonic and Templar temples.

The predominance of black and white as colours of uniformity could represent the increase in the strength of the power of the forces of division and the current dominance of the mind/moon.

Horned cows chosen as sacred to the moon in Asia Minor were black, white and red in colour, while the sacred bulls were preferably white to represent the full moon of fertility. (See Minos, Mino-taur, Nandi, Pasiphae, Mt Alban.)

While sitting at a bus stop in 2003, I happened to notice that the colours of new cars were mostly white, black, red or silver, hmm, coincidence? I took a walk around an electrical appliance store and noticed that the majority of the goods on sale were coloured white, black, red and silver, the same as the cars I had noticed from the bus stop, hmmmm, more coincidence? The flag of the NAZI Party is coloured black, white and red.

There is a jolly old fellow that most of us in the Western world adored when we were children. He wears clothes of red with white fur trim; big black boots, a belt with a big silver buckle and travels across the sky at night, just like the moon. The bad news is that the Father Christmas, alias Santa Claus was based on various characters such as the hobgoblin Pelz-nichol of Teutonic mythology (Furry Nick alias Old Nick) and the gift giving habits of Bishop/Saint Nicholas and his horned assistant Zwarte Piet. Originally based on the Hearth Gods that wore red and came down the chimney to keep naughty children inline, the modern day Santa is an invention of the minister Clement Moore who wrote 'The Night before Christmas'. The visual image was established by the artist John Nash in 1851. By the 1880s the image of Santa was firmly established and used later in commercial promotions like the advertising of Coca Cola in the 1930s and was subsequently used by many industrialists to promote mass marketing of consumer goods, boosting their own profits for the year. Not only has this jolly fellow been used to teach millions of children about the importance of mass consumerism and that material goods are to be associated with happiness, but he has also hijacked the celebration of the birth of the Son/Sun who rejected material wealth and wanted, as the Buddha did, freedom from materialism to be associated with happiness.

Was Santa Claus originally Satan Claws, also known as Old/Furry Nick alias Pelznichol alias Weihnactsmann alias Ruprecht or is the complete anagram Satan (Saturn) Lucas? (Compare Mon-santo.)

Santa Claus only appears on the last night of what was the old Roman Festival of Saturn, Saturnalia, which was held around the 17th to the 24th of December and coincided with the Greek festival of Kronia. It was an agricultural festival of drunken revelry, debauchery, feasting and gift giving. Saturn was also among the gods the Romans equated with Yahweh, whose Sabbath (on Saturday) he shared as his holy day. The 25th of December was of course the Son's day, the *'Dies Natalis'* of Sol Invictus, the *'Birthday of the Unconquerable Sun'*.

The Holly tree is the source of the wreaths hung up at Christmas to ward off the influence of evil spirits. Druid priests and witches from ancient times favoured the wood of the Holly tree for making their spell-casting magic wands, so is it no wonder that Hollywood is the place of magical illusion and spelling the future?

The White Lilly is the flower of death and funeral parlours and has long been associated with the night and the Moon. The lilly's white bell and its long red stamen are associated with fertility, the Fleur de Lis. It is a strong connector of names as you will see further in this book. (See Lil, Layl, Lilu.)

The fruit associated with the Moon is the Mul-berry (Moron in Ancient Greek; Morberie in Old English), which comes in two colours, black (with red juice) and white.

White animals were sacrificed to the moon gods. Doves, goats, sheep, bulls, and other animals were selected according to the purity of their whiteness and virginity. Blemished animals were discarded and only the purest (most clean) were worthy of being offered and given to the flames. This is why the colour white became associated with purity.

The Greek word for fire is 'pur', which later became pyr in Latin and fire in English, so to pur-ify means literally 'to give to the fire', or to burn an offering. This practice was done to honour and appease many gods around the world. (See purge, purify, pyre, pyro-manic.)

The Moon's attributed metal is silver, a white metal, second to gold, but not as perfect as gold. Tarnished silver quite often turns black. The atomic weight of silver is 108.0. (See Silenus, Selene, silver, argent, arguros, argurum, *'to argue with a silver tongue'*.)

The Moon is connected astrologically with Mercury the logical quick-witted communicator, trickster and patron of merchants, commerce, liars and thieves. (See quick-silver, Hermes, Thoth 7/11.)

The infant Hermes/Mercury stole a herd of sacred cattle from the Sun god Apollo as soon as he could walk, with a bit of quick talking he then traded his way out of punishment and became the messenger for the supreme god Zeus/Amon.

It is said that if a person has too much silver in their blood then the blood will turn blue. Silver cutlery was used as a status symbol by wealthy people (usually of noble birth). Having a silver spoon in the mouth for most of your life would quite possibly increase the level of silver in your body and help keep you healthy, as silver is an antibacterial agent. (See Blue bloods, Silver-solution therapies, Dragon of 'al Chem, chemistry.)

According to the Theo-sophists, the higher self of the Moon is 'Mars' the 'God of War', (red/iron = fer-ous), which represents a fer-tile (fer/pher = iron + tilious = obtain, Greek) masculine energy. The alchemical name for iron is 'Mars'.

The word fertile has associations with the old tradition of sprinkling blood from a sacrificed sacred king, sacred bull or a young male inter-rex on the cropping fields to encourage fertility. So gaining fertility is basically obtaining blood or iron since fer represents the red/rust colour of blood heamoglobin that contains ferrous iron. The name for iron ore is Haematite (from Ancient Greek, haima/heama = blood). (See ochre, milteios, miles.)

Iron is described as a whitish-silver metal that turns red when oxidised and is also known as the 'black metal'. A Black-smith works iron.

Fe is the chemical symbol for iron, which was associated with fertility and blood by the ancients. Compare fe-cund, fe-tus, fe-male, family (Femal-y? matrilineal bloodlines) and virile (from Germanic vir/wer = man), ferile (fertile). Note that F and W and V became interchanged in Anglo-Germanic words as in wolf and wolve, folk and volk, wise and vise.

Ferre/pher (to bear/carry) is related to 'ferry' in Ancient Greek. It was believed by some cultures that blood carried a person's spirit/soul and it is now known that it is the iron in the blood that carries oxygen (made available to it by the bodies supply of sol-fer) to the cells of the body. Since oxygen represents the essential breath of life is it a coincidence that the ancients believed that the 'spirit' was the 'breath of life'? (See Ki, Chi, Chiah, Chi-ron, spirit, spirare, respire.)

Charon/Ka-ron is the 'ferry-man' who under-takes the dead across the river Styx. (See carrion/caro = flesh, caries/ka-ria = death, feralis = corpses in Latin.)

The Theo-sophists believed that the peoples originating from the Moon were tall, long-limbed, had long faces and usually had a pale or white skin colour with dark or black hair. This could match up with the tall stature, long heads, noses and earlobes of nobility described in the mythology from Easter Islands, India, Egypt and South America, and the 'black-headed' founders of Sumeria who seemed to have appeared with their culture fully developed, presenting an anthropological enigma. Could the Sumerians have inherited their culture from a previous civilisation? The similarity of megalithic monuments in diverse locations around the world and the evidence of similar languages, art and cultural artefacts in areas of ancient settlements suggest a civilisation that had a global influence before the melting of the great ice sheets of the most recent glacial period. Before the ice melt and the subsequent rising of the oceans, there were many inhabited islands, cities and ports that are now submerged.

Up until very recently pale skin was highly prized as a sign of nobility or royalty as the lack of colour set them apart from lower classed people who had to labour out in the fields getting a ruddy suntan. (See rude/red, crude, redneck.)

Lighter skin colour is an advantage in regions closer to the poles as it aids in the production of vitamin D in low light conditions. Vitamin D is manufactured in the body when exposed to sunlight.

The Moon energy has been represented with an all seeing eye (NSA), an owl (ouil = eye), a crescent (meniscus), a pyramid with a missing capstone (imperfection), an obelisk/menhir, a creature with two heads/faces, the sickle of Kronos/Father time/Grim reaper, the horns of 'the heavenly bull', a hare or rabbit, a dove, a black or white disc, hunters of the night etc. (See Meniscus, Lillith, Di-anna, Te-hu, Columba, Janus, jonah, Ionah, Irene, Iahu the 'Exalted Dove' also a title of Yaho, the Native American Lulu = rabbit and Luyu = wild dove.)

In the New Testament, the dove represents the Holy Spirit (Anima Mundi) and is basically a symbol of purity and simplicity. The dove was sent by Noah to find land. When it brought the olive branch back to Noah's Ark it represented peace and an end of suffering.

The 'dove of peace' Irene was the Greek bringer of peace/death. She was also known as Epitymbria, 'She of the Tombs' that brings the end of suffering. (See epitaph, Pax.)

The Roman goddess of death was Venus Columba. Tombs were known as columbria (dovecotes). The spirit leaving the body after death was visualised as a dove (Columbus).

Father Time (Chronos/Kronus/Saturn) was an appropriate name for the Moon as most agricultural societies depended on the lunar cycles to keep time for their fertility rituals, planting timings and ultimately for their survival. (See Rhea Kronia, chrono-meter, Tehu.)

January, the first month of the year, is named after the Roman god Janus who was two-faced and stood in the doorway between humans and knowledge, life and death, physical and spiritual realms, holding the keys to the gateways of endings and beginnings of cycles.

To the Romans, Janus was the 'Keeper of the Gate'. In many traditions the 'Gatekeeper' was the teacher of higher knowledge who required students to totally submit/sacrifice themselves before they could pass through the symbolic Gate/Arch/Door in the ritual death of self 'to be born again' in an enlightened state. (See baptism.)

This theme has carried through to modern day religious beliefs and has been used by priesthoods and esoteric institutes to maintain their power by having the monopoly of the door to enlightenment.

Sheela Na Gig was the Irish representation of the cycle of death and birth. Her grotesque image can be found carved into the doorways of old Irish churches. Women were considered to be the true holders of the keys to heaven in Celtic Europe.

Could Janus be the arch-etype of the priestly Mon-archs? Has Janus been replaced by Saint Peter, the keeper of the 'Pearly Gates'?

The 'Holy Roman Church' teaches that Jesus gave the keys of heaven to the disciple Peter, who became the 'gatekeeper of heaven' and lets only the faithful through the *"Pearly Gates"*. The sign of the two keys (one gold and one silver) can still be seen in the Catholic Papal Seal.

Peter's original name was Simon, and the name given to him by Jesus is supposed to mean 'the rock', but the Greek word for rock is petros, could the name Peter have come from elsewhere? The name given to the 'opener' of heaven in 'The Egyptian Book of The Dead' was P-tah. Ptah opened the mouths of the dead with their 'pearly gates' of teeth to allow their soles to escape the body and enter the realms of Heaven. Jesus spent some of his early years in Egypt so he would have been familiar with this god. The teachings of Egyptian religions and religions from other countries were available to spiritual seekers in most of the Middle East. (See Pitr, Pitta.)

The Great Pyr-amid of Giza has been presumed to be more than just a tomb and was originally covered with 144,000 limestone facing blocks. It has been suggested that it may have been a place of initiation to higher knowledge. The king's sarcophagus could have been used as a chamber at the focus of the power concentrated by the pyramid's shape to enhance the spiritual awareness and astral travel abilities of an initiate through the gateway of simulated death (the Stargate?). The word pyramid apparently comes from the Greek word 'pyramis', the original Egyptian word was 'mer', which meant 'Place of ascension/transformation/baptism'. The word 'mer' can also mean water.

In ancient Egyptian tradition the word for t-omb is an equivalent of the word for w-omb, both of these are as gateways from one level of consciousness to another. In Quabalistic tradition 'Daath' (death) represented the higher knowledge, which could be the same as Daleth (doorway to the light/womb), the fourth letter of the Hebrew alphabet. (See Darth/dark.)

The Moon gods were commonly associated with death and the underworld as a gateway to transformation or purification of the soul through punishment and suffering. (See Hyades, Hades/Pluto, Purgatory, Hell, Fields of Elysium, Abaddon, Shoel).

The number 1 (odd) is a gateway to the duality of 0 the even number of the Cosmic Egg and 11 (the two pillars/gate posts) are symbolic of the arch/gateway of this universe. Two O's overlapped form the Vesica Pisces 'The Portal of Creation'.

The trinity of 1s (1-11) are representative of the Mexican Aztec 'Day of the Dead' which is held on the 1'st of November, as is the Christian 'All Saints Day'. (See All-Hallows day/Halloween.)

The Celtic Druid Samhain 'Festival of the Dead' also fell on the 1st of November (1-11) and is the origin of the bonfire and the burning of the human sacrificial effigy on Guy Fawkes Night. Guy Fawkes and his accomplices were Catholic agents working against the mainly protestant government of James I of Britain. They were actually hung up, disembowelled alive and quartered as was 'befitting all traitors' in old London. (See Gunpowder Plot 5-11-1605.)

On 'Armistice Day/Remembrance Day/Veteran's Day', the dead from World War 1 are remembered at the 11th hour on the 11th day of the 11th month (7/11).

Maybe the First World War that started in 1-9-1-4 and lasted for 4 years was in itself a mas-sacred festival of human sacrifice? (9-11-4) The trigger that started the First World War was the shooting of Austria's crown prince, Archduke Franz Ferdinand, by a young member of a secret organization called 'The Black Hand' (Mor Manus or Negro Mano or Dark Moon?).

The Second World War (World War II) started with the invasion of Poland on September 1, 1939 or 911939.

September is the ninth month of our current calender but really means the 'seventh' (septe) month. September/11 really means 7/11.

According to the occult Magi, the number 11 is the most powerful magic number, especially multiplied by 4.

The sacred magical numbers of Thoth/Hermes/Mercury include 7, 11 and 44. (See magic, magnet, magician, magnus, magistrate, major, majesty, and magistery.)

Most temples of ancient times had two pillars or columns standing at their en-trance. These were used to convey symbolic meaning and primarily to form the gateway to enter the temple. Phoenician temples originally erected one pillar of stone to represent Melqart (male deity) and a pillar of wood (the tree/plant) to represent Astarte/Asherah (female deity who bears fruit), who was also associated with groves of trees. At some temples the pillar of Astarte/Asherah was made of bronze for durability.

The traditional pattern shows that the pillar to the right as you would leave the temple is the masculine, and the one to the left is the feminine. This would represent the gateway of the joined couple (1 and 0, lingum and yoni) that brings the soul into the world as a child. So it appears that the temple itself is representative of the domain of the soul, which is projected into the world of matter though the gateway of the mother and the father.

In later Christian symbolism the pillars represented the virile sun as masculine and the sinister moon as feminine. This was in keeping with the beliefs of the Catholic Church.

The 'two of the same but opposite' is a powerful generator of energy as can be seen in electricity with the opposition of a positive anode and a negative cathode, to create a current. (See Anodos and Kathodos, Kata-holos, cata, Cat-holic.)

Two of the same but in different places exist with the symbolic erection of an Egyptian-like obelisk in Washington USA and the Obelisk in St Peters Square. Both of these stand in front of the Capitaline on the junction of a cross. An interesting feature of the Masonic Washington Monument is that its sides at the base measure 666 inches and it is 555.5 feet tall (6666 inches) a standard 10 to 1 ratio for Egyptian obelisks from the base to its peak. Both of these obelisks are not inscribed to the custom of the Egyptian monuments. It is also interesting that the pyramidal apex of the MWM is capped not with gold but a silvery-white metal that was more valuable than gold at the time of construction, Al-lu-min-ium. Why did the Alumni architect of the Washington Monument chose 666 as the number to use for its design? Could the Hidden One now have a seat in America? In the New Testament Revelations of Saint John it says that the 'number of the Beast' is 666 and represents 'the name of a man' or was it originally 'the name of man/moon'? The man-size sarcophagus in the 'Kings Chamber' of the Great Pyramid has an internal length of 66.6 inches or 5.55 feet.

To the early Christians Ceaser Nero was the great antichrist (Satan) of 'Roman rule' (the Devil) until his death in 68 AD, his name adds to 666 in Hebrew as QSR NRWN. The earliest found text of 'The Book of Revelations' gives the 'number of the 'beast' as 616. Was the Washington Monument designed by freemasons using the Sumerian 'Square of the Sun?' (36-111-666)? Sumerians and Babylonians used the sexagesimal number system (12/60).

The later translators of the 'Book of Revelations' may have thrown in the number 666 instead of 616 as a 'red herring' or decoy. Another theory is that 666 represents Babylon and the code number for the New Babylon, which was the Roman Empire. The context of 'Revelations' is very much in line with the Old Testament rather than the New Testament and may not have been written by Saint John. According to legend, St John was living in a cave on the island of Patmos when he wrote the Book of Revelations and the voice of God came from the *stone* above him.

All the numbers on a roulette wheel add up to 666. Many examples of famous names have been added up as having a numerical value of 666 including those of American presidents.

There are three obelisks symbolizing the trinity of the Anglo-American-Gallic alliance, the 'Cleopatra's Needles'. Standing in London, New York and Paris these obelisks are of Egyptian origin, carved from red granite and are fully inscribed. 2 uninscribed obelisks plus 3 inscribed obelisks = 5 (5 is a symbolic number used by the 'Il-lu-min-ati')

There are also a total of 5 Egyptian obelisks still standing in Rome.

Freemasons designed Washington City and its street layout contains the symbols of the pentagram and the compass and square. There are four main monumental buildings that form the points of a cross: United States Capital, White House, Lincoln Memorial and Thomas Jefferson memorial. At the centre of this cross stands the Phallus/Obelisk MWM. Is it just a coincidence that the US Capital building stands on Capital

Hill and that St. Peters Basilica stands on the Capitaline Hill? This is a very strange capital city for a nation supposedly founded on the values of Protestantism. The site of Washington was originally named 'Rome' in 1663 and had seven hills like it's namesake in Italy, complete with a river named Tiber, it was owned by Francis Pope. (See Washington Fasces, Rome Fasces, Fascism.)

The city of Astana in Khazakhstan is being reconstructed with occult symbolism in a big way; it's worth taking a look at its architecture. (See Kuala Lumpur towers)

For further research see, 9-11-01 & The World Trade Centre, 11-11, Stargate, Jachin and Boaz of the Temple of Solo-mon, the Freemason's Pillars of the Master and Apprentice, the Pillars of Hercules, the Pillars of the Temple of Heracles, the Pillars of Enoch, the Pillars of Edessa, *'The Two Towers'* by J. R. Tolkein, Endleoafan, Zero Point theory, 2011 and the Solar Magnus.

The Moon could easily be used as a symbol of the Father, the husband to Mother Earth and was regarded in Papua New Guinea as a woman's first husband. In the mythology of the Maoris of New Zealand, the Moon (Ma-rama) is the husband of all women. Rā is the Moari name for the Sun.

The words used for 'man' and the Moon are generally the same across the world. In ancient Egypt 'Min' was the name of an early masculine moon god and the moon god Amen was worshipped in later dynasties.

The Somali word for 'male' is mun.

In the East Sudanic language of Tama, 'ma' means male.

In Sanskrit the words 'ma, andro and soma' means moon, 'man' is mind, 'manava' means mankind and 'Manu' is the first man of the human race.

In the Tamil language, 'mantar' means people, men and 'mathi'means moon.

In parts of Africa and Asia 'mano' is used for man and moon.

The Gondi word 'manja' means man or person and 'Magh' is the full moon.

The Asian Yao people call themselves 'man' or 'mun');

In North America, the Squamish people of Canada use the word 'man' as husband.

The Indo-European word 'man' means man or human.

In South America, the Wanana word 'meno' means man, and 'manino' means husband.

The Kaliana use the word 'mino' for man and person and 'imone' means father-in-law.

In Guahibo the word for husband is 'amona'.

The Old English word for moon is 'mona'.

The Dutch word for moon is 'Maan'.

The Baltic name for the moon god is 'Meness'.

An Ancient Greek word for moon is 'mēnē' and the first human ruler of ancient Egypt was 'Menes/Mena'.

(See 'Lost Civilizations of the Stone Age' by Richard Rudgley, published by Century Press.)

The word 'Human' means any person of the human race 'hu-manus' in Latin. It could also mean in a humble way, those made from the soil deriving from humus (ground). The Old Testament tells us that hu-man was formed from the humid clay of the 'humus' earth.

'Hu' means 'divine word' in Ancient Egyptian. The Druids had a God named Hu, a famous hero of the Welsh people was named Hu and it is present today as the English name Hughe. The word human could have meant a handyman made from the 'divine word' as the word man is also used in reference to 'hand' (manus), as in man-ual or man-u-facture. Having a very developed and dextrous hand is very characteristic of humans, and the tools most essential for working and man-i-pulating our environments are our hands.

In Sanskrit language 'Hu' refers to the divine personality or god. 'Hu-ta' means *"to call upon, invoke or implore (the god/s)"* (Websters Dictionary 1913). Huta also means an offering, usually burnt.

According to the researcher and author Zecharia Sitchin, the Sumerian name for man was 'Lulu Amelu', which literally means 'primitive worker'. The Lulu Amelu seem to have been an improvement on the primitive Homo Erectus that may have been found on Earth by the Anunnaki. The modern word amel-iorate means 'to improve'; coupled with the word Lulu this could mean 'improve the mind'.

Loren Eiseley, a professor of anthropology from the University of Pennsylvania stated that .... *"man emerged from the animal world over a period of millions of years, slowly developing human features..., but there is one exception to this rule. To all appearances his brain ultimately underwent a rapid development and it was only then that man finally became distinguished from his other relatives."*

"Who forms Manu (the Man) and who forms his body? The LIFE and the LIVES. Sin the MOON." From *'Swayambhuva Manu'* (in *Manu*, Book I.)

Were we created in the image/zelem of Mano/Mas/Men/Menu/Menes/ Meni (Moon, mind, man) and made from a lump of mass? Did 'Lilith' (the beautiful 'Dragon Queen', first wife of Adam,) give Adam and Eve a Malus Pumilla/Melon (melon = apple/fruit in Ancient Greek) in return for her rejection for wanting to be equal and not subordinate as a wife to Adam under God's law? Lillith was condemned by God to roam the Deserts at night as a Screech Owl and Sucubus. (See melancholy, melodrama, melanoma, melas.)

"The Serpent of the Garden of Eden is frequently portrayed with the face of lilith....She was was often depicted as winged, with the body of a snake and was said to be the temptress of Eve". From *'Legends and Myths of India, Egypt, China & Japan'* by Rachel Storm, page 40, Hermes House 2007.

The apple symbolised the 3rd Dimensional core and the Hypersphere of the Fourth Dimension. The core cut width-way shows the pentagram and within it are the seeds of the future. The Hypersphere is said to be 26 times the size of the 3rd dimension, which was probably known to Pythagoras, Franklin, Newton and others of the esoteric trees of knowledge. (See Prisca Sapientia.)

Massa means lump in Latin and mass = moles = molecule in German.

Is the word molec-ule derived from Molec-h? Did Molech represent mass?

Molech/Melech/Moloch/Malik (the king, see MLK, Milcom, Milcah, Yaveh Melek) was a male-volent deity of the early Canaanite Semites, *"an abomination of the sons of Ammon"*, Kings 3:11:7 Old Testament, to whom they apparently sacrificed children by fire. Molech was represented in ancient times as a bronze bull-headed figure that consumed live children in its fiery bronze belly. Sounds a lot like the Greek Kronos/Cronus/Chronos aka Saturn, the father who swallowed his children. (See Satana-El, of Gnostic origin.)

Ammon was also the classical name of the Egyptian god Amen.

Molech was described as *"a Baal"* in the Old Testament, Baal to the Israelites was a word that just meant 'Lord' and was applied to any number of deities including Yahweh. With a name that has associations with mass, the moon and death, it appears that Molech was not really associated with the sun god Ba,al and that a 'Baal' was a term later used for any god that was despised and not approved of by the priests of the Hebrew god Yahweh.

Diodorus Siculus the 1st century Greek historian wrote: *"There was in their city (Carthage) a bronze image of Cronus extending its hands, palms up and sloping toward the ground, so that each of the children when placed thereon rolled and fell into a sort of gaping pit filled with fire".*

So Cronus/Saturn/Ba,al H-ammon/Grim Reaper is also Molech?

While the Romans laid siege to the North African city of Carthage, the priests of the city apparently sacrificed almost 400 young boys of the

Phoenician noble families in the manner described above in an effort to procure assistance from Cronus/Ammon. It didn't work, Carthage was flattened. (See The Punic Wars.)

In Numbers 8: 17-18, Old Testament Yahweh says; *"For all the first born of the children of Israel are mine both man and beast; on the day that I smote every firstborn in the land of Egypt I sanctified them for myself and I have taken the Levites for all the firstborn of the children of Israel"*.

The similarities between Cronus, Moloch and Yahweh are there because the Phoenician culture that settled in North Africa (and other tribes such as the Danaoi, Carians and Achaeans) were from Canaan, Palestine, Israel and neighbouring areas. These seafaring traders and refugees started colonies along the Mediteranean (such as Carthage, Troy and Venice) and as far away as Ireland, which still has traditions and legends in parallel to the Phoenician and Canaanite beliefs. Originally Ba'al and Moloch were not the same god, they were opposites, Sun and Moon, ben-e-volent and mal-e-volent, soul and mind.

"The Phoenicians could have carried Ba'al and Bel worship to the western and northern coasts of Europe. The Baltic Sea, and the Great Belt and Little Belt channels of Denmark, towns such as Baleshaugen, Balestranden, and many localities in the British Isles, such as Belan, and the Baal hills in Yorkshire were named after the influence of Bel and Baal worship" (Donnelly, 1949).

Ball Hill, Val Hill, and Baalbeg are examples of Baal place names in Britain. Baalbeg is a deserted village above Loch Ness in Scotland. Other nations and tribes from the Mediterranean also travelled far and wide.

See Bel-fast, Belgrade, Tribe of Danu/Tuathe de Danaan, Danmark, Danaona, Cessair, Brutus of Troy founder of New Troy/London (Fortress of the Moon)? Princess Scotia, Zara-gosa in Spain from Zarah daughter of the Hebrew King Zedekiah? Sarina apparently an old Phoenician port and mining centre in Queensland, Australia. (See *'A Brief Summary on The Sarina Sites, Central Queensland, Australia'* by Val Osborn, www.phoenicia. org and Rex Gilroy.)

According to the beliefs of the Mormons, ancient Hebrew people sailed to the Americas. A large stone was found near the town of Los Lunas in New Mexico that has the Ten Commandments inscribed upon it in Ancient Hebrew text. It does not seem to be a fraud. On the mountain above Los Lunas are traces of ancient ruins on a plateau with petroglyphs indicating the very important Hebrew day Tishri 1st, or Rosh HaShanah, of the year 107 BCE. (See 'America B.C.' by Dr. Barry Fell, New York: Pocket Books, 1989.)

The theory of the international movement of ancient peoples to the New World may be backed up by the finds of other stones and artefacts marked with Egyptian inscriptions in other parts of the Americas. The integration of Egyptian and Hebrew words into the old languages of the Americas is also evidence of Old World trading, expeditionary or migration activity. Some of the words used by the Algonquin tribes of North America and the Moaris of New Zealand have remarkable similarities to ancient Mediterranean and Asian languages. There is little known about the once mighty Opec culture of South America. Besides their impressive pre-Aztec monuments they left statues, possibly self-portraits that depicted people with distinctively African facial features.

Father Crespe, a missionary in Cuenca, Ecuador amassed a collection of gold artefacts brought to him by local Indians from underground tunnels. Some of the artefacts in this collection are inscribed with illustrations, hieroglyphics and letters common to the Old World civilizations. Depictions of Egyptian type pyramids are present and elephants even though they had been extinct in the Americas for at least 10,000 years. (See The Crespe Collection.)

Over 14,000 years ago people of the 'Solutrean Culture' ventured from Western Europe to populate the Northern Americas contributing to the establishment of the Clovis Culture before being wiped out by a great conflagration caused by a close passing comet around 10,900 BC. They left evidence of their origins in their flintwork.

OK, enough divergents, back to the subject at hand.

The moon was used as a symbol of 'El' the 'Bull of Heavan'.

El was the title given to Yahweh of the Semitic Hebrews, El means Lord and also meant 'The king' and `The bull', which was symbolic of the supreme deities during the Chaldean astrological age of 'Taurus' (approximately 4430-2270 BC). As the precession of the equinoxes moved in reverse through the houses or ages of the Zodiac 'The Bull' was banished. Mithra killed the Bull and fertilised the Earth with its blood (the same fate that was bestowed on most sacred kings of ancient times) to make way for the age of the Ram/Aries (approximately 2270-110 BC). During this period worshipping symbols associated with The Bull such as the Golden Calf, were severely discouraged. The Jews still use the ram's horn/Shafar in their worship rituals.

The Egyptians also changed their focus of worship from the Bull to the Ram. (See Aram, Rama, Rammanu, Ramesis, Theban Zeus with ram's horns.)

The God Dionysus was infamous as one of the sons of Zeus. His mother was Semele ('moon') although he was born from the thighs of Zeus with horns and had serpents for hair, restored Ammon to his throne, wandered about with his teacher Silenus (a moon deity) and a group of saters/satyrs and maenads, got drunk, went mad and committed many murders, maddened his enemies through mind control, became feral, terrorised the world into worshipping him and then sat at the right hand of Zeus with the 12 gods after taking Hestia's (Earth goddess) seat. Was Dionysus a chip off the old moon or a branch off the old bush? (See *'The Greek Myths'* by Robert Graves, Folio Society edition 1996 and Pentheus.)

Kronos/Chronos was originally a child of the Earth, a Titan/Gigas/Gaiant who separated the sky god Ouranus from the Earth with his crescent sickle (meniscus). Kronos devoured his children after he was told that one of them would be greater than he. As time went by Kronos was dethroned by his son Zeus/Jupiter (who escaped being swallowed) and moved further out into the cosmos to finally occupy his position as the furthest of the five planets. This planet became known by the ancient astrologers by the name of the Roman Saturn who was originally a god of agriculture, wealth and pleasure. Saturn became the satan to the Sun. To modern astrologers Saturn has two sides: one is dark, male-volent, restricting and chastising and the other is light, wisdom, effort and cleverness. Saturn the 'Lord of the Rings' was depicted by the Sumerians as a disc with a ring around it even though the ring can only be seen through a telescope. (See munera, Lua Mater, Rhea.)

Saturn's sacred number was 30, and in late Roman mythology was said to rule over the bone/grave yards. The Roman Saturn was associated in Greek cosmology with Chronos (Kronos/Cronus) the 'Grim Reaper', and 'Father Time', usually depicted holding a sickle and an hourglass. The Egyptians had Te-hu the Moon as timekeeper. (See hu-manus, chronometer.)

Lu-lim/Saturn, retained his double-faced lunar personality of teacher and judge. Saturn is known in Hebrew mythology as the home of the 'Archons' of Jewish mythology and has a peculiar artificial looking moon 'Iapetus', which was featured in Stanley Kubrik's film 'A Space Odyssey, 2010'. (See Hypostasis of the Archons.)

The Chaldeans, who once lived in the country that we know as Iraq (Sumeria, Babylon, Mesopotamia) knew our Moon as the masculine and most powerful Moon god Sin/Nannar 'Brother of the Earth', 'Father of the Sun' with his consort Ishtar. (See 'Genesis of Eden Diversity Encyclopedia' by Chris King.)

The sacred number for Sin was 30, his symbol was the crescent moon (meniscus) and his sacred mount was Mt Sinai. The sacred number for Saturn was also 30.

Judas accepted the payment of 30 pieces of silver from the priests of YHWH who were intent on suppressing the Son. The number 30 and the metal silver are symbolic of the Moon gods.

The Egyptians may have known 'Sin' as the Moon god Yah or Lah (see Yah-weh, Al-lah) who had almost the same titles attributed to him, such as 'Father of the Sun', 'Father of the Gods'. The earliest references to Yah refer to the moon in its physical form. Yah or Lah was introduced to Egypt and was mentioned in the ancient writings of Exodus so the Hebrews who migrated to and in time left Egypt could have been worshipping this God. Before the Isrealites left Egypt their god was also known as Iouiya or Yaouai pronounced Yahweh, meaning 'he who lives'. (See *'The Egyptian Hieroglyphic Dictionary'* by E. A. Wallis Budge and *'A Dictionary of Egyptian Gods and Goddesses'* by George Hart.)

"The mountains quaked before the Lord, the one of Sinai, before the Lord, the God of Israel". Judges 5:5, Old Testament (KJV).

The Hebrew word Halle-lu-yah or in Greek allelu-ia, means 'praise Jah/Yah/Ia', as Y, J and I are interchangeable as in IHVH/JHVH and YHWH (Hebrew usually drops the vowels). Roman Latins and Greeks used a V as they did not use the W in their alphabet, so Yaveh was the same as Yaweh.

The word Halle-lu was used among the Bedawi people and in Abyssinia as a salute to the New Moon. (See Briffault, v3 110.) The Egyptians also used the word Hallel as 'praise'.

Alphabet derives from the Greek Alpha Beta, which derives from Aleph (ox/mighty), and Beth (house/family) in Ancient Hebrew. Aleph is where we get the word Eleph-ant.

As you can see A and E become interchangable as in El and Al both of which mean 'Lord', mighty or powerful.

The invention of the first alphabet is attributed to an Egyptian named Menos (moon) but the origins of the alphabet may be much older. The alphabet we use originally had 22 letters based on 7 shapes (22/7=pi) our current alphabet has 26 letters and is based on the formal Roman Font.

The pre-Hebraic name for 'God the father of all things' was Yah/Jah/Ja/Ia and the original name for the 'Mother of all living things' (Eve) was Havah/Hawah/HVH (Yah's consort at the time). Combine the two together and you get (JHVH), which sounds very much like Jehovah

(JHVH). The word 'Jehovah' may have come into use around 1278 AD and was adopted as a new name for God in German Protestant bibles during the Lutheran Reformation in 1518 AD, spelt as 'Iehovah'. The letters Y, J, and I are as before interchangeable phonetically.

During the Lutheran Reformation, Martin Luther exposed the truth of one of the biggest scams of all times, the 'Indulgences' sold by 'Pardoners' of the Catholic Church.

El was the earliest name of God found in the Ancient Negev script used by the Hebrews, meaning 'Lord' or 'The Mighty', represented by the Bull/Ox head/Aleph/Al/El symbol, when turned around became the letter 'A'. Later inscriptions like those found on the 'Lachish Ewer' of the Late Bronze Age show the name 'El Yah the Ram' along with the name of 'Elath' (Asherah) as a female consort. The inscription on this ewer shows the Menorah as 'the tree of Elath' aka 'the Tree of Life' according to the 'Yah of Gat' translation by Harris and Hone, April 1997.

In Greco-Roman myths, the Moon was also associated with female deities. (See Semele, Selene, Dianna, Io, etc.) The Moon is associated with the monthly men-struation periods of women. Women were the source for the ancient monarchical revitalising ritual of consuming hormone rich menstrual blood (Starfire/Am-b-rosia) provided by virgin temple priestesses, keepers of the 'eternal flame'. (See mens = months = moons, Vestal Virgins, Scarlet Women, Vam-pires/Oupires = overlords, umpires, empires.)

In the Tantric tradition of Am-rita Kala, the fountain of youth springs from the Suvasini, the 'sacred women'. (See Kadru, Amrita. Dhanvantari.)

Could Lu Lu have been a model of the Supreme Gods of the mythological 'Silver-Age', including the Father of the Old Testament? Are we in the 'Age of Iron'/Mars, the aggressive aspect of the mind? Does the dark side (subconscious) of the mind keep its hold on power by hiding the truth and creating il-lu-sions?

The Moon, as seen from the Southern Hemisphere.
This image has been slightly adjusted to enhance the features.

THE EARTH

(Female energy, blue, wisdom, matter, body, life, symbolizing the creation of the universe and the integration of soul and mind energies).

From space, Earth appears as a luminous blue planet whose nature combines life and death, creation and destruction, the mother of all living things. Her names include Airtha, Apia, Anahit, Anaitis, Bhumi, Kali, Kuna, Ge, Gaea, Gaya, Gaia, Geo-rtha, Geo-rgia, Geomatre, Rhea, Terra, Era, Ertha, Hertha, Nerthus, Nana, Jorth, Sarpa-rajni, Maia, Maka, Maya, Mia, Pachamama etc.

(See gay, gaiety, Gaiants/Gia-nts/Gigants, geometry, Sheela, terrain.)

In astrology the Earth is represented as a circle with a vertical and horizontally beamed cross inside; in some ancient cultures the beams of the cross are diagonal. In some traditions a wheel with 8 spokes represents the Earth and Venus as Isis/ Ishtar/ Asherah/ Ashtoreth/ Astarte/ Ashratu/ Atirat/ Elath/ Sud/'Wife of the Moon'/'Queen of Heaven', 'Asherat of the Sea'.

The Earth's diameter is 7926 miles, 7+9+2+6 = 24 hours in one rotation, 1 hour = 60 minutes, 1 minute = 60 seconds, 60 x *432* = 25,920 years as the Precession of the Equinoxes. 2+5+9+2+0 = 9.

12 hours x 60 minutes x 60 seconds = *43200*.

The Earth turns 366 times (days) per orbit and is 366% larger than the moon.

The Earth is in what scientists call 'the Goldie Locks zone' where the planet is neither too far away from the Sun or too near, it is just right to support life and with the stabilizing effect of the Moon maintains a 22.5-degree pitch that creates a habitable environment for life to exist.

According to Theosophists, the blue planet Venus is the higher self of the Earth and the natural Earth peoples were short, round-faced and of darker skin colour.

Venus is the only planet in our solar system to scribe a concentric pattern with its elliptical orbit around the Sun: this is the Pentacle or Pentagram, the ancient symbol of feminine power commonly seen on tarot cards, which has been wrongly associated with evil, witches and Satan worship (unless inverted with the middle point down resembling a goats head). The Pentacle can be seen in English royal symbology as the Five Petalled Rose, a possible remnant of matrilineal genealogy. Many secret organizations tap into the power of the Earth and the Goddess by using the pentagram, which can also be a five-pointed star. The most powerful organizations operating as one on this planet are using the pentagram star as their linking symbol. (See Tudor Rose, War of the Roses, Rosicrucians, Rose Line, Templars, flags of the world and military symbology.)

Copper is the feminine metal, golden pink in its polished form. As it tarnishes and corrodes it takes on colours of the Earth: blue, green, red and brown. The alchemical name for copper is 'Venus' and Venus is the representative of Earth.

The word copper possibly originates from the Old English words copa/cuppa, meaning cup/container/cask (see cupa/cooper), which could originate from the ancient Greek words Copia meaning abundance or Kuprus meaning Cyprus where copious amounts of the metal were found in abundance. (See Cornu-copia, chalice.)

For Earth's soil to be fertile essential minerals must be available. Plants and livestock need a correct balance of sulphur, iron and copper to be healthy.

The use of NPK (superphosphate fertilisers) *"lock up"* minerals and trace metals creating an imbalance. (See *'Natural Horse Care'* and *'Healthy Cattle Naturally'* by Pat Coleby.)

The metal bronze (copper with tin and zinc added) is usually given the last place in the trinity of award metals that we use e.g. gold, silver and bronze. (See brass, brassy/brazen also associated with the female deities.)

Blue and green are the traditional colours of Earth. As seen by astronauts blue and green dominate the Earths surface and Earth has been called the blue planet because of the great cover of oceans and seas that our planet supports. The planet Venus is also seen as the blue planet.

Blue was the colour associated with feminine energy and was the favoured colour for motherhood and nativity.

Historically, until recent times female infants (Gai gürls) were traditionally dressed in blue clothing and male infants (Knave gürls) were dressed in red/pink.

Green was the traditional colour of Mother Natures's fertility. This colour was commonly associated with Wicces, Wiccas, Druids, lepre-chauns, faeries (fairies, Faeroes), and others living close to the Earth including Pagans (villagers/villains/viles), Pict-Sidhes (Pixies/Pictavi).

The use of the colour green was not popular with the early patriarchal church in England and is associated with a famous excommunicated and outlawed gnoble who was known as Robin of the Hood, a steward of the forests of Essex. (See *'Realm of the Ring Lords'*, by Sir Laurence Gardner, Viking books, 2001.)

The Earth has always been associated with the symbolisms of motherhood, the feminine force, fertility and the womb of life (mother = mater = materialis = matter, matrix).

Sometimes the sea is related to the womb (Mary = mare = mari = marine = sea/mer), which has similar saline qualities and the sea is where life on Earth is supposed to have originated. The blood of humans is basically salt water;

tears and sweat are also salt water, saline. (See Mummu Tiawath, Tiamat, Miriam, Meri-Amon, Merri, Merrow, Isis, Ishtar, Venus, Asherah 'Lady of the sea, the wife of El/YHWH and queen of heaven', Mulaprakriti etc.)

Approximately 70 per cent of the Earth's surface area is covered by seas; the rest of the surface being land. This is roughly the same proportion of liquid to solid in most living organisms.

Mary, 'Mother of God' also known as 'Star of the Sea' and 'Queen of Heaven', is often depicted as wearing a blue gown in Catholic iconography, reminiscent of the sea and holding the Christ child. In some artistic portrayals of Mary such as the 'Madonna of the Magnificent' by Botticelli, Mary wears a black robe with a scarlet tunic. These garments symbolise her original status of priestess and princess of the 'Royal House of David'.

Isis and other goddesses were also often depicted as a mother holding a child. (See 'Madonna and Child', 'Mother and Child', Sirius, Mama, Black Madonna and the Hindu Mari.)

In some Catholic iconographies of Mary she stands on the globe of the moon with a serpent embodied within it. The moon was intimately connected in all the Pagan myths with the Dragon, her eternal enemy. The Virgin, or Madonna is standing on the mythical Satan as the moon serpent/dragon crushed and made powerless under her feet. This is because the head and tail of the Dragon in Eastern astronomy represents the ascending and descending nodes of the moon, which were also symbolized in ancient Greece by the two serpents.

In mythological and religious stories the Earth Mother usually becomes the consort for the Sun as the Father dies or disappears from the story (see Horus, Oedipus). This tradition is continued in Christianity using the symbology of names: Mary Magdalene (high priestess of Dan) becomes companion to Jesus replacing his relationship with his mother Mary. It is written that Mary Magdalene travelled to and settled in Provence in France to escape the persecution of Christians. Josephus, the son of Jesus and Mary became the source of the historical Mero-vin-gian branch of the royal bloodlines. (See Tamar, Josue Del Graal, Merovaeus, King Dagobert,

Cathars, Albi-gens, Elphame, Sangraal, *'Holy Blood/Holy Grail'*, *'Da Vinci Code'*.)

Very ancient Europe did not worship gods; the first practice of worship was apparently centred on Mother Earth/Great Mother, the loved one who brought new life into the world. A being who could create life would have been held in high esteem by those in wonder of the mystery of procreation. As successful procreation was beneficial for the continuance of the genes of a tribe the mothers of the tribe would most likely to have been well looked after by the other members. The 'Venus Figurines' and Fertility Goddess figurines representing female figures have been found widely across Europe and into Russia possibly giving evidence of an ancient 'mother cult-ure'.

Women did not rule the matricentric Mother Earth societies as all were equal as children of the mother, but women were held in respect as equal to men, and men had respect as equal to women in power. In this type of society peace and equality were prominent aspects of life.

Ancient royal burial mounds of Europe, sometimes built in the shape of a woman's pelvic area and thighs seem to symbolize the return of the dead to the Great Mother's womb (see Norns Tump, Gloucestershire England). Many common graves from the same era have been found with the dead placed in a foetal position.

In the later eras of matricentric societies the culture changed from a no-deity Mother Earth culture to an anthropomorphised deity culture with the Sun, Moon and Earth given human characteristics. During these eras the influence of the Mother Goddess became important as can be seen in the worship of the Greek Hestia, the goddess of the hearth.

The broom became an important tool for keeping the hearth tidy and working, and to sweep the ashes on to the coals to preserve the home-fire when it was not in use. As women mainly used the broom it became a symbol of their magic. During the times of the Inquisitions, those that still worshipped the goddess Dianna were accused of flying with her through the night sky in her nocturnal hunting parties on brooms.

The Sun actually became less important than the Moon as the Moon gained status in its relation to women, menstrual cycles and its power to lift the tides, eventually taking over in its importance as the trinity of Hera/Eurynome/Iahu. At the same time the patriarchal cultures were developing among the northern horse herd (Cen-taur/Taur-ag) peoples. (See pre-Hellenic cultures of ancient Greece.)

The Moon as Hera the queen of the heavens and cruelly jealous partner of Zeus gradually dominated the matri-archal religions, gaining power through superstitions and fear, creating inequality and division between the sexes. It was during this age that the status of the men of these cultures was diminished to the level of subservience. The queen chose a new 'sacred king' (Hero) each year who was given a subservient position and could not act without the permission of the queen or the priestesses (see qena, kuna, kunti). At the midsummer festivals the 'sacred king' was ritually killed during the fertility rites and the next Hero was chosen.

Even though the Mare Priestesses associated masculinity with the Sun at this time, the Moon became dominant over the minds of humans, also showing itself as the power of the patriarchal tribes that warred against and eventually subdued the competing matriarchal cultures. The Moon/mind seems to play one side against the other to achieve its sinister goals of division. (See French Celtic La Lunada.) Femininity and Earth also has its dark side, for example see Tiamat, Sheela Na Gig, Hecate, Gorgons and the Hindu Black Kali.

Look for the Hittite Appu and Amazons/Moon Women (from ama/annia = female/mother?) who settled in Alb-ania and Lybia (an ancient name for the African continent). A-mason would also mean 'not masculine'.

In Albania some women still take on masculine roles. In Kanun tradition, women who become men are called 'virgjinesha', or 'sworn virgins'. Virgjinesha will take an oath (swear) to become a man. From the day they take this vow, which is sometimes at a very early age, they become men. They dress like men, act like men, walk like men, work like men, talk like men, and their families and community treat them as men. They will never marry and will remain celibate for the rest of their lives.

'Albania' is also the Latin name for Scotland.

'ANNA' is the North American Algonquin name meaning mother. 'Anatu' is the ancient Sumerian/Babylonian name for 'The Great Lady of Heaven', Anu's consort.

Columba the dove of mythology was universally associated with and sacred to the 'Great Mother' goddesses and 'Queens of Heaven' as femininity and maternity. The dove (Ionah/Jonah/Ityn) was sacred to Astarte, Cybele, Isis, Venus, Juno, Mylitta, Semiramis and Aphrodite. The dove is also an emblem of wisdom; it represented the power and order by which the lower worlds were maintained. The dove also held an important part in sacrificial and funerary rites. (See *The Woman's Encyclopaedia of Myths and Secrets*, by Barbara G. Walker.)

'The Great Mother Lodge' is in Queen Street, London. The ancient name for England was Albion 'The White Land' as the first view of England on a boat from Calais is the brilliant white chalk cliffs of Dove-r.

The goddess Brit-annia/Barat-Anna, the Akkadian and Phoenician 'Great Mother of air, sea, light and fire' is represented on the reverse side of the British (UK) 'penny'. She was depicted sitting, holding the shield of the 'Sol Invictus' (light and fire) and the Trident (sea), pointing to the sky (air) with her left hand. Britanniae was the Roman term for what is now England, Ireland and Scotland and it was Emperor Hadrian who first had coins pressed with the image of the goddess that symbolised the British isles.

Up until just recently in our history the Earth was regarded as the centre of the universe and the prominent view was that the sun, stars and plants revolved around the flat Earth. These were the views of the Catholic Church based on the teachings of Aristotle and Claudius Ptolemaeus whose theories were agreeable to scriptural interpretations. Galileo Galilei challenged the church with his view that the dogma of a geo-centric universe was incorrect? Galileo referred to the work of Nicolaus Copernicus whose book 'De Revolitionibus' was banned by the church until 1835. Galileo was imprisoned and persecuted by the church even though the roundness, size and atmospheres of the Earth and the helio/

solar-centric nature of our solar system were known and documented by ancient cultures many centuries before. (See Copernicus, the Map of Piri Reis, the teachings of Hermes etc.)

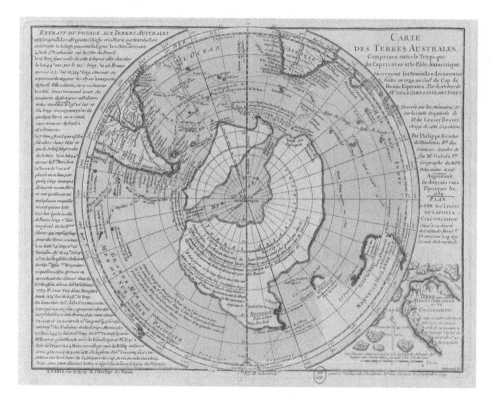

The Philippe Buache map of Antarctica, made in Paris in 1737, a century before Antarctica was discovered. Copied from maps surviving from ancient times, it shows Antarctica as separate landmasses, a fact not established until 1958 through ice soundings, but known to ancient navigators who may have visited Antarctica during a period of a warmer climate. From 'Mysteries of Forgotten Worlds' by Charles Berlitz.

The 1958 survey showed that Antarctica is actually a group of islands connected by a mile thick ice cover.

EARTHS PEOPLE

A surprising result of this research has been finding out that the peoples of Europe and Asia Minor seem to be related to tribes with common origins. Maybe the Genesis story of Noah's three sons Shem, Ham and Japheth (another Trinity) fathering the 3 racial types yellow, black and white-skinned was possible? This trinity leaves out the fourth skin colour Red that we associate with the American indigenous groups.

When I was still quite young I was confused about the colours that were supposed to designate each of the racial types, it just didn't make sense. When my fellow dark-haired white-skinned friends are exposed to the sun they turn a good shade of red before going brown (probably of the Mesopotamian Elvin strains?). I notice that those friends with yellow hair and white skin usually tan to a lovely golden colour (of the forest dwelling fair-skinned Faer-y strain?). My red-headed friends go red and back to white-pink quickly as they don't seem to have protective pigments so they may be of the underground miner goblin/Kobelin strains or descendants of Princess Scotia, whose people colonised Ireland and eventually settled in Caledonia/Scotland.

I also met people who have jet-black hair and very white pigment-less skin, which I am told is almost as rare as an albino person. White skin was a standard sign of Lords and nobility in many cultures including our own and was still desirable amongst royalty up until the last century.

Could the racial types have originally been categorised in reference to the colour of their skin? Or was it originally in reference to hair as yellow, black, brown and red headed?

If the colours were in reference to skin colour it would have to cover the four groups we were taught to believe about in school, white, black, yellow and red, and in church the three races sired by the sons of Noah having skin colours of white, black and yellow.

The Chinese are still said to be the 'yellow-skin race' but this is not true, there is a diversity of colours in the population of China. The Chinese saw the world divided into the cardinal parts:

North-black. South-red. East-blue. West-white.

The lands of China were central or Huang, which means yellow. China is known as Zhongguo (central country). Huang (yellow) is a common surname in China.

The Yellow Emperor was the legendary first Emperor of all China; his name was Shih Huang Ti (Huang = yellow, Ti = deity). Huang Ti was responsible for consolidating the 'Great Wall of China'.

The Chinese identified their Five Races Under One Union as Red - Han, Yellow - Manchu, Blue - Mongol, White - Hui and Black - Tibetan.

The races that supposedly have yellowish skins (xanthodermic) are widespread across the world and include Mongol, Eskimo, Peruvian, Hottentot, Quarani, Lapp, Turk and Ugrian peoples. These people have a skin colour more akin to a light tan or 'wheat colour' than what we would call yellow.

Among the natives of North America ('red-skins'), stylised medicine wheels are typically depicted with four colours associated with the cardinal directions:

North: White
South: Red

East: Yellow
West: Black

The original Shemite/Semitic people supposedly sired by Noah's son Shem: the Babylonians, Assyrians, Sumerians and Phoenicians were black-headed (black haired).

The Hammite people from Noah's son Ham/Chem, ancient Egyptians, Berbers and Tuaregs were also black-headed.

The Japhite people from Noah's son Japheth the Basques, Etruscans, Georgians etc. were also black-headed.

They all were originally from the white-skinned, black-headed Al-bin/El-vin family of Noah. So where did the yellow, brown and red-headed people come from? Could the yellow race originally have been the yellow haired race of the fair-skinned Faeries from Faeroes?

Where did the 'black-skinned' people come from maybe the Sirius system, like the African Dogon people? Did the author of Genesis get it wrong? Are the black-skinned people the original natives of Earth? Did black skin evolve within 6000 years from the bloodline of Noah's son Ham?

In "The Books of Enoch', Noah's ancestors had the glorious 'badge of priesthood' upon their chests, which could have been traces of 'scaly skin', the mark of the giant 'Nefilim/Nephilim', 'the shining ones', 'The Watchers'. It is possible that Noah himself had a patch of scales on his chest that he did not want his sons to see, from Genesis 9:21, Old Testament. (See Melchizedek.)

Hebrew mythology describes the appearance of the first men; *"man was of exceedingly great stature", "the dimensions of man's body were gigantic", "his body was overlaid with a horny skin".*

"The first result was that Adam and Eve became naked. Before, their bodies had been overlaid with a horny skin, and enveloped with the cloud of glory. No sooner had they violated the command given them than the cloud of glory and the horny

skin dropped from them and they stood there in their nakedness and ashamed".
From *'The Legends of the Jews'* by Louis Ginzberg.

Could it be that Noah came from a bloodline of humans that were interbred with intelligent reptilians from another planet as suggested by the mythology from Sumeria as translated by Zechariah Sitchin? In many texts worldwide, the rulers, demigods and priest castes came from a union of humans and serpents or dragons. The offspring kept some of the physical traits of their giant human Nephilim godparents. It seems that the Nephilim returned after the flood as ancient records describe humans of giant proportions or strength. Goliath is the most well known of these giants and most people have heard of Hercules and there were others like the Rephaim 'King Og' of Bashan who was said to have slept on an iron bed four metres long.

Enoch was visited by two angels/seraphs (messengers) of the Lord;

"And there appeared to me two men, exceedingly big, so that I never saw such on earth; their faces were shining like the sun, their eyes too were like a burning light, and from their lips was fire coming forth with clothing and singing of various kinds in appearance purple, their wings were brighter than gold, their hands whiter than snow." 2 Enoch 1:6.

The Aryan Hindu noble warrior Karna of the Mahabharata was born of the sun god Surya and a human mother Kunti. Karna was born with a natural suit of golden armour (scales or horny skin?) and earrings that were a sign of his divine origin. Indra tricked Karna into cutting off the armour that he was born with and *"..then it was given him a devastating weapon that could only be used once"* (a bomb?).

Did Huang Ti have golden scales too?

In Japan there is the legend of Akagire Taro whose mother loved a Dragon from the sky. The direct descendant was a great warrior of the Genji clan named Saburo Ogata, who inherited the scales of his ancestor and bore them with pride. Another great warrior with 'horny skin' was Ferdia as stated in the Irish 'Book of Leinster' in 'The Cattle Spoil of Cualnge'. (See also Sigurd of the German 'Thidreksaga'.)

Could it be possible that the people of Earth were improved, bred and educated by interstellar 'gods'? The idea that visitors from other places than Earth could have taught our ancestors technologies that were very advanced, is a popular concept, but is there any evidence?

Clay pot electric batteries containing electrodes from the Iraqi desert dated at 2500 B.C.

A small 6-inch model plane, with fuselage, wings and tail, discovered in a tomb near Saqqara, Egypt, dated to approximately 200 BC.

1000-ton precision cut blocks of stone in temple foundations at Baalbek that even modern engineers would find difficult to handle without massive machinery.

A gigantic cut stone stele base found in the Yangshan Quarry, Nanjing, China, weighing 16,000 tonnes.

Massive carved stone blocks found at Sacsayhuaman, Peru.

A 3000 year-old frieze from a temple in Abydos Egypt depicting rockets, airplanes and even a helicopter.

An aluminium belt in a Chinese Chin Dynasty general's tomb from 300 AD. (High voltage electric power is required to extract aluminium from bauxite ore).

The Ashoka Pillar, an ancient pure iron column in Old Delhi that has never rusted.

The 'Iron Man of Kottenforst'.

The 'London Hammer' found in Texas USA.

An ancient skull of an auroch from Russia that was pierced by a bullet? The auroch apparently survived the shooting as the hole showed signs of healing. Ancient human skulls have also been found with the same type of holes seemingly made by high velocity 'bullets'.

Artefacts from many thousands of years ago have been found in unexpected places like the 'Grooved Spheres' of South Africa found in Precambrian rock 2.8 million years old.

The 'Dropa Discs' (10,000 BC) that tell of a space voyage.

The 'Ica Stones' of South America.

The precise geometry of the 'Nebra Disc' astronomical calculator dated at 1600 BC.

The 'Antikythera Astronomical Computer', found in a sunken wreck of an ancient Greek ship. This machine employed toothed wheels of a fine clockwork nature manufactured centuries before the development of this type of technology was officially recognised.

The 'Giant stone balls of Costa Rica'.

The amazing mathematics and size of the Great Pyramid of Giza and the Pyramid of Cholula.

The ingenious engineering of Machu Pichu.

The elongated skulls of Peracus.

The mysterious skull of the 'Starchild' from Mexico.

The mysterious buildings of the ancient pacific island city of Nan Madol.

The incredibly precise stonework of pre-Inca architecture.

The accurately machine cut (?) stones of Pumapunku.

The mysterious great stone boxes in the Saqarra Serapaim.

A 3D stone slab map showing the ancient form of the Ural Mountains found near Chandar Bashkiria that was constructed using unknown technology. This map dubbed 'The Map of the Creator' may be 120 million years old.

The above are just some examples of technological and cultural enigmas from our past.

There are three massive stone platforms that have been identified as being possible places for the descent and ascent of interplanetary vehicles in ancient times. These are the temple foundations of Baalbek, Pumapunku and the Temple Mount (Mt Moriah) in Jerusalem. Babylon 'The Gateway of The Gods' was known in ancient times as the place where the gods descended and ascended to the heavens.

An undersea UFO base has been said to be responsible for the strange phenomenon in the Bermuda Triangle. According to ancient Sumerian mythology, the god Oannes/Uanne of the 'Annedoti' brought civilization from the Persian Gulf or Erythrean Sea. The Annedoti were amphibian and would retire each day to sleep under the sea. Oannes is depicted with a fishlike hat, much like the headdress of modern day bishops and dressed in scales. The Chinese Dragon Kings, the Lung Wang were said to be human-like dragons that lived under the sea. (See Dagon of Mari, Neptune, Viracocha, Mermaids, Moruach.)

According to royal historian Sir Laurence Gardner, the Gaelic word leprechaun, which is said to emanate from luchorpan (small body), is originally from the Latin leprecorpan (lepre = scaly + corpan = body). The Greek word for body is corpus. 'Chaun' is pronounced the same as 'corn', which also means a thickening or hardening of the skin, so maybe leprechaun actually means a 'scaly hard skin'.

Why have the records of royal bloodlines from ancient times to present day been so well protected and preserved?

Why do the royal families, the Jews and the Mormons keep an extensive genealogy?

THE SERPENT

According to archaeological evidence, prehistoric people revered the animals they were familiar with. These people revered the Bear, the stag, the bison and other forms of life that they hunted and admired. The most common animal that held an esteemed position in sacred lore was and still is the snake. The earliest evidence of snake worship found is in Africa (70,000 years) and Australia (at least 40,000 years) in the form of reverence for a great python. The snake is the earliest known animal to have been given sacred status. The great snake has been revered across the world in many forms and in some parts of the world is still an important godlike figure. The Snake symbolised wisdom, regeneration and the creative force. Snake culture is still strong in India, Native North America, South America, Aboriginal Australia and many parts of Asia. (See The Rainbow Serpent, the Hindu Naaga and the Hopi Solyalangeu.)

Snake worship is a common phenomena associated with widespread ancient pyramid culture of South America, Egypt, China, Tongatabu, etc. According to the ancients the snake belonged to the element of fire.

"The first and highest divinity is the snake with the sparrow hawk head; when it opens its eyes it fills the whole of the newly created world with light; when it shuts them the darkness spread over everything". Areios of Heracleopolis

The historian Sanchuniation of 1250 BC wrote;

"The snake has a speed which nothing can exceed, because of its breath. It can impart any speed it likes to the spirals it describes as it moves...Its energy is

exceptional... With its brilliance it has illuminated everything." (sounds like a comet?)

The word 'serpent' is generally associated with the word 'snake' and the word 'dragon', but are they both from the same origin and has the meaning of each word been adjusted for political or religious reasons?

The Serpent in Christianity became the symbol of evil, and of the Devil only during the middle ages. The early Christians, had their dual Logos: the Good and the Bad Serpent, the Agathodaemon and the Kakodaemon. This is shown in the writings of Marcus, Valentinus, and many others, and especially in *'Pistis Sophia'*, a document of the earliest centuries of Christianity.

Vampires/Oupires = overlords (upir = upper = above, umpire). Vampires would be a good research subject at this point with the well known Vlad (the 3rd) Drac-ula ('Son of the Dragon') who was a Voivode of Wallachia (near Transylvania) and Draco (Dracon = dragon) an Athenian lawmaker who prescribed death as a punishment for nearly all offences (Draconian means very strict, cruel). (See 'The Masters of the World' by Robert Charroux, Dusseldorf, 1972.)

In other traditions a cover-up seems more sinister with associations of reptiles, serpents, Saurons, krakens and dragons:

The Sumerian Anu-nnaki from the Dragon Queen Tiamat, Zu,

the Ubaid Dragon Lords,

the Pen-Dragons of the ancient Royal Scythian culture,

the Sauro-mata (of the lizard mother),

the Sar-matians (of the sarpa mother),

the Dragon Society of ancient Egypt,

the Egyptian 'Serpents of Wisdom' Djeheuti, Djedhi, Ejo,

The Royal Dragon Court of Europe,

the Grand Dragon of the Ku Klux Klan

the Dragon origins of Chinese Royalty, Lung Wang, Huang Ti, Emperor Yu, the Dragon King Ryu-wo and the four Dragon kings, Ao Shun, Ao Ch'in, Au Jun and Ao Kuang,

the Mayan Bearded Serpent God, Viracocha/Kon-Tiki, Quetzalcoatl,

the half human-Dragons of Greek and Sumerian mythology,

the half Dragon Athenian founder Cecrops,

the Serpentine Indian seven-headed Nagas and Sarpas,

the Mexican sorcerer Nagals,

the African Chitauri,

and the Mesopotamian Nammu all make interesting research for those interested in the Reptilians.

(See 'Flying Serpents and Dragons: The Story of Mankind's Reptilian Past' by Rene A. Boulay.)

The Chinese regard the Dragon as a symbol of wisdom and fertility, a benign creature. The earliest depiction of a 'Chinese dragon' was found in the excavation of a 7000-year-old Chinese Neolithic tomb of the Yangshao/ Huaxia culture. The figure of a dragon was laid out with mussel shells next to the remains of an adult male; on the other side was the figure of a Tiger. The same totemic symbols were found in the Zhou dynasty Zeng Hou'yi royal tomb.

An ancient creator deity of China was Nu Gua, a friendly half human half serpent who had the ability of shape shifting. She created humans from clay, taught them irrigation and tamed wild animals.

Another friendly serpent was Mucilinda the king of nagas who sheltered the meditating Bhudda during seven days of rain.

A Dragon is a reptile is a Liz-ard is a lac-er-ta, which means hidden/ covered from ancient Greek. (See 'Lac-er-ate' meaning tear apart/divide.)

In the 'Le Morte d'Arthur' by Thomas Malory, Arthur was the illegitimate son of Uther Pen-Dragon. In British mythology Arthur became the king of the El-vin/El-fin/Al-bin 'Ring Lords' of The Round Table/Circle of Knights after drawing a sword from a block of stone placed therein by Merlin. The 'Ring of Iron/Knights' was held together by the symbol of the marriage of Arthur and Gueneviere, the 'Ring of Gold'.

When the Ring of Gold was broken by the affair between Sir Lancelot and Gueneviere, it resulted in the disintegration and dispersal of the Ring of knights from the 'round table' and the return of Excalibur (Arthur's source of power) to the Lady Du Lac, the 'Lady of the lake'.

(See Modred, Mor-gana, Mer-lin, Myrddin, lake/loch = basin or lac, hidden/covered or occulted, Loch Ness, Mo-loch, 'Pater Coliavificit Artognou'.)

In the house of Vorsung during the marriage festivities of the King of Gothland, there entered an old man dressed in a cloak. He drove a sword into a log of wood right up to the hilt. He voiced a prediction that the one who could draw the sword out would be a great hero and then disappeared. The old man was Odin and the sword was Gram that Sigurd used to kill the Dragon Fafnir who guarded the golden treasure, the sword of Chrysoar and later, the sword Excalibur. (See the *Volsunga Saga, Durandal, Arthur and the Knights of the Round Table, The Hobbit, Jormungand.*)

In Tolkein's 'Lord of the Rings' he describes how the Sauron (Latin, Saur = lizard) had gained control over kings by giving each of them a 'ring of power' and retaining *"one ring to rule them all"*. This is not far from the truth as rings of power formed the controlling system of most institutions. The Scythian lords who revered the dragon lord 'Afrasiab' ruled with the formation of rings of council.

An assembly of Western religion is known as a 'Church/Kurche/Kirk', which apparently comes ultimately from the Greek word Kuros meaning 'power' or was it the word Kirkos, which means a 'ring'? Does this refer to the Papal Ring or the Ring of Cardinals?

In the book *Tragedy and Hope* by Prof. C. Quigley (MacMillan Books), he describes a secret organization founded and funded by Cecil Rhodes. This organization was intended to bring civilization to all backward countries in the form of the British Culture but has morphed into an extremely powerful organization intent on bringing their own form of ruling organization to the world. Prof. Quigley has described the organization that was based on the structure of the Jesuit Order as a hierarchy of rings within rings with round-table meetings. There maybe a ring that still rules them all; this carries the power to control mankind's future if the soul is locked up and subdued. This all-powerful ring only retains power if its true purpose and identity is kept occulted (hidden/covered). (See the Council of Foreign Relations, Bildeburg Group, Trilateral Commission, Brotherhood of Babylon, The Club of Rome, The Round Table, The Society of the Elect.)

The Red Dragon emblem of Wales apparently originated from Scythian troops conscripted by the Roman Empire, who were employed in and eventually settled in the British Isles. Scythian chiefs were titled the Pen (chief/head) Dragon. Scythian warriors apparently wore armour and the 'Phrygian cap' made up of small pieces of metal shaped like scales. These fearsome warriors could well have been described with the Latin words lepre-corpans.

The Scythian warriors introduced the use of the 'Draconarius' that struck terror into the hearts of those who stood against the Roman Cavalry.

'To lac-quer' means to cover or hide with resin - from rosin - the red/rose coloured sap of the Dragon trees; Lili-acious and Calamus Draco. (See Lilly, Fleur-de-Lis, Dragon's Blood, Le Serpens Rouge.)

Lac/Albin (see lac-tose, albumin, albino) also means Milk/white, which could also refer to white-skinned peoples, e.g. Aryas/Arians and Caucasians who originated from the Caucus and Arial Mountains. (See The Shining 'luculent' Ones, Albigens, Mt Ararat, Noah, Milcah.)

The Sanskrit word Arya (of noble birth), means the same as El-vin and Al-bin, El and Al means Lord, 'vin' and 'bin/ben' means birth/born of. (See vine, vini, gin, gen, gene, Bin Laden.)

Lac also means Lake, a bright red pigment made by combining metallic salts with cochineal. (See Mordant, Lacone, Lacuna, Lacus, Lactalbumin, Lac-e-de-amon.)

If only I had the records of the gno-mes, the ones who kept the know/ gnow-ledge. (See gno-sis, Gnostics, ledger.)

'Nomes' was an administrative term for sub-regions of ancient Egypt. Nomes were also government administrators and record keepers of the early Dynastic period of Egypt.

Lizard (saurus) could have also meant a Lis-ard (desirer, of sinfulness), or was it Lith-oid (like stone)? 'Stones' was a common English word for testes the source of male fertility.

Snake = oph-is, oph-thalmus = eye, does the snake and the eye seem to have something in common?

In Hebrew, NaHaSH means to see clearly, to find out, a shining one, serpent. In Sumerian the word Nachash meant one who knows or bears knowledge/wisdom. (See Ophion, S-ophia, Python, Boreas/Borealis, Typhon/typhoon/Typhus, Sia, see, seer, seraph).

The Python was the gi-gant serpent of Hellenic Greek mythology that guarded the Oracle at Delphi a virgin priestess seer who sat on a tripod stool in a trance breathing noxious gasses from a crevasse beneath her. Ancient legends tell that the Sun god Apollo killed Python and released the virgin Oracle and Perseus rescued the maiden Andromeda who was chained to a rock as a sacrifice and destined to be lunch for a sea monster. Here we have the basic elements of the present day Christian story of 'Saint George and the Dragon'. (See Acta Sancti Georgii, Mor Gewargis Sahdo, Indra, Marduch.)

The 15th century word sapient means wise, knowing or sagacious, as in Homo Sapient (self knowing or aware of self) and is the closest word I have yet found to serpent. It is of Late Latin origin and is supposed to come from the word sapere, which means 'to taste'. So what 'sapere' has to do with wisdom is a mystery, which is yet to be solved. (See sage, saga.)

The word 'serpent' did not appear in Latin until the 13th century and was not used by the authors of the Bible before that time. Serpent supposedly comes from the word serpere (to creep), which is very close to sapere (snakes and lizards constantly use their tongues 'to taste' the air), and is supposed to be related to the Greek herpein. (See herpes.)

Knowing the mediaeval Catholic passion for wiping out blasphemous ancient knowledge it would not surprise me that there is a greater story that has been hidden by this possibly planned confusion of words and meanings that requires further investigation. The Sanskrit word for serpent is Sar-pa, I think that this is the origin of sapere and serpere, but this is still to be proved. The Sanskrit musical notes Sa and Pa symbolize Earth and Sun. Sarpa-rajni (Serpent Mother/Queen, from the Nivids, Rishi Kutsa) was an ancient Hindu title given to Earth as the mother of all 'sarpat' animated or creeping things. (Compare Tia-mat, Sauro-mat.)

The Hebrew word NaHaSH is related to the name of the Vedic King Nahusha, who achieved a high status amongst the gods of India, but due to his arrogance was cast down and became a python, a beast of the fields. (See Mahabharata, Nehushtan.)

A parallel to this story is the tale of the Biblical King Nebuchadnezzar who becomes the great king of Babylon with God's help. Because he believed more in his own power he was cast down and made to be like a beast of the fields to display God's might. (See Daniel 4:33, Old Testament, Saddam Hussein.)

Nahushta was a Semitic serpent god and appeared as a bronze serpent on a wooden stake/staff ('stauros', 'Tao') in the Old Testament story of Moses and the plague of snakes (Seraphim) (2 Kings 18:4, Old Testament). Some Gnostic Jews worshipped the serpent god Nehustan for the first few centuries AD. They were known as Naassians, which means 'snake-worshippers'.

(See Gnosticism, Ophites, nehoshet, nehasim, Ningiszida, Wadjet, Wadd.)

Moses from mose meant 'son of' or 'seed of' in ancient Egyptian. The Biblical Moses was called Mosheh in Hebrew which means 'drawn forth' as he was drawn forth from the waters of the Nile river and raised up to be a Pharaoh; he was a renowned magician and prophet. He carried the staff of the serpent (Numbers 21:8, Old Testament). He received the serpent staff in the epiphany of the burning bush (Exodus 4:2-4, Old Testament), and the sign given to Moses and Aaron when their rods (staffs) were turned into serpents/tannin (Exodus 7:10, Old Testament). (See caduceus, uraeus, The Rod of Asclepious, The Staff of Mercury, The ASVATTHA, Musa, Mises, Egyptian 'mose', Thut-mose, Balagir, Nemo.)

Moses was instructed to have a brazen serpent made and mounted on a staff as an antidote for the bite of the 'seraphs' (Numbers 21 O.T.). The word 'seraph' from Hebrew, meaning 'to burn', has been interpreted as a snake or fiery serpent, but in Hebrew mythology seraphs are the mythical beasts having six wings and many eyes that guard Gods throne. The Seraphim are considered in Christianity to be the highest-ranking angels, 'the burning/shining ones'. (See Sar-aph.)

"And as Moses lifted up the serpent in the wilderness, even so must the Son of Man be lifted up; that so whoever believeth in Him will have eternal life." John 3:14, 15, New Testament KJV.

The 'brazen serpent' that was lifted up by Moses called Nehustan had been crafted by the Midianite miners of the Sinai deserts. This artifact was destroyed many centuries later in the reign of Hezekiah. (See. *'Genesis of Eden Diversity Encyclopedia'* by Chris King.)

A similar 'brazen serpent' was found in the ruined temple of Hathor at Serabit el Khadim on the Sinai Peninsula. This copper and gold effigy of a snake was also made by the Midianite miners. It is interesting to note that both Moses and Mercury were both messengers of their relevant supreme god and both carried the serpent staff. Moses is also famous for having been a Hebrew child who was set adrift in a basket, discovered amongst the rushes then raised amongst Egyptian Royalty. When the Hebrew people were enslaved by Babylon their written records were destroyed or left behind, they had to rely on oral history to reconstruct their bible. The tales of ancient Babylon may have been incorporated in Hebrew mythology at this time. The Moses story may have had its prototype in the Babylonian myth about King Sargon I. of Agade/Accadia who according to a tablet of King Nabonidus lived circa 3750 B.C.

"A curious legend is extant respecting this king, to the effect that he was born in a city on the banks of the Euphrates, that his mother conceived him in secret and brought him forth in a humble place that she placed him in an ark of rushes and closed it with pitch that she cast him upon the river in the water-tight ark; that the river carried him along; that he was rescued by a man called Akki, who brought him up to his own trade; and that from this position the goddess Ishtar made him king." From *'Babylonian Life and History'*, page 40, by E. A.Wallis Budge.

The word Reptile could have originated in the 'Garden of Eden' as Reptilius (Anc. Greek, Rep = rib + tilius = obtain/cultivate), the one who took Adam's rib to construct Eve or it could refer to the fact that snakes obtained a lot of ribs? Coincidences abound! (See Rephaim or warrior gods, descendants of the Nefilim.)

It is said in Genesis that when God punished the serpent he told him that from now on he would crawl on his belly, so does this mean that the snake used to walk on legs as a dragon or man would?

The Anaconda of the Amazon rain forests still have traces of what were once hip and leg bones.

Nowhere in the early Biblical texts is it said that the serpent in the Garden of Eden is the Devil. This association was not made until St Augustine suggested it in the 3rd century A.D., thousands of years after the supposed seduction.

Maybe the Serpent was actually a 'sapient', a person of great knowledge or wisdom, or a Dragon? In every continent serpents were revered as spiritual creator beings of light and fire, and bearers of knowledge and wisdom, far more than coincidence. The serpent may have originally been a dragon of high status that was then brought low or demoted to a low rank as punishment for insubordination. Such was the fate of Prometheus for giving the knowledge of light and fire to mankind or King Nahusha for forgetting his proper place. Maybe the serpent was the reptilian Anunnaki god Enki who gave the fruits of wisdom and knowledge to man and foiled Enlil's attempt at removing mankind from their Garden of Eden with a flood. Enki was known as 'The Great Administrator' or in Sumerian languge 'Satam'. I can bet Enlil felt like strangling his half brother.

The entwined twin serpents on a staff known as the 'Caduceus' of the medical profession, was also the symbol of healing and Enki the healer, serpent and half brother to the Dragon Lord of the Earth, Enlil. (See DNA, genetic engineering, double helix.)

Gnostic tradition has associated Jesus with the serpent that gives wisdom to mankind and the snake has commonly been closely associated with Sun worship in world mythology.

The Vatican's main hall is the Basilica. The word 'Basilica', originating in 16th century Latin, means 'King's Hall' from basileus meaning 'King', the same as the name Basil. The word Basil-isk (meaning a 'serpent') is a 14th century word originating from the Greek Basiliskos, which means 'Royal Child'. So Basilisk would mean a 'young royal serpent' or 'royal child of wisdom'? Maybe the Basilica was named in reference to the fact that the first Pope was not Peter, but Linus the son of the Pen-dragon of Britain, King Caractacus who lived under restraint for seven years in the 'British Palace' in Rome.

In 2170 B.C. the Royal Court of the Dragon was established in Egypt under the pharaoh Ankhfnkhonsu, which provided an institution to preserve the work of the Dragon of Al-Khem/Te-hu-ti also known by the Greek names Thoth or Hermes. The word chemistry comes from the word alchemy, which in turn comes from Al-Khem, the Great Work of the Dragon. The most famous books attributed to him are the Emerald Tablet and the Divine Pymander. Reptilian shapeshifters were apparently mentioned in his works although I haven't found the reference yet. (See Kemetism, 'The Book of the Secret of Creation'.)

Is it really possible that Earth was visited by reptilian-like humanoids from elsewhere, maybe Sirius the 'Mother and Child'? Or were they inhabitants of the constellation Draco who had very advanced technology and had passed this knowledge and some of their DNA on to the mammalian humanoids they found here on this planet?

Some unearthed figurines from the Ubaid culture are in the form of the 'mother and child' and have unusual heads resembling reptiles. Similar figurines were found in China.

The Dogon people of Africa have a traditional story that tells that their ancestors originally came from the Sirius star system. Possible proof of this is in the fact that they knew about the Sirius system having a solar arrangement of two suns travelling around each other, one of these (Sirius B) is much smaller and darker and is not visible to the naked eye.

How did the Dogon have this knowledge? Were they brought here as servants to the lords? Astronomers measuring the oscillations of the larger visible star detected the smaller twin star only a few decades ago. (See Dagon.)

In the popular science fiction movie series 'Star Wars', the wise elder and teacher of the young Luke Skywalker the son of Darth Vader (Dark Father) was Obi-wan Ken-obi, a Jedi master. Obi-wan continued to help against the forces of the Empire even after his death, a transition into another state of being. Was it just coincidence that George Lucas chose these names or did he want to preserve the knowledge that these names are connected with Sun, Earth and serpent worship, and are symbolic of ancient wisdom? (See Obis, Obi-wan, Obion, Obeah, Orb, Aub, Sith/Syth.)

Were the likes of Jesus and similar identities who were sacrificed for the sins of the world and resurrected actually students of the Djehdi mystic magi schools of ancient Egypt? (See Tammuz.)

Most of these people in addition to Pythagoras and Simon Magus, were apparently able to perform miracles that were also attributed to Yeshua/ Iesus/ Issus/ Issa.

Jesus was thought to be the reincarnation of the Old Testament El-isha, who also performed a number of impressive miracles including turning water blood red, reviving a dead boy, feeding a hundred people with a bit of leftover food, filling empty jars with a tiny amount of oil and floating an iron bar on water. (See the 'Book of Kings', Old Testament.) Reincarnation was an accepted part of church teachings until it was declared false by the Second Council of Constantinople in 553 AD.

Is it possible that the true Serpent, 'the one that sees clearly' is the giver of wisdom, light and love and that it is the Dragons from the sky that have had domination by fear and cruelty in this world?

Comets that have passed the earth close enough to cause fear and damaging effects were described as dragons in various cultures around the world.

If the Serpent is the one who could see clearly the true nature and identity of the Dragon then he would be a threat to the one who wants to have control over the Earth. The Serpent and his followers would be killed by those of the Dragon, but the Serpent who sheds his skin and appears to be reborn is a powerful symbol of regeneration and will always return. The poor old snake has received the brunt of human ignorance across the world with his head being bruised in mythologies from Mesopotamia to South America. How much longer will these creatures be made the scapegoat for the Dragon's hidden agenda of ruling this world?

Ouroboros, the wholly serpent of regeneration.
This design is based on an old German woodcut.

TRINITY

Before the movement of cultures who worshipped the patriarchal Aryan Sky Gods, the Trinity of the visible moon phases represented the ages of woman-hood in the Matriarchal cultures:

New Moon (the young maiden growing), Full Moon (fertile motherhood) and Waning Moon (the aging wise crone). (See Cronus, Crow.)

In later European mythology the moon commonly had three aspects represented as a trinity of goddesses such as the three Mo-era (moon phases):

"Diana in the leaves green, Luna who so bright doth sheen, Persephone in hell."
John Skelton.

Or the Fates of the Greek myths:

Clotho (the Spinner), Lachesis (Destiny) and Atropos (the Inevitable, who cuts the thread of life).

The Great Southern Arab Culture had the trinity of goddesses, who later became the Daughters of Alilah the Arab Moon god:

Al-Lat (the Goddess), Manat (Fate/Destiny) and Al-Uzza (the Powerful One, Moon goddess).

In keeping with the 3 females tradition Catholicism has 'Les Saintes Maries de la Mer' (the Saint Marys of the Sea):

Mary Magdelene, Mary Salome and Mary Jacob also known as Mary the Gypsy/Egyptian.

After the Mother-worship cultures had been subjugated by the conquering Patriarchal cultures the phases of the moon could have been reinvented to represent the three ages of man (similar to the Son, the Father and the Holy Spirit of Catholic belief):

The Son, The Father and The old wise-ard (wizard, see withered).

The Egyptians originally worshipped the Sun as Re/Ra and its trinity of daily phases as:

Kepri (the crawling dung beetle), Re-Heracte (the Sun at noon or Hawk) and Atum (the old lion or the old man).

"The gods of Egypt grouped in sets of three, and each city had its own trinity. In Thebes it was Amun-Ra, Athor, and Chonso, or father, mother, and son. Sometimes, however, they were arranged as father, son, and mother. In Nubia, the trinity is Pthah, Amun-Ra, and Horus-Ra, and these are the three gods worshipped by Rameses II. At Abousimbel the king also worshipped Amun-Ra, Horus-Ra, and Horus of Lower Egypt. At Wady Seboua; Pthah, Kneph, and Athor. At Silsilis; Amun-Ra, Horus-Ra, and Hapimou, the Nile. At Philæ the trinity the king worshipped was Osiris, Isis, and Horus, a group common to most parts of Egypt. Other groups were Isis, Nephthys, and Horus or Isis, Nephthys, and Osiris; and with a national love for mysticism the priests often declared that the three, in some undescribed way only made one person". From 'Egyptian Mythology and Egyptian Christianity' by Samuel Sharpe, London J.R. Smith (1863) ch: 2, p: 13.

The idea of a trinity was not a new idea for Catholic theology and the idea of trinities continued near and far from Egypt.

In the Catholic traditions the Holy Trinity appears as the godhead of *Father, Son and Holy Spirit/Ghost.*

In the New Testament the importance of the number 3 continued with

The 3 Kings visited the Christ child.
There were 3 gifts of the Magi. Christ was born to be God-King-Sacrifice.
Jesus was tempted 3 times in the wilderness.
Peter denied his association with Jesus 3 times.
There were 3 crosses at Calvary and there were 3 appearances of Christ after his
3 days of death.
There were 3 Marys and there are 3 virtues being Faith, Hope, Charity.
Jesus lived for 33 years and performed 33 miracles etc.

The New Zealand Moari's Great Spirit is a trinity of

Sun, moon and earth,
past, present, and future,
symbolised by raising three fingers.

In Hindu tradition from the Hindu Tri-murta:

Brahma (the universal creator), Vishnu (the sustainer) and Shiva (the destroyer)
each with their Shakti or female counterpart; Saraswati, Lakshmi and Kali.

Also of the Hindu religion:

Mitra (Sun god), Varuna (sky/water god) and Indra (serpent slayer, warrior)
and the Yaska's trinity of *Agni, (light/fire), Vayu (air/storms) and Surya (Sun).*

There is the ancient Naacal trinity of 'AUM':

Ahua (masculine, father), U (feminine, mother) and Mehen (the son, man.

The Mesopotamians had the trinity of:

Ann (father), Bel/Illil (storms, fertility) and Ea (helper, healer) of Accadia and
Anu (father), Enlil (storms, land) and Enki (sea, healing) of Sumeria.

In Norse mythology with Odin/Woden (see Sacred Oak, wooden) as the chief god, the trinity was *Woden (chief /father), Thor (thunder) and Freyr (fertility)*

(See Wodensday, Thorsday and Freirsday)

The Scandinavian Three Norns:

Mani, Nyi and Nithi.

PreAztec culture of South American mythology has the trinity of

Xochiquetzel (Earth/Mother) attacked by her daughter Coyolxanhqui (Moon) who is eventually killed by Huizilopochtli (Sun) the son.

In Buddhist tradition there are

The Tri-ratna, The Three Precious Jewels and the Buddha, Dharma and Sangha.

Toaist's have The Great Triad of *Heaven, Man and Earth.*

PreChristian Romans and Greeks had the trinity of

Jupiter (Zeus), Juno (Hera) and Minerva (Athena).

The Avesta of ancient Iran had the trinity of *Ahuramazda, Mithras and Apam Napat.*

The ancient trinity of the Druids consisted of

Yesu, Beli and Taran.

The Celtic Bridgit is threefold and there are the Celtic Three Blessed Ladies.

An ancient symbol of female trinity is the Tri-quetrais consisting of three interlaced vesicas forming the shape of the Power of Three or the threefold nature of existence; soul-mind-body, life-death-rebirth, past-present-future, beginning-middle-end and the creative forces of thought-word-deed etc...

Many of the ancient traditions had innumerable Triads, often a threefold aspect of the same divinity such as the Egyptian Thoth the Thrice Great Tris-megistus.

"Three is the mystery, come from the great one,
Hear, and light on thee will dawn.
In the primeval dwell three unities,
Other than these none can exist.
These are the equilibrium, source of creation,
One God, One Truth, One Point of Freedom.
Three come forth from the three of the balance,
All Life, all Good, all Power.
Three are the qualities of God in his light-home
Infinite Power, Infinite Wisdom, Infinite Love.
Three are the circles (or states) of Existence:
The Circle of Light where dwells nothing but God, and only God can traverse it,
The Circle of Chaos where all things by nature arise from Death,
The Circle of Awareness where all things spring from Life.
All things animate are of three states of existence,
Chaos or death, liberty in humanity, and felicity of Heaven."

From the 11th Emerald Tablet of Thoth the Atlantean.

The relationship between the Moon, Earth and Sun corresponds with the myths of the common Father, Mother and Son trinity. A few examples are:

Anu + In.anna + Enki,
El + Asherah + Ba,al,
Enlil + Ashteroth + Ish.Kur,
Sin + Ishtar + Shamash,
Osiris + Isis + Horus,
Amun + Mut + Khons,
Yaweh + Mary + Jesus.

Another trinity pattern that becomes visible is the patriarchal trinity involving the father and the two sons or associates who have characteristics in opposition. This could be a symbolic patriarchal reflection of the creation of matter from the singularity(1) of the one into the duality of positive and negative, Yin(2) and Yang(3), etc.

In Genesis we have the trinity of Adam with his two sons, Cain and Abel.

In Sumerian mythology it is Anu with his sons, Enlil and Enki. Enki had his opposing sons Bel and Marduk.

In the Hindu Trimurta, Brahma is combined with Vishnu and Shiva.

The Norse legends had Odin, Baldor and Loki.

One of the little-known trinities was described by the Greek philosopher Pythagoras: He divided the universe into three parts, which he called the Supreme World, the Superior world and the Inferior world. The highest was the Supreme World, a plane of subtle spiritual essence that everything existed within and the domain of the Supreme Deity. The Superior World was the home of the immortals who existed above the material plane but whose activities affected the lower plane. The Inferior World was the material plane where creatures were formed of material substances and laboured in the material world. This plane was the home of mankind who being temporarily of the Earth could rise to the higher planes by reason and philosophy.

Many more Trinities can be found in unexpected places such as nursery rhymes and old sayings like *"bad things come in threes"*, *"three blind mice"* or *"third time lucky"* etc.

EVIDENCE FROM
JEWISH TRADITION

The Judaic Traditions are extremely important for understanding the western religions, the nature of YHWH (God) and the true nature of the Holy Trinity. The Biblical Old Testament that we are most familiar with is an almost direct copy of the Tanach/Tanakh or Hebrew Bible. The Torah is the first five books of the Jewish sacred writings (Pentateuch) and tradition including oral law, the book of instruction, the core sacred writings of the ancient Jews, traditionally written by Moses under divine inspiration. The written law of the Hebrews as given by God through Moses is known as the Canon of the Twenty Four Books. There are other books of Judaic Traditions, the Talmud book of laws, the Haggada book of Jewish legends, the Midrash book of tales and laws and the Kabbalah which has within it three books;

The Book of Concealed Mystery,
The Greater Holy Assembly and
The Lesser Holy Assembly.

(See *'The Kabbalah Unveiled'* by S.L. MacGregor Mathers (1912), the *Jewish Publication Societie's English translation of the Tanach'*. Also The Abjab and The Grimores.)

The Menorah is the traditional symbol of the Nation of Israel, the lamp with 7 lights kept in the Tabernacle.

Menorah appeared to be another moon word so I had to take a closer look at it. It was originally an oil lamp fuelled with 'olive oil', but is described as a 'candlestick'. The word 'candle' comes from the word 'candere' (to be white). A maker of candles is a 'chandler' from 'chandelle' (candle) originating from the Hindu 'Chandra' (the moon). (See Chandelier.)

The word 'menorah' itself is supposed to derive from the Hebrew word for lamp 'ner' as in me-ner-ah, but this does not fit (and seems to be a decoy to avoid its astrological origins) as the central syllable is correctly nor and the beginning and ending syllables are not explained.

Looking back to Ancient Hebrew, the word for light is 'orah', which could explain the last part of men-orah, which is probably derived from the ancient root word 'ora'. The word 'ma'or' meaning lights/shining in Hebrew is derived from 'mah'ora' (moon as illuminator). (See ora-nge, aura.)

The first part of the word menorah is 'men', which could also be derived from the Hebrew root word 'mem' (water/blood/moon/chaos). There does not seem to be a connection here with the more modern Hebrew word for moon 'ya re'ach' (xry) until you look at 'ach' (x = kinsmen) since 'acher' (rx) = 'men' ('Strong's Numbers' 0312). The name of the city 'Jericho' derives from the word Ýareach.

Does Men-orah mean moon-light? Or does it mean Moon-Sun? The last part of the word is probably from the same root word that aurum comes from (aura/ora/sun/gold), and the original Menorah was made of a single piece of gold.

The central lamp (the head/resh/sun) of the 'yarek' (stem of the Menorah) is called the 'shamash' and was used to give light to the other oil lamps on the six branches.

The word 'yarek' (lunation) is derived from 'ya re'ach' (wandering moon).

Shamash/Sama was the Sun god of ancient Babylon, the 'servitor' or helper, as was Enki/Ea in the Sumer times. (See Utu, Sama-ritan, Chemosh.)

While the Hebrews served their time in Babylon (Bab ili) they would have been exposed to Babylonian beliefs and traditions that were handed down to them by their Sumerian predecessors.

"Together with Sin and Ishtar, Shamash forms a second triad by the side of Anu, Enlil and Ea. The three powers, Sin, Shamash and Ishtar, symbolised the three great forces of nature; the sun, the moon and the life-giving force of the earth. At times, instead of Ishtar, we find Adad, the storm-god, associated with Sin and Shamash, and it may be that these two sets of triads represent the doctrines of two different schools of theological thought in Babylonia which were subsequently harmonised by the recognition of a group consisting of all four deities." From www.wikipedia.com, ref; *'Encyclopaedia Britannica 1911'*.

In the ancient Ras Shamra Texts;

Yarikh was the Moon and Nikkal was his consort. The sun goddess, Shapash 'Light of the Gods', helped Anath in her retrieval of the dead Baal from the underworld and intervenes in the final conflict between Aliyan Baal and Mot/Mavet (Death/Devil).

Is the Moon of both genders? Does the Moon have its feminine side too?

The Hebrews knew the presence of God on Earth, as the Shekhinah/ sh'kinah. This represented the Holy Spirit, the Dove and the Mother Goddess mentioned in the Targun Onkelos.

The Shekhinah manifested to communicate with humans when God did not present in person such as when Moses received his instructions on Mt Sinai (Mt Horeb) through the burning bush and was told that God's name was 'Ehyeh asher Ehyeh', which is interpreted to mean 'I am that I am'. While man is in proximity to the Shekhinah, the connection to God is more readily experienced. In Hebrew script 'am' means mother, A is aleph, which means mighty/strong/powerful/leader. M is the letter 'mem', which means water/blood/chaos/moon. In East Sudanese 'ma' means 'male', in Sanskrit 'mah' means mighty and moon. (See Al-Mah, L'Alma.)

Shekhinah in the Hebrew language is a feminine term and denotes the female aspect of God's presence. The Gnostics considered the Holy Spirit to be 'Sophia' the 'motherly mystery of God'. (See Matronit, Maggid, Paraklete, Ruach, Shakti, Sephira, Saraswati.)

The fact that the Holy Spirit/Shekhinah is apparently female gives further evidence that the original Trinity was 'The Son, the Father and the Holy Mother'. The God Yahweh had female consorts, the Goddesses include Asherah, Anath, Lilith and Shabbat Hamalka the 'Queen of the Sabbath'.

In the Hebrew Kabbala, the lamps of the Menorah represent the 7 days of the week, the 7 eyes of God, the 7 lower Sephiroth of the Tree of Life and the 7 heavenly orbs that were visible and recognised by the ancient astronomers.

Each of the planets, the Moon and the Sun were represented by a letter from the Hebrew alphabet having a numerical value, all added in total to 1000 and each of these orbs had a specific colour e.g.:

Sun = Resh with a value of 200 and the colour Yellow;

Moon = Mem with a value of 40 and the colour white;

Mars = Yod with a value of 10 and the colour red;

Mercury = Lamed with a value of 30 and the colour blue;

Venus = Shin with a value of 300 and the colour green;

Jupiter = Kaph with a value of 20 and the colour purple;

Saturn = Taw with a value of 400 and the colour black.

The number 7 was a common sacred number among the early cultures of Europe and Asia Minor. The lunar month is divided into quarters, each having 7 days, and Sacred Kings were sacrificed on their 7th year of their reign. In ancient Egyptian religion the Menhorac were the 7 Moon priestesses that served the goddess Hathor/Asherah.

There are also the 7 steps (hall of the Great Pyramid), 7 Chakras (India), 7 Pillars of Wisdom, 7 Barrows (England), 7 Sacred Truths, 7 Hathors (judges/Krittikas), 7 Sisters, 7 Titans, 7 stars of Pleiades, 7 churches, 7 gates of Shoel (the world of the dead), 7 stars of Orion, 7 hills of Rome, 7 Tablets of Creation, Snow White and the 7 Dwarfs (Khnumu), 7 deadly sins, 7 Rishis etc.

To the ancient Sumerians 7 was the sign of divine perfection and 3 the sign of completeness.

Menorah

MOLAD

According to the Old Testament, the Israelites celebrated the New Moon 'Molad' Holy Days with a festival of worship (why?). Apparently the lunar calendar was held sacred to the Israelite God.

"The Molad is counted as the day that the moon is not visible from any point on earth. The moon is dark the day before and the day after. This moment is called 'the birth of the new moon'. It is the official beginning and end of the moon's cycle. The Molad or 'astronomical new moon conjunction', sometimes identified as the 'mean conjunction', is usually postponed during the year by a day or more, causing the Hebrew calendar to actually count from the visible crescent moon for their holidays." From *'Understanding the Jewish Calendar'* by Rabbi Nathan Bushwick.

Seventh Day Adventists believe that because most Churches of God go by the Hebrew calendar, which in turn follows the Jewish tradition of postponing the true 'new moon conjunction', these same Churches of God are also postponing 'God's true Holy Days' of the 'dark-moon' (mor-mon). The Sabbath and the Catholic Mass is traditionally celebrated on Saturn's day not the Sun's day. (See Sabbat, Sabbatical.)

According to Marcello Craveri, Sabbath *"was almost certainly derived from the Babylonian Shabattu, the festival of the full moon, but, all trace of any such origin having been lost, the Hebrews ascribed it to Biblical legend."* (See *'The Life of Jesus'* by Craveri, Marcello (1967) Grove Press. p. 134.) This conclusion is a contextual restoration of the damaged Enûma Eliš creation account, which is read as: *"Sabbath shalt thou then encounter, mid(month)ly"* the time of the full moon, the lunar month was started at the first day the new moon became visible.

The new moon and the lunar calendar is also important to the Muslim faith. God commanded Muslims in the Holy Qur'ân to fast from dawn to sunset during the month called Ramadan (see Holy Qur'ân 2:185, 187). The beginning and end of the month is determined by the crescent (2:189)

The Crescent or Meniscus

TREE OF LIFE

The ancient Jewish mystical doctrine of the Tree of Life is a chart of reality, including the material universe and its microcosm, the human body. God is the macrocosm the Macroprosoprus and his expression in this world is the Microprosoprus or man.

The Tree is based on ten sephiroth, stages in which God manifested itself in creation. Masculine qualities are placed on the right, feminine qualities on the left. They are combined in the central sephiroth:

The highest is the trinity of:

Kether (crown, central); giving rise to
Chokmah (divine wisdom, female); and
Binah (divine intelligence, male).

A gulf separates this supernatural triad from the lower sephiroth, which consists of:

Chesed (Com-passion, female) a constructive and loving principle;
Geburah (Ag-gression, male) associated with vitality, action and energy; and
Tiphereth (Aesthetics, central) the life force symbolized by the Sun and the heart.

Lower on the tree is:

Netzagh (Victory, female) instinct, passions, forces of attraction and
Hod (Glory, male) representing imagination, thought and conquest,

Yesod (Foundation, central) is linked with growth and decay, the Moon that links the Sun and the Earth.

At the base of the tree is:

Malkuth (Kingdom, central) is Matter, Earth and the Body.

Please note that aggression does not necessarily mean hostility or violence. Aggression from Latin ag = to/forward + gression from gressus from gradi = to go/step, eg. to go forward, as opposed to regression meaning to go backward. (See progress.)

In the Kabbala, the male side is compared with the 'Pillar of Severity' and holds the planets Saturn, Mars and Mercury. The female side is compared with the 'Pillar of Mercy' and holds the planets Jupiter, Venus and the stars. The 'two pillars' (and pentagrams) also appear in the Tarot Cards. (See also Prajapati, the Flower of Life, The Seed of Life, The Egg of Life and Pleroma.)

Before the Seed, the Flower and the Tree of Life came the 'Germ of Life' of 6 circles, which when drawn starts with one circle representing 360 degrees then the second circle adding up to 720 degrees. The third circle totals 1080, the fourth brings the total to 1440, the fifth to 1800, the sixth to 2160. Seen these numbers elsewhere? Is it coincidence that each of these numbers add up to 9?

9 times 6 circles equals 54, which adds to 9 the Trinity thrice 3 3 3.

The Flower of Life containing the Seed of Life and the Tree of Life.

EVIDENCE FROM QUANTUM PHYSICS

Most of us know the theory of the big bang and this theory is well accepted as the most plausible explanation for the creation of the universe, but is there a more plausible theory?

"Before the world was created, the Word already existed; he was with God, and was the same as God. From the very beginning the Word was with God. Through him God made all things; not one thing in all creation was made without him. The Word was the source of life, and this life brought light to mankind. The light shines in the darkness and the darkness has never put it out." John 1:1, New Testament.

A 'word' is sound (sund in Old English).

The sacred word of Eastern meditation Om/Aum is said to be the vibration of the living universe and the first word to be uttered by God to create the universe. The creation of the universe could have started with a resonant and continuous 'hum' instead of an explosion.

It has been known for many centuries that the material of the universe is made from different frequencies of sound; every atom vibrates at a certain frequency according to the material it makes up. Sounds resonate to create the music of life.

"One must examine the sounds to understand the tones; one must understand the tones to understand the music. He who understands the music can penetrate the laws and he who knows the laws and the music possesses the secret of life." Da Dai Li Gi, from the ancient *'Book of Customs (Laws)'*.

Modern scientists have only been rediscovering what has been known to Pythagoras and other teachers of ancient times. (See Atomos, Atomism, Democritus, Lucretius, Atomic Theory, Atum.)

"If you wish to understand the universe, think of energy, frequency and vibration". Nicola Tesla.

"Atoms are actually harmonic resonators, proving that physical reality is actually governed by geometric arrays based on sound frequencies". Polish physicist Andrew Gladzewski researched atomic patterns, plants, crystals and Harmonics in music. (See Cymatics, John Keely, *432*, sonic geometry.)

The first atoms of matter (mass percieved as physical) of the universe were of heavy hydrogen (deuterium) and then helium.

Hydrogen (hydro = water, gen = birth, born) molecules are the only molecules made up of the duality of two atoms.

"Water is the base of all matter," Thales (Greek philosopher, 624-546 BC)

"In the beginning when God created the Universe the earth was formless and desolate. The raging ocean that covered everything was engulfed in total darkness and the power of God was moving over the water." Genesis 1, Old Testament. (See Egyptian Nef/Neph.)

The hydrogen atom has 2 terminals, the electron + proton = duality.

Other atoms consist of:

electrons-----protons---neutrons; which have virtual particles called
leptons-------quarks"--gluons; plus the 3 forces of
electricity----nuclear*-- gravity; which correspond with
energy--------mass------ matter;

```
antimatter--dark matter--matter;
gas,----------liquid-------solid;
gold-----------silver------bronze;
soul -----------mind-------body;
sulphur--------iron--------copper;
head ---------chest-------ab-domin;
crown---------stem-------roots;
flame---------stone--------tree;
fire------------air----------water;
Sun -----------Moon-------Earth;
Son -----------Father------Mother, etc. = The Trinity Matrix.
```

"Three sub-quarks make up a quark and three quarks make up a proton (nine sub-quarks).

*Nuclear is divided into a duality of forces, the 'weak force' and the 'strong force'. (See 'The Higgs Field' as theorised and proven by Peter Higgs of the Edinburgh University.)

In the early 20th century two leading theosophists Annie Besant and Charles W. Leadbeater, predicted subatomic particles and their triune structure using 'clairvoyant vision' decades before scientists proved them right.

The duality of 'visible matter' and 'dark matter' permeates this trinity and can be combined with 'anti-matter' to form a trinity of matters.

Another trinity that is said to be prevalent in our universe is the interdependent trinity of space, time and matter. Space is a measure that cannot exist until at least two particles of matter exist and time is a measure that cannot exist until matter is observed to move through space, which also gives us the measure of speed, as speed equals time over distance. In this case matter is the only actual thing in existence since the others are really only observed measurements.

Our universe is 3D/three-dimensional depending on the expression of space as the three dimensions of length, depth and width of mass/matter. Time is supposed to be the fourth dimension but this cannot exist without mind memory and the observed movement of matter. Time is basically just the mind's record of the position of matter at any given moment. Time needs movement and a conscious observer and time is a point of view constructed by the mind of the observer based on experiential deduction of recorded events. Time cannot exist without consciousness and memory. Time is a sense, not a physical phenomenom. Speed, movement and mass equals continuous but timeless change if no records are kept. Like watching a video on a screen with a remote control, hit the pause button in any given moment and you only have what is now, hit the pause button later on and you still only have what is now. If no memory records are kept you only have what is now.

All physical form is made up from energy vibrating at different frequencies and only appears to be solid. Energy cannot be destroyed: physical forms transmute from one form to another if their frequency is changed, e.g. ice, water, and steam.

You are made up of organs, which are made up of cells, which are made up of molecules, which are made up of atoms, which are made up of quarks, which are made up of energy. You are energy!

"We are all made from 'First Generation Subatomic Particles', duplicating these are the 'Second Generation Particles', which are unstable and decay into first generation particles, but are replicated again by the 'Third Generation Particles'". Physicist Isidor Rabi.

Carbon, the main element of life forms, is formed within large stars from the precise collision of 3 Helium nuclei that become stuck together. The astronomer Fred Hoyle first noted this process in the 1960s: he found that carbon could only be made in significant quantities at certain well-defined resonances of energy from sheer chance. In later detailed studies Hoyle discovered other coincidences, which seemed to be a *"monstrous series of accidents"* and commented that it was as if *"the laws of nuclear physics have been deliberately designed with regard to the consequences they produce in the stars".*

Beyond the realm of physical particles it is calculated by physicists that a field of energy exists in the form of 3 layers of wave frequencies forming a woven matrix of crossing ripples that forms the fluid that permeates and suspends the entire universe of matter. This concept was symbolised in world mythologies as the Spider/Arachne. (See web, weft, warp, weave, wave and The Gauge Field Theory, Max Planck.)

Where flows of hydrogen cross, Suns are born.

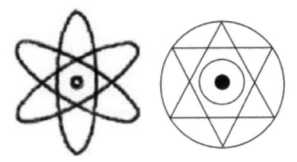

More stuff to think about.

There are 3 basic colours within our visible spectrum.

Yellow (spiritual), red (aggressive) and blue (passive).

Mixed in the correct proportions become:

Yellow + red + blue = brown, (the average colour of animals, including humans);
Yellow + blue = green, (the average colour of plants);
Yellow + red = orange, (aurum, gold, saffron, Eastern spirituality); and
Red + blue = purple, (monarchs, priests, merchants, emperors).

There are 3 main parts to an animal e.g. head, chest and abdomen, which corresponds with a plants crown, stem and roots. The Head is usually thought of as the main centre of sensual perception and nutritional intake, the chest contains the pumping mechanisms, and the ab-domin absorbs fluid and nutrients. Considering that the Sun is our main source of energy as light, the Moon has a lifting effect on liquids and the Earth supplies our fluids and nutrients there could be a pattern in progress here.

The ancient text of the Ayur-veda ('science of life') teaches that the human form is made up of the trinity of Doshas or mind body principles. According to Ayurvedic teachings the balancing of these three principles is necessary for the healing of the body, mind and spirit and the return to wholeness.

The trinity of Doshas:

Vata, representing... movement, energy and spirit.
Pitta, representing... transformation, change and mind.
Kapha, representing... structure, order and body.

According to Bhuddist belief there are three levels of mind:

Mano Vijnana the Individual Discriminating Mind.
Manas the Intuitive Mind.
Alaya Vijnana the Universal Mind.

Within all living beings, all three energies (soul, mind, body) need to be balanced for the being to be healthy, and so it should be with a whole society. A dominance of one energy force can lead to dis-ease, stress and an imbalance.

1+0+8 equals 9 which is a 3x multiple of 3 the number representing The Supreme Balance which is 3 3 3 a trinity of trinities. In Hindu belief the number 108 is auspiciously important. 108 is a 3 figure multiple of 3x36. 108 is represented in the 'japa mala' or string of 108 beads worn by devotees reciting the 108 names of God and chanting The Gayatri Mantra and is the forerunner of the 'Rosary'.

Why is it that our theologians refer to the western religious system as mono-theism instead of solo-theism since mono and solo are supposed to mean exactly the same thing?

Why do we have mona-steries instead of sola-steries? Because the Moon (mind) rules, O.K.? (See Mona/Monas, which means 'moon' in Old English.)

The word 'monastery' could have originated from a place or observatory dedicated to studying the moon and stars/asters, as in mona-aster-y? Yes its mona not mono, please take a look. According to the authorities the word monastery originates from the Latin word monasterium from the Greek word mon-azein, which supposedly means 'to live alone' (in a monastery aloneness is rare). However, the Greek word azein is supposed to mean 'hard to breathe' and zein means 'grain'. 'Hmm', is this meant to be another cover-up or what?

The female equivalent of a monastery is a convent from the Latin word 'conventus', which means 'to be together', related to convention.

The first recorded mono-theistic or I should say 'solo-theistic' religion was founded by the rebellious Egyptian Pharaoh Aakhun-aten, 'the Son of God/Aten'. Aakhunaten shunned the worship of Amen and the mass of lesser gods, establishing an arcadian religion dedicated to the one-god. His son in law Tut-ankh-aten gave-in to the priests of Amen and restored the pantheon of the 2000 gods, renaming himself Tutankhamen.

The name of the Biblical King Solo-mon could mean the 'one-moon', 'one-mind', 'one-god' or 'sun-moon'. The seal of Solomon (Star of David) is made of two overlapping triangles. One is pointing up, the other is pointing down, this can be given many meanings such as *"as above, so below"* or the representation of the duality of the masculine (up/sword/lingam) and the feminine (down/cup/yoni) as in Hindu tradition. In Bhuddist tradition this is the Dharmadaya, the six pointed Chakra.

Leonardo da Vinci apparently used Old English as a code to hide the true meanings of some of his words from the authorities who were more familiar with Latin. In light of this, Mona Lisa could mean desirous or desirable Moon. Mona means moon (masculine) and Lisa could be read as Lis-a or L'ISA.

Lis and list (from the Old English *lystan*) are words for desire or sexual passion derived from an old agricultural term 'list' meaning a ridge raised with a plough or the act of raising a ridge while ploughing. In ancient times, ploughing the earth was associated with sexual penetration of the earth with the plough to fertilise and seed the soil. A 'list' of words resembles the straight lines of furrows in a ploughed field. (See list, lis-some, list-less, lis-ard, Fleur de Lis, lust.)

The astral or emotional body stays connected to the physical body for 3 days after death. There is scientific evidence that the brain, even when all other systems are failing takes 3 days to register complete shutdown.

The Trinities are essential for the universe to exist! All parts are not and never can be evil; all is God, all is Good. The concept of evil and sin are human inventions and are only committed by humans.

As the Ancients knew, there is neither good nor bad qualities inherent to the parts of these Trinities, they are merely functional in maintaining the existence of the universe and life. Just like the parts of a machine, everything has a part in the great play. It is the disharmony of these forces that is perceived as destructive. Balance is essential even though the concentration of energies seem to ebb and flow in a dance of the universe.

The human mind is powerful and the concentration of thought in one direction only, can topple the three-legged stool we are all sitting on.

The ancient Greeks knew far more than what we give them credit for and they made an attempt to pass on their knowledge through a vast educational campus in Alexandria, Egypt. It stood for hundreds of years before succumbing to destruction through ignorance and fear by the speakers of Latin.

The first burning of the Great Library of Alexandria occurred when Julius Caesar burned the ships in the harbour while fighting against the army commanded by Cleopatra's brother. The fire spread through part of the city where the library stood and caused extensive accidental damage. Catholic zealots led by Bishop Theophilus in AD 391 on the orders of Emperor Theodosius, carried out the final and intentional burning of 'heretical works' representing thousands of years of knowledge and art. It is said that this destruction allowed the Church to hide the true history of mankind.

Maybe the Great Library of Alexandria and all its stored knowledge was burnt to hide the truth or thwart 'Yetzer harah' 'the sin of knowing'/free will, from the Kabalah? (See Abjad, Grimores.)

I think that if you research the Trinity pattern yourself you will see all the connections and discover more.

Following is a montage of extracts from religious, scientific, mythological and many other types of books (too numerous to give references as yet) put together as one theory...

Tri-quetrais

TRINITY OF EXISTENCE

Religious stories are probably models of the original pattern of creation.

Religious figures and heroes may have existed physically as the original pattern expresses itself throughout the universe.

The combining of religious stories and the models used to explain the original pattern has caused a knotted mass of false information, false gods, false beliefs, destructive actions, pain, grief, guilt and fear.

Stripped to the bone, these leave the original pattern, which can be expressed as:

Pole 1. + Pole 2. = The Field 3.

1. Consciousness + Thought = CREATION
(awareness)

2. Truth + Lie = PERSISTANCE
(communication)

3. Static + Motion = ENERGY/MASS/MATTER
(action)

That is: 2 poles (terminals), similar in nature, but opposite, having a state of tension = CREATE + PERSIST = ENERGY/MASS/MATTER

(The original trinity?)

The DUALITY could be the energy-flows to and from the opposing poles (terminals) and having the qualities of repulsion plus attraction, which would result in a state of tension...

REPULSION + ATTRACTION = TENSION.

The combination of this Trinity and the Duality could be imagined as a triptych formation consisting of two poles held in tension by a double-helix with a circular or egg-shaped field between them (you can see similar patterns in the towers and domes of sacred architecture and as towers and circles in cathedrals and mosques).

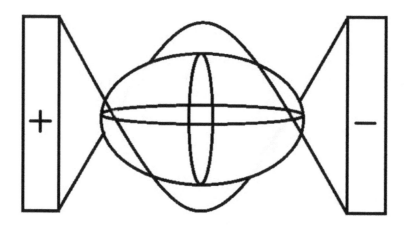

Pole 1 (Soul?) represents a manifestation of the original, the thought potential, Consciousness. It was probably static, stable, with no movement, continuously true until thought occurred.

Pole 2 (Mind?) represents the thought (concept) and could be the result of an effort by the Consciousness to be conscious of itself by making a thought image of itself. A thought could have been made to create a thought-place, a likeness of Consciousness, to observe the original thought-place/ Consciousness. Conscious mind is paired with its other polarity, the subconscious mind that binds mind with the illusion of mass and matter.

To hold the two poles apart there had to be a difference, an alteration, as they would be both occupying the same space. Accordingly, two forms cannot occupy the same space at the same time, as they become one. The difference had to be enough to keep the two apart, e.g., an error or lie, a difference of polarity. (See Christian Science, Quantum Physics, matter/antimatter, quasi-matter, the Looking-glass Theory.)

The Field 3 (Body, the Ovo?) represents the creation, a full spectrum of energy frequencies (e.g. notes) of matter in all dimensions (e.g. octaves). The creation contains the purest energy to the densest matter, space and life (universe, uni = one + verse = a turning or 'one sound', Om).

The Double Spiral (helix) represents the flow of energy to and from the poles. The flow of energy passing through the field of creation from column 1 starts out as the purest energy and gradually condenses into dense matter as it approaches pole 2.

The energy from pole 2 is probably released from matter into its pure form, which then flows back to pole 1. These two flows of energy could represent the two types of emotional flows present in humans and other living beings: emotions of attraction (e.g., love and compassion) and emotions of repulsion (e.g., fear and anger). The flows of energy work together to create static tension that holds matter in its form and space in what physicists call the 'fabric of space'.

Mass is, just a form. It is energy taking any form such as light, electricity, radio waves or any denser material in various volumes and frequencies. As a being accumulates experiences they are recorded and held as patterns of energy/mass forms/memory. Energy/mass forms can also manifest as emotion. Mass is energy in motion (E/energy + Motion = emotion).

Matter is energy condensed to exist as a perceived solid in the 3rd dimension. When quasi-particles come into the 3rd dimension they come through as pairs of positrons and electrons, mass becomes matter.

Energy can be released from the state of matter. Matter can be brought back to energy if it becomes stilled, as in the combining of a positron and an electron (the combining of 2 through the gateway of 1), which wholly transforms them into energy '0' which is in itself a duality (see 'Zero Point'). This is the type of event that could occur in the crushing effect of black-holes. The only thing that escapes black-holes is energy/mass below the frequency of visible light. This means that black-holes could be like huge recycling units sucking in debris and converting the matter back into energy-mass waves.

E/energy = MC2/mass or the energy contained within any object can be measured by it's mass times the square of the speed of light (speed of light =186,624 =*432* squared). (See Albert Einstein's 'Theory of General Relativity' and the 'Theory Of Special Relativity' and Wave Particle Duality.)

MATTER IS A PRODUCT OF THOUGHT?

It has often been said to me *"If a thought is made it will attract what is thought of"*. It is well known that a person becomes what they believe themselves to be, or will attract situations according to their thoughts. A living being consists of matter plus thought-consciousness.

In the old texts Enoch (Noah's ancestor) was lifted up to heaven and was told to write down the '64 Keys of Knowledge' of the Elohim in his own handwriting to take back to Earth. To preserve the knowledge Enoch engraved the information onto the 'Pillars of Enoch', two obelisks male and female erected in the valley of Sidhim. In time, the two pillars were lost but part of the knowledge was preserved on one of The Emerald Tablets. This carried the information about the Universal Law of Attraction, which has been handed down through the ages to those who became most wealthy elite leaders and scientists of history. The information is now available for all who wish to see it, even though it has been suppressed in the past. (See *'The Master Key System'* by Charles Harnold.)

Another view of divine knowledge;

"These ancient mysteries were originally given to humanity by the Hierarchy, and were–in their turn–received by the Hierarchy from the Great White Lodge on Sirius. They contain the clue to the evolutionary process, hidden in number and words...They veil the secret of man's origin and destiny." - Alice Bailey, *'The Rays and the Initiation'* New York: Lucis Publishing Co., 1955.

Thought-consciousness (being/soul) is separate from matter and will not conform to the laws of the physical universe unless it believes it is of the physical universe (believing it is matter).

"I rightly conclude that my essence consists in this alone, that I am a thinking thing... and although perhaps ... I have a body with which I am closely conjoined, I have, on the one hand, a clear and distinct idea of myself as a thinking, non-extended thing, and, on the other hand, a distinct idea of my body as an extended thing; it is therefore certain that I am truly distinct from my body, and can exist without it." Descartes *'Meditations'*.

If an individual being can affirm that it is thought-consciousness then that individual might have the choice of being in a physical body (in-carnate) in one form or another, or not being in a body (dis-incarnate), mind over matter.

The old view of the action of matter in the universe was established by the great mathematician and scientist Sir Isaac Newton as being like a big clockwork mechanism. His system followed set rules, however he did recognise that there was a supreme intelligence that he called 'The Grand Architect'. Newton worked on the theory that the universe is set out and constructed to mathematical formulas, described this Being as 'The Grand Architect' after he was astounded by the regularity of his research results. Sir Isaac Newton is best known for his recognition of the force of gravity.

Modern scientists such as the great physicists Albert Einstien and Niels Bohr realised that we are as individuals part of this Grand Architect and do have considerable effect on our reality.

Scientists have come to recognise that the whole universe is not just a random act, but is a complicated matrix of well-balanced design; even when it is supposed to be chaotic, it still follows a pattern.

More and more scientists, especially those dealing with quantum physics such as David Bohme, Frithjof Capra and Arthur Young believe that consciousness has a major part to play in forming physical reality. Many studies are appearing that suggest that consciousness could be the ultimate cosmic reality. They believe that a comprehensive theory of matter will have to include consciousness as an integral constituent. (See Stanislav Grof, *'Beyond The Brain; Birth, Death and Transcendance'*, State University of New York, 1985.)

"Human beings can function as vast fields of consciousness...transcending the limitations of the physical body and its senses, of Newtonian time and space, and of linear causality". Stanislav Grof.

Thanks to Victoria Lepage.

DOES MASS MATTER?

The 'fabric of space', is said to be made-up of one hydrogen atom per cubic metre of space. If this is true then the hydrogen particles would have found their equilibrium between repulsion and attraction and can be used as a measure of gravitational effect. This is relevant as space can be defined as merely the observable distance between two or more observable points. Basically space is not empty; it is filled by an extremely thin hydrogen and helium gas at a temperature of 4° (degrees) Kelvin above absolute zero.

I imagine a perfect space as filled with one-meter cubes of latent energy with an atom of hydrogen at each corner. This matrix of squares makes a massive volume of elastic space. Each atom is connected to every other atom by their electromagnetic field, so space is not really a vacuum but a vast complexity of particles with a weak electromagnetic connection that is constantly stretched tight by the pull of our expanding universe. To bring the atoms together to form a larger mass would require a considerable force to overcome the equilibrium of uniformity. Pulling on two atoms to bring them together would create a warping in the spaces between the other atoms for many kilometres and they would snap back to their original positions if you let them go. A great turbulence similar to swirling your hand around in a bucket of water would be needed to bring enough atoms together so that their combined magnetic fields or gravity would be strong enough to resist the pull of the web.

Dark matter (negative) repels matter (positive) because they are totally different frequencies.

Matter of like frequencies GRAVITATE: like attracts like. ANTIGRAVITY could be simply a persistent difference of magnetic frequencies = REPULSION.

Caution! THOUGHTWARP-. Just as an air bubble rises up through water to air, or a rock sinks towards rock, matter vibrating at a different frequency to the surrounding matter would move away towards a field of substance vibrating at the same or similar frequency. It may not be just because one has more or less mass than the other, although perhaps greater mass could theoretically amplify this effect.

Entering a large object of matter into space would draw the hydrogen atoms to it as the object's matter, which is basically made up of hydrogen, would be vibrating at a frequency similar to the frequency that the hydrogen particles would be, causing the hydrogen atoms outside the object to compress the space between them with a decreasing effect further away from the object.

The space between the hydrogen molecules would be compressed closer to the object, creating denser space. This would create an effect similar to Einstein's 'curved space' but, not so much as a salad bowl as he described it but as a subtle compressed sphere around the object reaching far out into space in all directions thinning out with distance.

Now Einstein's 'Theory of General Relativity' says that light travels in a straight line if no gravitational forces are present. This has been used to find dark objects in space as the gravity from these objects condenses space around the object causing light passing the object to bend. This is the same effect as when light passes through a lens. Since the space around the object is denser (the distance between particles are reduced) we get the same effect that we would get from light travelling through curved surfaces (e.g. lenses) of different layers of atmosphere of different densities, it appears to bend. You would see this at the rising or setting of the Sun or the Moon: they appear larger closer to the horizon as the atmosphere produces a lens effect

It is not quite correct to say that space becomes curved but more that space becomes either condensed or stretched. Space between the hydrogen molecules would become condensed around objects and stretched further away to an almost immeasurable degree. It is almost like pulling very gently on a spider's web.

Alternatively, any object in space could be drawing in hydrogen atoms in a continuous flow so instead of a static condensing of space it could be an acceleration of space towards an object, like what is supposed to happen in the black-hole theory, with the object gradually accumulating more mass. Our own Earth could be growing each minute from the atoms it is pulling in to itself.

Think about this: if space was a total vacuum before the 'Big Bang' then the moment of creation should have been called the 'Big Suck'! You need a dense atmosphere to experience a bang, since sound is carried by air, liquid or solid of some kind.

The effect of space condensation on time (Gravitational Time Dilation) is interesting as time requires the observed movement of an object between two observable points with space between them, so the further you get from the centre of a planet the less gravity there is, so the further apart particles are and more space is between them. Therefore it would require a slightly faster speed for an object to travel from one point of observable space to another compared to an object closer to the centre where gravity condenses space more. This phenomenon was first proved in the 70's with an atomic clock kept at a static location on the ground while a second synchronised atomic clock travelled in a jet liner high above the Earth's surface. When the jet landed it was found that it's clock was slightly behind the one kept on the ground. Matter towards the centre of a large body like our planet would appear to move slower and matter would appear to move faster towards the outer, much like looking at a wheel rotating. The rim of a wheel always appears to move faster even though the hub and the rim are turning at the same 'revolutions per minute' RPM. The matter on the rim would travel through a far less condensed space than the matter at the hub. Therefore the matter at the hub travels through far more space (condensed) and uses less speed but more time to travel a comparative distance than matter at the rim which uses more speed but less time to do the same RPM in less condensed space. So according to GTD, the further you would travel from the centre of a planet, the greater speed required to travel between the same distance between matter (less condensed) means you would experience less time for the same distance covered, then the less you would age in comparison to those travelling at the hub in more condensed space. In theory, the faster you travel away from the planet the less time you would experience because in fact you would be travelling at a slower RPM than those at the hub even though you record the same speed through space as those at the hub.

Confused yet? Don't worry about it too much, unless you are planning to travel across the universe and back to see if you can reverse aging wrinkles or to be there for your great, great grandchild's birthday.

What has all this got to do with religion and God? Some religions teach that this world is an illusion and the more you take a look at physics and science in general, the more you will see that even Buddha was teaching the truth and that no thing or idea is as solid as we think it is. If you change your mind you can change what you perceive as reality, even what you call God.

Think about this: have you ever seen the trick of getting a shelled boiled egg into a bottle without damaging the egg or the bottle by using air temperature differences? Imagine a white goose inside a green bottle. Now, how would you get the white goose out of the green bottle without breaking the green bottle or killing the goose? Some people take a long time to figure this one out.

THE CHARACTERS OF
RELIGIOUS STORIES
AND MYTHS

Many creation stories worldwide start with the great ocean (Great Mother, Tiawath, Eurynome, Chaos etc.) and the spirit, god or goddess or animal that causes the forming of land or the birth of the Earth sometimes from an egg. The Sky is then separated from the Earth.

The ancient Greeks/Helens held that Chronus used the sickle/scythe (of the Crescent Moon?) to castrate Ur-anu-s/Our-anu-s/Anu (Sky) and separate him from Earth, and incidentally created the 3 female Furies. The female warriors of some Scythian tribes (including Amazons) apparently used to carry small sickles into battle for the purpose of castrating their male victims, as is still done apparently in some East African tribes. The Hurrians and Hittites said it was Kumarbi who did the deed with his teeth or with a saw. The Chinese credited the god P'an Ku/Pangu with separating Sky and Earth. In Hindu mythology Dyaus (Sky) and Prithivi (Earth) were separated by Indra and the Greeks had Atlas to hold them apart.

Combining the Christian stories and the Hebrew traditions from which Christianity sprang from it could be said that the Creator, consisting of both male and female principles, makes the universe Mother and ethereal Father and then projects itself through the etheric Father (the gateway), to the physical Mother, manifesting as the physical son/child. The Sun child displays gentleness and compassion and the ability to heal, and usually ends up getting killed by a jealous rival (see Judas and Jesus, Loki and Baldor, Cain and Abel etc.), he has not sinned, he does not need to be purged of his sins in Purgatory and is usually brought back to life after 3 days.

Many gods worldwide experienced death and resurrection, which can be directly linked to the setting and rising of the Sun and the Moon, and the renewal of the cycle of the seasons.

The priests change the stories to suit the purpose of accumulating followers by binding people to them emotionally. Religion = rebind, from Latin re + ligere, fascism, or was it originally re + legion?

These priests use division and manipulation to create conflict, pain, suffering, sacrifice and obedience. They use punishment and fear to control, but promote the belief in miracles to attract people who will believe they can survive only if they stay loyal to their God. The 'God' gives wisdom to be effective in civilisation and war.

These 'Gods' are of the mind's creation and are either personifications of the aspects of nature or the personification of mans nature. The gods are just 'faces' manufactured by the mind and can only survive if the minds creation persists in the collective minds of man and accumulates mass/mind. Their followers identify heavily with mass and go about creating more mass by making more minds agree with their reality. This gives more energy to the mass of minds that believe and worship a god and of course more wealth to the priests.

If these gods are not worshipped then they have no 'mass' as nobody will be perpetuating their existence with 'mind mass' (i.e. emotional energy)

The hero character is usually the Son of God, The Messenger, the Prophet etc... He is a born human who understands and expresses the truth of what he sees. He usually opposes the established order and teaches a new way, a gentler and more compassionate way, and presents the idea of unity and freedom for all people. This character teaches healing and that truth and unity is essential for the survival of the spirit. He demonstrates that the spirit can overcome the physical laws and that all beings are able to choose between life or death, freedom or enslavement, pain or pleasure, release or entrapment. He teaches how to release thought-consciousness from the trap of mass/matter through acceptance and forgiveness, letting go, detachment from matter and painful mass/emotion. The hero usually experiences a journey, a temptation, a form of self-sacrifice and a return from the realms of death. The true form of this character does not want to be worshipped; he just asks that his teachings be heard and remembered.

The third character is usually presented as the Mother of the Son of the God. The Mother is a virgin or one of purity, who suffers all the pains of motherhood including the grief of losing her child or partner. She can also be sister to the father or partner to the son. The Mother is usually worshipped as a deity in her own right and usually is given a name associated with the Earth or the sea, the womb of creation and life.

In many religious patriarchal trinities the third character is the opposite of the son or another son with opposing characteristics and nature. In Hindu mythology Shiva 'the destroyer' is the opposite of Vishnu 'the preserver'. In Hebrew legend it is Cain who opposes Abel and in Christian mythology it is Satan who becomes the opposer of Christ and so on.

The symbols that represent these characters or aspects are nothing more than symbols so it would be silly to worship the Sun, Earth and Moon as Gods.

The unseen character we do not hear much about is the one who created all of the above, it seems to have no real name, 'the unknowable one' and 'the nameless one', 'the Great Mystery', 'the Great Spirit' and 'the Eternal One'. This being could be described as the 'Universal Creator'. The Egyptians gave this concept of the 'Creative Force being' a title 'Neter' as did the Jews, 'Kether', the Hindu 'Brahm' or 'Mahat' and the Chinese Yu Ch'ing. These are just some of the names given to the unity, the ultimate one the creator.

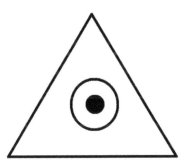

An ancient universal symbol of the creator or creative force is the eye (circumpunct) within the triangle. This could also represent the spirit/life within all of us that is experiencing existence within the 3D universe. Some occult organisations call this the 'All Seeing Eye' and use it to qualify their actions and beliefs as legitimate in purpose and can be seen on the Freemasons US Dollar bill among many other places.

A phenomenon that resembles the 'All Seeing Eye' has also been seen on the planet Saturn;

"It looks like a hurricane, but it doesn't behave like a hurricane…. Whatever it is, we're going to focus on the eye of this storm and find out why it is there." Andrew Ingersoll, Cassini imaging team, California Institute of Technology, 2007.

HEAVEN AND HELL

What we call 'heaven' could be the state of having freedom of choice, free from the entrapment of the mind mass. To be able to experience creation to its fullest, a being would have to be free to choose its pursuits and form its reality according to what it experiences as true and not what others tell it to believe as true. In this state we enjoy experiences that we want to experience, this is pleasure. What we call 'hell' could be the entrapment in mass/matter. In this state we are forced to experience things we do not want to experience but having little choice in the matter we experience pain.

Thought-consciousness beings are very inquisitive and willing to experience the material world and can get trapped if the true nature of self is forgotten. Entrapment forces the separation of a being from its source, like trapping an antelope separates it from its family, its herd, its source. Once trapped in feelings like greed, hate and selfishness, the beings go through the cycle of the mass/matter universe, like getting caught in the cogs of a machine, unless another being reminds it of its true nature and shows the way out of entrapment and painful experiences. The life experience of Guatama Buddha was based on releasing oneself from pain and suffering through the practice of detachment, detaching oneself from the desires, beliefs and limitations of the material world.

Heaven has meant different things to different cultures each having their own idea of heaven. Some spiritual leaders think that the heaven (or hell) that you will experience will be the one that you were taught to expect as you create the reality you expect to see.

In ancient and modern myths, the world of the dead has three layers, as in Dante's 'The Divine Comedy' there is a Paradise, a Purgatory and the Inferno (lake of fire). Purgatory is where the spirit was cleansed (purged) of 'sins' (mass?) before moving on to paradise. Are blackholes like purgatory or are they the ultimate lake of fire? Maybe matter is drawn in with souls trapped in the mess of the end time Inferno and crushed back to energy/ mass, which is released to start again, recycled into a new universe?

Hell/Hades was the name of the underground world; from the Indo-European word 'Kel'. Hel was the Nordic-Germanic goddess of the grave and 'helan' was the word used for 'a covering' or 'a concealment' (a grave). In the New Testament the word translated as hell was the Aramaic 'Gehenna' or in Hebrew 'Ge-ben-hinnon' which just referred to the smoking rubbish pit outside Jerusalem where local refuse, the bodies of animals and sometimes the unclaimed bodies of executed sinners were dumped and burned.

Basic Pattern

The basic pattern of the Trinity as described in ancient religious texts is the primary pattern of existence. It starts with a singularity that either becomes or creates a duality, both giving rise to a trinity. In modern terms we could describe this pattern as Spirit creates mass and both of these create matter. This Trinity could be imagined as a downward pointing triangle with the singularity or Creator/energy at the top left corner opposite a duality/mass. Both of these at the upper side of the triangle interact to instantaneously form a third entity, the universe/matter.

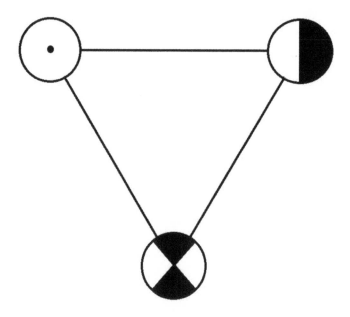

After considering that the singularity or Creator is always referred to as an infinite being and that the duality and the universe is supposed to come to an end we could turn the triangle to the traditional position of pointing upwards with the Spirit/Creator/Chrestus/unity at the top and the duality/mass/masculine energy at the bottom right corner with the universe/matter/feminine energy opposite to it. In the physical world all things below are a reflection of things above, this triangle would be Sun at the top and the Earth and the Moon at the bottom corners.

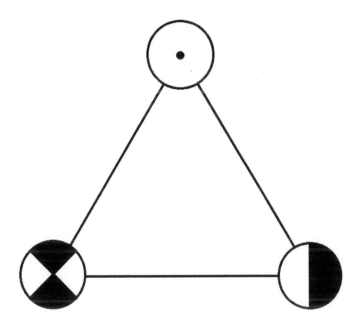

But there is also a fourth aspect and that is what we call life. So what is life? If we look at the basic pattern of the Trinity from the view of Christianity we have the Trinity of Father, Son and Holy Ghost. This trinity as I have shown is a reflection of the ancient trinity of Father, Mother and Son. Looking at this trinity as a downward pointing triangle the Father/duality and the Mother/matter unite to give birth to the Son. The Son or child is the projection of the Spirit into the physical realm; the Spirit/Creator interacting with the physical becomes soul/chi/life/breath in a physical body.

The two triangles joined together form a diamond shape with the Spirit/Creator at the top, the Father to the right, the Mother to the left and the creator projects itself down though the middle of the gateway formed by the Father and Mother to express itself in physical form as a living being. This living being contains life, the soul that contains and represents the Spirit, the soul is an individual and separated portion of the wholly spirit, like the individual cell is a small and separate portion of the whole body.

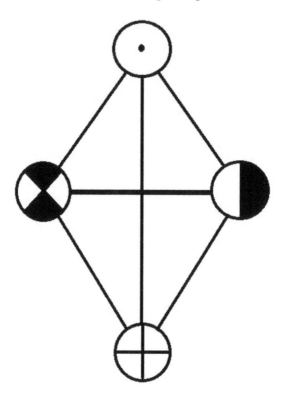

The pattern has been symbolised in many ways one of which we often see as the Star of David with the two triangles overlapping. Another ancient symbol for the pattern is the Flower of Life using circles instead of triangles. This pattern starts with a singular circle that then joins an overlapping circle to form a portal, the Vesica Pisces is followed by a third circle overlapping the first two forming a triangle, the Seed of Life. This basic pattern is then duplicated and joined to the original and it becomes the Tree of Life and is then again multiplied until the complete pattern of the Flower of Life emerges just as a living body grows from the multiplication of cells.

These observations of the basic pattern of the Trinity may seem simplistic, but that's what the basic pattern seems to be. The extended patterns can be calculated using numbers, as in mathematics, numerology or in 3D using geometry. The pattern is present in music, astrology and anatomy, in fact every part of existence.

Our lives are based on patterns and the basic pattern is played out again and again. If you want to understand what is happening in the world around you, look to the basic pattern, it is the template.

The Father

(Old English fæder, Old High German fater, Old Norse fat-hir, Old Frisian feder, Latin pater, Greek pāter, Sanskrit pitr)

Many gods were given the title of Father and it was a title bestowed on respected elders and chiefs of communities.

God was originally from the word for good in Old English (see God/Goda/ Gad = the good) and Father was a general term used for any community leader, even the ancient Scythian chief God was called Papas. (See Papa, Pa, Pasa, Baba, Padre, Pope, Pop = Father.)

This world is greatly affected by the belief in the Father of three religions that originate from the one source. Each of these holds onto worshipping the one god, but whose extremists are in constant conflict against the followers of the other two. Who is right, who has God on their side? Will they never be at peace with each other until they give up their religions?

This situation is summed up by the words of a famous author,

"The great unmentionable evil at the centre of our culture is monotheism. From a barbaric Bronze Age text known as the Old Testament, three anti human religions have evolved – Judaism, Christianity, and Islam. These are sky-god religions. They are literally patriarchal- God is the Omnipotent Father - hence the loathing of women for 2000 years in those countries afflicted by the sky-god and his earthly male delegates. The sky-god is a jealous god, of course. He requires

total obedience from everyone on Earth, as he is in place not for just one tribe but for all creation. Those who would reject him must be converted or killed for their own good. Ultimately, totalitarianism is the only sort of politics that can truly serve the sky-god's purpose." -Gore Vidal.

Who is the Father of the Old Testament? Who is the Father of the New Testament? This is a very important question as the illusion hinges on this enigma.

"You will know a tree by the fruit that it bears".

It is really hard to figure out what or who is the Father of Jesus. Jesus is said to have told his followers that his father was a god of love and mercy yet the God of the Old Testament was anything but. There are so many contradictions to filter through. Remembering that the Bible was written, modified and transcribed by mortal men with the aid of a mind it seems that the texts have been written in such a way that the truth is in plane sight yet hidden.

Truth can be found by looking at consistencies and the personalities of Yahweh and Jesus are found to be consistent amongst the contradictions.

Yahweh is consistently a god of patriarchal wisdom, power, war, judgement, punishment and conditional mercy. He has little compassion and is short on patience; He loves in a dominating and possessive way and is prone to angry and very destructive outbursts, showing traits of sadistic behaviour. His actions cause more division than unity and segregation of his people from other races.

The characteristics of Yahweh are in keeping with the moon gods of old and the kingdom of the dark and division.

"Woe unto you that desireth the day of the lord! To what end is it for you? The day of the Lord is darkness and not light". Amos 5: 18, Old Testament.

"The Lord has said that he would dwell in the thick darkness" 2 Chronicles 6: 1, Old Testament.

"He made darkness his secret place; his pavilion around about him were dark waters thick clouds of the sky." Psalm 18: 11, Old Testament.

On the other hand Jesus is compassionate, patient, kind, forgiving, understanding. He does not judge, his love is unconditional and is non-hierarchical or non-dominating. His wisdom is inclusive of both genders and of all people from all races. His emotional outbursts are mild and non destructive. His actions and words are aimed at encouraging unity, reconciliation and light.

"Then spoke Jesus again unto them, saying, I am the light of the world: he that follows me shall not walk in darkness, but shall have the light of life." John 8: 12. New Testament, KJV.

"This then is the message which we have heard of him, and declare to you, that God is light and in him no darkness at all". First Epistle of John 1: 5. New Testament, KJV.

(This is a set pattern and anything written that contradicts this should be looked at carefully.)

Here we have two very different personalities reflected by two different testaments (covenants), which throws up again the question of who is the Father of Jesus?

"Who ever has seen me has seen the Father". John 14:9, New Testament.

In his discussion with the Priests Jesus said; *"...You neither know me or my Father, if you had known me you should have known my Father also",* John 8:19, KJV. And to the priests who worshipped Yahweh he said;

"Ye are of your Father the devil, and the lusts of your Father ye will do. He was a murderer from the beginning, and abode not in the truth, because there is no truth in him. When he speaketh a lie he speaketh of his own: for he is a liar, and the Father of it", John 8:44, New Testament KJV.

There is far more to this text and it is important to read the whole lot so it is not taken out of context. The church that approved the texts that ended up in the bible seems to be controlled by the 'ruler of this world' so all is not as true as it seems to be.

The Christian evangelist Kris Vallotten, in his recorded sermon 'Living in Grace Land Part 2' also likens the Old Testament with the 'Kingdom of Darkness' and that the New Testament is like the 'Kingdom of Light'. The Old Testament was governed by the Laws of Moses (Mosaic Law) and was based on judgement and punishment, 'an eye for an eye and a tooth for a tooth'. The New Testament is based on the laws of forgiveness, compassion and non-judgement; 'do to others, as you would have them do to you'. Whoever still judges and condemns another is still in the kingdom of darkness and is living by its laws and has not entered the new kingdom. It's a matter of changing your mind that depends on which kingdom you live in. If you judge other people then you will be judged, if you forgive other people then you will be forgiven, this is basically the law of karma, whatever you sow, you shall reap.

In the book of Genesis, God is described as 'Elohim', this term is plural, referrring to more than one entity. The God of the Old Testament seems to have a split personality or two faces, said to be the merciful and generous God by those who appeased him and then proving to be a jealous, angry and vengeful tyrant interested only in disciplining his 'chosen' people and destroying those who did not bow down and fear him.

"And when the lord your god has delivered them over to you and you have defeated them, then you must destroy them totally. Make no treaty with them and show no mercy" Deuteronomy 7: 2' Old Testament.

"And it came to pass on the morrow that the evil spirit from God came upon Saul". 1 Samuel 18: 10, Tanach (Old Testament).

"I am the lord and there is none else. I form the light and create the darkness, I make peace and create evil, I the lord do all these things". Isaiah 45:7, Old Testament.

The Old Testament/Tanach has very little reference to the devil or a person called Satan. In these texts the God (Yahweh) is the author of good and evil.

If Yahweh were the 'creator of all things' he would have even accepted the gentiles as Jesus did. He apparently created them, didn't he?

The Father in the religious stories seems to have a habit of taking over (eclipsing) and making use of the glory of the Sun. This can be seen easily with Amen taking the throne of the Sun even though he was a moon deity, a modern version of the story being Father Christmas taking over the celebration of the Son Jesus, turning Christ-mass into a Luni-mass. Maybe that's why it is known colloquially now as the 'Silly Season' and causes so much domestic stress.

There is a distinct pattern of the Moon gods hijacking the Sun's throne and glory:

"The light of the moon shall become like the light of the sun." Isaiah 30:26, Old Testament.

By all accounts, Yahweh's behaviour and that of his followers could be used as a role model for the Devil himself. In Mediaeval folklore, the mythical Satan was Gods right hand man, his lieutenant, until Satan opposed God, taking half of the angels, but in the story of Job you will find that the satan was still God's dark-side or Azzaz-el.

Considering what I have discovered earlier in writing this book, God is the Universal Spirit, the original creator and the first polarity of unity. To create the universe it needed an opposite (a satan) to create division so there would be 'space'. The opposite would have to be a likeness of equal strength and power, powerful enough to oppose the creator. The opposite would have to be a clone, an identical twin in appearance, but different in nature. If this is the case that God created a twin, then it would be very difficult to tell them apart until you got to know both of them and if the clone was trying to deceive you into thinking that it was the original then you could be in for a tough time.

It would be the same dilemma of dealing with two personalities in the same body. Who would you be talking to, Al or Ben, you would only know by working out their intentions. Al wants to take over the body completely because he thinks that Ben is a sook for not wanting power, vengeance, war and destroying cities full of people; while Ben wants to have a cooperative relationship with Al, so they can both benefit from each other's strengths.

It is only by knowing the characteristics of each entity that you would see the subtle differences between them. They both have the same face, the same voice. Wow! It's hard to tell them apart. If the real God has no shadow and is the 'Father of Light' as told by the disciples John and James, then the clone would have a shadow and half of him is in darkness as is the Moon and all men *"made in his image"*. Man was created in the likeness of Yahweh so it makes sense to look at the construct of humans to see the nature of the God of the Old Testament/Tanach.

If it was the clone that inspired the writings in the Old Testament, it made it clear that it was going to judge and punish until those who were not totally loyal to it were destroyed. It can be seen that it accused, judged, numbered, weighed and divided until Jerusalem was destroyed and the Hebrew race was divided and dispersed across the world. Satan was said to be 'the accuser' but how many times in the Bible did he actually accuse anyone? How many times did Yahweh accuse anyone?

Could it be that the God of the Old Testament was the satan, the 'Prince of Darkness', the 'ruler of this world' but not the creator of this universe? Is he the descendant or reincarnation in character of ENLIL or Saturn (whose father was Ur-ANU-s)? Nothing much has been seen of Yahweh since Exodus or heard of since Jesus arrived on the scene. Christ like Horus was supposed to have conquered and thrown the Set/Satan into imprisonment for a thousand years. Maybe Yahweh is still pulling strings and controlling the MATRIX under a new disguise until the final day when his followers will judge themselves and let go of their old mentality, freeing themselves from the bonds of this illusion.

Why did Jesus tell the Priests that they did not worship his Father and that the one they worshipped was the satan?

Is Yahweh like Osiris, whose name was not to be said out loud for fear of the punishment of death by stoning? How many people were cruelly stoned to death for just uttering the name of 'the one who shall not be named and therefore kept hidden'?

Why is it that Catholic priests and clergy are called Father even though Jesus reminded the people that his God said that he was the only one to be called 'Father'?

The earliest Christian sects; the Gnostics and the Cathars believed that there were two Gods, one that was good and was the Father of the New Testament, represented by Christ's teaching, and one that was of the Old Testament, the Lord of this world, the Demi-urge. Were they killed off by the Catholic Church for knowing the truth?

This idea is similar to the Zoroastrian dualistic concept of a good God (Or-mazd/Mazda, Mithra) and a bad God (Ahri-man/Angra, angry?). I think that these two aspects could be present in the one God Yahweh, as each is an aspect of the duality that is reflected in the creation of life, but it is said in the New Testament that God, the Father of Jesus, has no darkness in him, could this be the Sun? Could it be that the Sun and the Son are of one and the same spirit?

In the New Testament, Jesus said that *"the only way to the Father is through me and that if you do not know me, you do not know my Father"*.

Is the real Father of Jesus represented by the Sun, having a temperament and personality the same as was demonstrated by Jesus, or was Jesus referring to the Moon that reflects the light of the Sun? No, half the Moon is still in darkness. *"God is light, and there is no darkness in him."* First Epistle of John 1:5, New Testament, KJV.

So why is the Father of the Old Testament so different from Jesus? Maybe it's not his real Father, or just one aspect of the Father, or were the translations made to fit a preconceived idea of religious order?

In the New Testament parables Jesus (Yehoshua/Yoshua/Joshua = God's helper) describes the Lord Father as a farmer (a renter of land) while Jesus is called the Good Shepherd. This theme can be found in other texts such as the story of Cain the farmer and Abel the shepherd and the story of Enlil and Enki. The Shepherd was the one who cared for the welfare of his flock/people; the Farmer was concerned with the profits his crop would bring. In Old Gaelic the word 'cain' meant payment of farm produce as rent.

Were the priests of Yahweh riding on the glory of Jesus and creating an Earthly Empire that went against most of what Jesus taught? I may be wrong, but I believe that the still powerful 'God' Yahweh or YHWH / Yaouai / Yahoo / Yawa / YaHshua / Iah / Jah / Ja / Jehovah / JHVH / El / Adhonai / Hashem / Eloh / Eloah / Elah / ElShaddai / Elyon / Elyeh / Ilu Kurgal etc, (the seventy two names of God) is really the personification of mind, mass, male-volent energy that exists and dominates by the energy force of those who believe in it and is NOT the creator of this universe but just an aspect of the real Creative Force turned into a personality cult by minds trying to harness the energy of man. There is so much evidence to believe that this view is correct.

This 'yidam being' could also have the same origin as the ancient Moon gods Nanna, En-lil, Sin, Al-ilah, Yaho, Yahu, Yah and Lah. Abraham's god could have originally been a god known in Babylon as Ya'u who is said to have also blessed Ishmael and his sons. Abraham was originally a citizen of Babylonia.

The historian Lydus insisted *"the Chaldeans called their god Yaho"*. Yaho is also mentioned by Diodorus Siculus, the Valentinian gnostics, the Kaballa and Yahuq pre-Islamic Arabs.

From what I have read from the Greek historians, the Arabs worshipped two main deities before Allah; one was the Moon god Alilah/Alilat accompanied by his consort Ishtar and the other was Oratalt. The Moon crescent and the star of Ishtar is on the Arabian flag.

Is the name 'Allah' a general word meaning 'Lord' and used the same way Christians and Jews use the words God, Father, or Lord, which are general terms for worshipped deities?

The name Allah is made up of two words Al and lah. 'Al' as we have seen is the equivalent of 'El' and 'Il', which means 'Lord'; 'lah' is the equivalent of 'Yah'. Al-lah is the same as El-yah or the title meaning Lord-God.

The Aramaic words 'Alaha' and 'Ilahi' are equivalent to a Hebrew word for God 'Eloha' and the Arabic 'Ilah'.

"Etymologically, Allah is probably a contraction of the Arabic al-ilahh, "the God," although the Aramaic Alaha has also been proposed. The origin of the name can be traced to the earliest Semitic writings in which the word for god was Il or El, the latter being the Old Testament synonym for Yahweh. Known to Arabs even in pre-Islamic times, Allah is standard Arabic for God and is used by Arab Christians as well as Muslims." (See 'Encyclopaedia Britannica Micropedia'. Vol. 1; page 250.)

"The god Il or Ilah was originally a phase of the Moon God, but early in Arabian history the name became a general term for god, and it was this name that the Hebrews used prominently in their personal names, such as Emanu-el, Israel, etc., rather than the Bapal of the northern semites proper, which was the Sun. Similarly, under Mohammed's tutelage, the relatively anonymous Ilah became Al-Ilah, The God, or Allâh, the Supreme Being." (Carleton S. Coon, 'Southern Arabia', Washington, D.C. Smithsonian, 1944 p.399).

In the ancient Tamil language (said to be 'the mother of all languages') Al is the word for 'night, negative, not, hidden from view'. The word Allah in Tamil means 'The God you can not see'/ who is not visible, who has no form'. The Tamil word for 'no' is 'ille'.

Reading through the Holy Qu'ran shows that the God of the Hebrews is the same as the God of Muslims. The Holy Qu'ran tells the stories of the well-known figures of the Old Testament/Tanach, eg: Abraham, Joseph, Moses etc, and tells that the God of these patrons is also Allah. The Holy Qu'ran also describes the birth of the prophet Jesus and again describes God as Allah. So we can only assume that God is Allah is also Yahweh is also God. Abraham and his son Ishmael built the most sacred shrine of the Arab world, the Kaaba. Covered in its shroud it resembles a black cube.

I was told that the written Hebrew word for Yahweh is also the word for Allah if turned upside down. Interestingly it does seem to work if you take the Hebrew tetragram, reverse it and invert it, then link up the letters as you would in Arabic.

Could one God control three of the most powerful religions on Earth? Are you God-fearing? Under what name do you fear the Father? Yahweh, Jehovah, Allah or God? Is it possible that the original God and Goda were the two forces of duality, male and female brought into existence by human belief in a creator?

(See also Gott, Goda, Gode, God, Gud, Gad, Gade and Ghohd = unity, the Persian Khoda and Hindu Khooda.)

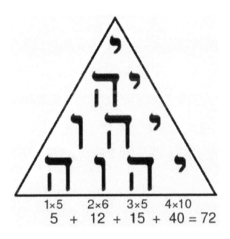

Yahweh Gematria.

The Son

(Greek Huios, Latin Filius, Hebrew Ben/Bar, Old English sunu, Old Norse sunr, Gothic sunus, Old High German sunu, Sanskrit sūnu,)

There have been many representations of the Sun as a deity and many representations of the Son of the Sun as a man-god. Since this book was based on the Christian Trinity, I'll start on the one named Jesus (Greek) or Yehoshua/Yeshua (Hebrew) aka Joshua (English).

Jesus probably did exist as a real flesh-and-blood person as his teachings were revolutionary, even verging on sacrilegious and too different for the culture of his time, even though there is almost no historical evidence outside the Bible? Is it a coincidence that Jesus was crucified in his 33rd year after performing 33 miracles? Could he have been just an ordinary guy whose story was 'beat up' to make him look like a superhero for the political agendas of the rulers, or was he a good-hearted magician of extraordinary abilities? The Holy Quaran says that Jesus was a great prophet, nothing more, but he was quite possibly the true descendant of King David, which would have made him heir to the throne of Israel. It is most likely that he was at least one of the mannequins for the 'Sons of God' story and thought of as an incarnation of the 'Great Angel' (Enoch ascended). It wasn't until the Council of Nicea in AD 325 that Jesus was officially made equal to God by the Catholic Church.

It could be that any historical records pertaining to this Yehoshua could have been destroyed during the destruction of Jerusalem or hidden so that the fact that he was just a man and not of divine origin could easily be negated.

In the New Testament, Matthew 1:23, it is said that Jesus was to be called Emmanuel ('God is with us'), but Jesus is the Greek translation of Yeshua/Joshua. Emmanuel is possibly derived from the Ancient Egyptian words Amun u El which is 'Amun/Amen is God' and refers to the Hidden God... or does it really mean The Moon is lord, was it Em-manu-el? The original translation spelling is Immanuel and because of the variants within our language base could mean 'God in man', Em/Im (in) manu (man) el (God) or Im (not) manu (moon) el (God). (See impossible, imposing, empower, etc.)

The Biblical story of Jesus is symbolic of astrological events.

Jesus the Nazarene ('the lamb', son of the Ram?) made his entrance early in the astrological age of the Fish/Pisces (approximately 110 BC-2050 AD). Early Christians adopted the fish as their symbol and became the 'fishers of men' (Nazoraeans). Did the town of Nazareth exist at the time of Jesus? (See Natzrat, Nozrim.)

The Hindu god Vishnu who was originally a solar deity, one of the Hindu 'Trimurta' and 'protector of the world' first appeared as 'Matsya', the fish.

The Bible mentions that the Messiah (King, annointed one) was to be called 'the Lion of the tribe of Judah'. This could be a reference that Jesus was to be born under the Zodiac sign of Leo the lion, which is the sign of the Sun and the sign of kings. The astrological time of Leo, July 23 to August 22, is far more plausible as the birth month of Jesus as this is in the warm season of Israel and was the time that shepherds would have been out with their flocks at night. December in Israel is in the season of winter and bitterly cold winds, a bad time for people to be travelling to cities to be counted in a census or for shepherds to be out in open fields at night. It has been determined by astrological dating that the actual birth of Jesus could have occurred on the 29th of July 7 BC. (See 'Signs In The Sky' by Adrian Gilbert, Three Rivers Press, 2000.)

Other researchers say that Jesus was born 1st, March 7 BC, which was not the traditional birth month for Hebrew royalty. The King/Herod of Biblical infamy died in 4 BC so this date of 7 BC for Jesus' birth puts them together in the correct time frame. It is also possible that the 3 'wise men' visited Jesus and presented him with the 3 royal gifts on his 3rd, birthday, thereafter the Holy family moved to Egypt. The census or counting actually occurred in the year 6 AD under the governor Cyrenious; Jesus would have been 12 years old at this time and would have ritually been 'reborn' in a ceremony that is known as Bar Mitzvah. At 12 years of age Jesus would have started his education in the temples.

It is possible that Jesus was linked with Enki/Ea, the ancient Sumerian god of waters, wisdom and bene-volence towards humans who appeared as a fish to give warning to Uta Napishtim about En-lil's plan to destroy troublesome humanity with a Great Flood. Uta Napishtim took Enki's advice, built an Ark and filled it with pairs of each animal just as Noah did. In other countries of the world there are ancient myths of a Great Flood (Deluge) and of great ships landing on foreign shores. Some of the ancient civilisations that originated these myths are found in China near Takla Maklan, in South America, in Egypt and Mesopotamia, all of these cultures built stepped pyramids.

There are no known verifiable historical records that the Christ was crucified and this is used as an argument that he did not exist at all, but his influence and punishment was apparently recorded in the Tacitus Report 115 AD in *'The Annals'* translated by Alfred John Church and William Jackson Brodribb:

"Nero fastened guilt and inflicted the most exquisite tortures on a class hated for their abominations, called 'Chrestiani' by the populace. Chrestus, from whom the name had its origin, suffered the extreme penalty during the reign of Tiberius at the hands of one of our procurator, Pontius Pilatus, and a most mischievous superstition, thus checked for the moment, again broke out not only in Judaea, the first source of the evil, but even in Rome, where all things hideous and shameful from every part of the world find their centre and become popular." (Note there is no mention of the name 'Jesus' here.)

If Jesus really existed then Jesus (Yehoshau Ben Panthera?) was not himself a Sun God. He was born a Jew, studied as a Jew, most likely joined the ranks of the Essenes and studied at the Egyptian Panther or Djehdi schools of mysteries and healing, travelled widely and taught the healing arts for the rest of his life. There is no hard evidence that Jesus actually died on the stauros or the cross. Most of the story of Jesus may have been made to conform to the traditional story of the Sun Gods for political reasons since Sol Invictus was the favourite religion of the late Roman Empire. Many records and documents were destroyed during the sacking of Jerusalem and this may account for the lack of evidence. I think that the priests of Yahweh got their revenge on the Roman Empire for destroying their power base in 76 AD by infiltrating and gradually taking over Rome itself under the guise of Christianity.

The real story of Jesus will never really be known as there is insufficient evidence from historical records. It is possible that any surviving historical references that mentioned he was just a man instead of a deity would have been destroyed by the past authorities of the church in Rome. The miracles he was supposed to perform were probably taken from the models of previous 'Sons of God' and may have never happened as written. The miracles had similar features to the acts of Buddha (from 500 years earlier), whose abilities also included walking on water.

The Biblical story of Jesus is supposed to be almost word for word the same as the story of Horus according to the *"Book of Vivifying the Soul Forever"*, which seems to be a figment of someone's imagination as I can't find it anywhere. I believe this was an invention of the eccentric author and self styled Egyptologist Gerald Massey?

The Persian/Roman Sun god Mithra was born in a cave to Ana-hita a virgin 'Mother of God'. His birth was celebrated on the 25th of December; Attis of Phyrigia was born to the virgin Nana on the 25th of December. They were crucified, placed in a tomb and resurrected after 3 days. If there were a real Jesus his story would have been modified to fit the traditional template story of the 'Sons of God' to serve political purposes. The story of Krishna is also of the Sun god model as told in the Bhagava Gita of 4000 BC(?).

The astrological story of the 'Son of God' starts with a birth on the 25th of December to a virgin mother Virgo (the zodiac 'House of Bread', in Hebrew is Beth-le-hem). The birthplace or rising of the Son is marked by the rising of the 'Star in the East' (Sirius) this event is preceded by the rising of the Three kings (or Belt of Orion) leaving the Serpens Capus (The Reptiles Head, Herod or Herrot).

The 'Sons of God' show their wisdom and understanding of the scriptures at the age of 12. At the age of 30 they are baptised and then began their ministry. They usually have 12 disciples (the 12 houses of the Zodiac?) who accompany the Sun. They perform miracles, healing the sick, walking on water and increasing the quantities of food, oil and wine. The Sons were known as The Lambs of God, The Good Shepherds, The Truth, The Light, God's Anointed Sons, etc. In their 33rd year they are betrayed, they die on the shortest day of the year in the Northern Hemisphere (22nd of December, Winter Solstice), buried for the 3 days that the Sun seems to remain still, and then resurrected (or reborn) on the 25th of December, the day that the Sun begins it's return journey. Even in some versions of his myth, 'Dionysus' was also said to be a Son of God, born of a virgin mother on the 25th of December.

Jesus may have been nailed to a tree (or post) as is written for opposing the priests, but he may not have died. Some of the early Christians and Gnostics such as Irenaeus and Basilides believed he survived or was never crucified. So if Jesus didn't die on the 'stauros', what happened to him? An important 2nd century founding father of the church Bishop Irenaeus never mentioned the crucifiction. He stated that the ministry of Jesus lasted for twenty years in the Holy Land. Jesus then went to Asia with his brother Judas Thomas where he died at an old age. (See *Against Heresies* by Irenaeus and the *Acts of Thomas*.)

Records in India tell of Jesus as Yus Asaf, Yusu, Yusus or Issa who ascended to the 'heaven on Earth' we call Kashmir, high in the mountains of India. His mother Mary and other brothers had gone before him. Jesus's last resting place could be in Mohalla Khaniyar, Srinagar at the Temple of Rozabal.

In the 'Tafsi-Ibn-i-at-Tabri', Ibn-I-Jarir says, *"Jesus was like unto the Holy Prophet. He and his mother, Mary (as a result of Jewish persecutions) had to migrate from Palestine and leave for a far off country and he went from country to country"*.

In the Holy Quran 23: 50 it says, *"And we made the Son of Mary and his mother a sign and we gave them shelter on lofty meadows and springs"*.

Even today there is a valley in Kashmir called Yusu Margh ('meadow of Jesus') where the people of Yadu (Jews) are still found. Jesus' mother Mary may have died at Murree near Rawalpindi, her tomb is called 'Mai Mari da Asthan' meaning 'the resting place of Mother Mary'.

If Jesus were a real person, would he have real descendants? According to the Greek Bible translation he was called 'Rabbi' 16 times. The word Rabbi has been translated as 'master' in the King James Version. According to Hebrew law a Rabbi had to be 30+ years of age and married. Mary Magdalene was the most likely candidate and legend says she was sent to France bearing the child of Jesus. In 318 AD the Desposyni sent a delegation from France to Rome. They talked with Bishop Silvester about restoring Jerusalem as the seat of Christianity and recognising the original Christian doctrine. They also requested that one of the bloodline of Christ be made Bishop of Jerusalem; they were turned away without success. Since the destruction of Jerusalem many of the Davidian bloodline were hunted down and killed by authorities of The Holy Roman Empire.

Whatever is said, it doesn't alter the fact that the humanistic ideas of compassion, equality, kindness, and gentle strength that some of the prophets taught is still very important if we want the human race to survive.

It seems that Jesus (if he did exist) was driven by the desire to see kindness and compassion being the norm for human behaviour, which is totally different from the indifference of the material world and the violent rage of the God of the Old Testament. Could this trait of Jesus be recognition of the unity of all things and the desire of the True Creator to reunify with the fragments of its self that were separated by the force of division it created?

Where Jesus quotes the Old Testament prophecies, he actually changes the words or leaves some out to make the prophecy more benign. The Old Testament teaches that 'an eye for an eye' is the law, but Jesus taught that you must 'love your enemy' and if he strikes you then 'turn the other cheek'. The New Testament is about reconciliation, forgiveness and mercy, which is different to the attitude of judgement and vengeance of the Old Testament. In the New Testament, Jesus asked us to give up the old way and take up the new way that will bring peace and goodwill. 'You will only be judged by your own conscience made aware by his words'.

Could the one who created the universe be longing to be whole again?

I can understand the desire to be whole once more, to feel united once again with all life as one, it would feel like returning once again to the people that you love dearly who love you so much no matter what you have done or said, sincerely and unconditionally, the feeling of joy and the release of the grief of separation. This to me is re-ligion, acceptance, returning home, reuniting! We can only achieve this through tolerance, forgiveness and education, not by hate and destruction. Vengeance makes more vengeance.

I think that Yeshua (Jesus) and the 'comforter' Mohammed were trying to help correct this situation of division by teaching the truth about the Creator as a good and merciful God and not the God(s) that the priesthoods had created by persisting with worshipping the Moon Gods (Pitris) as they still seem to do. It seems that older ideas and traditions were maintained by the few who were reluctant to change to the new ways. Mohammed achieved his aim of clearing the vast number of pagan deities that the Arabs worshipped and reducing worship to one God, but the influence of the old moon-god is still being felt.

Those who serve the god of division unfortunately have also used the Koran to support the justifications for the grabbing of power through hate, vengeance and suppression of women. Unfortunately the Bible and the Tanach have also been used for the same purpose. Suicide bombing by terrorists and imposing religion by conquest is actually against Islamic law.

"The sword could never be used to force Islâm on others, compulsion in religion being forbidden in clear words (v. 4). Fighting was undoubtedly allowed but it

was expressly allowed only as a defensive measure against those who were bent upon annihilating Islâm by the sword, not to compel people to accept Islâm (vv. 5, 6). When persecution ceased and everyone was at liberty to profess whatever religion he liked, the sword had to be sheathed" (v. 7). From a translation of *'A Manual of Hadith'*, chapter 19 'Jihad' by Maulana Mohammad Ali M.A., LL.B. (1944).

'Jihad' means the striving or struggle to spread the faith as a missionary effort or in the 'defense' of Islam, not the use of violent intimidation to convert nonbelievers and certainly not the mass slaughter of civilian men, women and children.

There are also many so-called 'radical Christians' who have the extreme wish of clearing the Earth of all who do not believe in Jehovah, this was the way of Yahweh/Adonai, but this is not the way of the Christ.

I think the teachings of Jesus/Yeshua and Mohammed/Muhammad have both been misinterpreted and their teachings corrupted and used to benefit mass-orientated merchant priests to continue the same power base and aggressive behaviour that had existed previously. We do not need to fight each other, we are all of the same family, hate begets hate and vengeance is the food of evil. Religion is being used to recruit those who can be sucked into being pawns for the vindictive, the power and glory hungry servants of the mind.

The New Testament of the Bible was put together a long time after the death of Christ; many scripts were left out. Why? (See The Apocrypha.) The Holy Koran/Qurán was written down 600 years after the death of Jesus, at this time the corruption of Christianity had already well taken hold in the form of the unholy church, the Kata-Holis.

600 years is a feature of the Naros/Neros solar-lunar cycle that brings forth a prophet each 600 years.

Why were a lot of essential facts left out of the story of Jesus, and are only recently being rediscovered through the studies of the Dead Sea Scrolls, the Nag Hammadi Codices and other writings of the Essenes, Gnostics and modern historians? Is it because the priests of the 'Hidden One' wanted to establish absolute unshared control under the guise of 'The Only God'?

The Creator expresses itself through the Creation (male and female, Moon and Earth) and the expression would be its spirit child on Earth. The 'Sons of God' show the true God and it's nature of being and is as consistent as the trinity of Sun, Moon and Earth.

"Every good gift and every perfect gift is from above and comes down from the Father of lights with whom there is no variableness, neither shadow of turning". This quote from James 1:17, New Testament, has to refer to the likeness of the Sun, as it is the only body within our solar system that has no *"shadow of turning"* since it is our source or 'father of lights'. (See the Egyptian Aten)

In all the legends about the Sun gods there is the prophecy that the Sun-god will return, but when? Egyptologists who studied the Great Pyramid say that the internal features of the Great Pyramid show a timescale of events as in prophesy. In the book 'The Great Pyramid Decoded' by Peter Lemesurier, Element, Dorset, 1995, the author seems to predict the year 2034 for the return of the Christ. This may not mean that Jesus will return, but may mean that the spirit of the Highest/Chrestus will be present on Earth, possibly incarnated in someone with an unlikely name like Joe Bloggs. It could also mean that the Christ energy will again become strong enough to make its presence felt.

The Mayans had a very good understanding about the major cycles of our universe and recorded the cycles on a large stone disc that we know as the Mayan calendar. The Mayan time scale shows that we are at the start of the current age or creation cycle, the age previous to the one just finished ended with a great flood. The dead from this catastrophe are remembered by the Aztecs on the day that is our 1st of November. This commemoration day may have been shifted by the Catholic missionaries.

Each Mayan age consists of 13 baktuns equalling 5,125 years on the Gregorian calendar. The end of each age is a chance for individual transformation, to choose between going the way of 'One Hunahpu' who sacrifices his 'lower self' and becomes whole, or stay on the path of the 'Seven Macaw' the master of the world of division and separation.

The current age started on the 21ˢᵗ of December 2012, which was the exact date of the Galactic Alignment of the December solstice (12/21.11:11 universal time), which occurs roughly short of every 26,000 years (one precession of the equinoxes). This was the year of the Triple Cross (XXX) when the Earth and the Sun lined up to appear to be in the exact centre of the Milky Way (our galaxy). The ancient Mayans regarded the Milky Way as the Great Mother, the Sun representing Hunab K'u is returning to the mother's womb to be born again.

According to the original Mayan *'Book of the Jaguar Priest'*, the 11ᵗʰ Katun or period from 2013 to 2033 will be the birth throes of a new age of enlightenment and truth, a period of difficulty and opportunity. The old beliefs will be washed away and the start of the Golden Age will begin. This coincides with the Hopi prophesised 5ᵗʰ Age, the 'Age of Illumination'.

Here's something interesting; if the Mayan Long Count Tun or year of 360 days is multiplied by the traditional expected lifespan of humans of 72 years the result is 25,920 or just short of 26,000 days.

An astrological Age is a twelfth part or 2,160 years (30 degrees) of the Great Year of 25, 920 (360 degrees). Dividing 2,160 by 30 equals 72. Dividing 25,920 by the Chaldean base time measure of 60 equals *432*.

The Hindus also have a progression of ages similar to those of the Mayans. Apparently we were experiencing the last of the cycles Kali Yuga (3102 BCE to 2025 CE =5127 years?) the 'Age of Destruction' and are now moving back into the first of the cycles Satya Yuga the 'Age of Truth'. (See *'While the Gods Play: Shaiva Oracles and Predictions on the Cycles of History and the Destiny of mankind'*, by Alain Daniélou, Inner Traditions International, 1987.)

Well, it seems that experts on this subject still do not agree on the many interpretations of the time length of the yugas and that the truth of the Hindu calendar is also in doubt.

The Sanskrit scholar and nationalist leader of India, B.G.Tilak had mentioned in his book, *'The Arctic Home in the Vedas'* (1903), that:

"The writers of the Puranas, many of which appear to have been written during the first few centuries of the Christian, era, were naturally unwilling to believe that the Kali Yuga had passed away... An attempt was, therefore, made to extend the duration of the Kali Yuga by converting 1000 (or 1200) ordinary human years thereof into as many divine years, a single divine year, or a year of the gods, being equal to 360 human years... this solution of the difficulty was universally adopted, and a Kali of 1200 ordinary years was at once changed, by this ingenious artifice, into a magnificent cycle of as many divine, or 360 X 1200 = 432,000 ordinary years."

The original Yuga Cycle doctrine appears to have been very simple: A Yuga Cycle duration of 12,000 years, with each Yuga lasting for 3,000 years. This cycle is encoded in the 'Saptarsi Calendar', which has been used in India for thousands of years.

"Each of these periods of 12,000 years brings a complete change, both externally in the material world, and internally in the intellectual or electric world, and is called one of the Daiva Yugas or Electric Couple." From *'The Holy Science'*, Yukteswar (1894).

The complete Yuga Cycle closely approximates the Precessional Year of 25,765 years, which is the time taken by the Sun to move backwards, through the 12 zodiac constellations.

Apocalypse, from the Greek 'apokaluptein' meaning to disclose or to reveal does not mean worldwide disaster.

The 'Age of truth' may bring the light of the Sun and reveal many things hidden, major, major Wikileaks!!!.

MIND

Mind seems to be made up of energy-mass; mind is memory. Memory is a record of experiences, a disturbance of the energy-field creates a form that can be experienced, observed and registered by a being as an occurrence in a certain space and time within matter, energy and space. Memory is stored in the subconscious mind and accessed through the conscious mind.

Each of these occurrences registered in sequence build up as memory-mass. If the memory contains trauma it has captured a great deal of energy-mass as a painful en-gram (written-in) with emotional charge that is usually avoided by the memory systems as being too fearful and therefore the experience is hidden from conscious memory, which is traumatic amnesia. Hypnotists can also place an engram in the mind and give suggestions that stop a person's conscious memory from finding it. The commands within the hidden engram affect the person without the person knowing the source of his/her actions.

The engram can be found by carefully releasing the mass of emotion held around it and opening the closed off memory for the conscious mind to deal with. (See memes.)

Inflicting pain or emotional trauma on a person increases the production of denser mass (unconsciousness) and reduces a person's ability to think or act rationally.

(See 'The brain's record of visual and auditory experience; a final summary and discussion' by W. Penfield and P. Perot in 'Brain' (1963) 86: 595-696,

'Dianetics, The Modern Science of Mental Health' by L.R Hubbard 1950, 'The Science of Mind' by Ernest Shurtleff Holmes [1926], compare 'The Mayummari' Model of Therapy for Child Abuse Victims', 'Mayummari', NSW Australia, 'EVOLVE YOUR BRAIN' by Dr. Joe Dispenza of The SHOCKphilosophy Institute of Advanced Manifestation.)

The human brain is associated with the Min-d/mem-ory/men-tal and is a model of division, having 2 sides (left and right) and 3 levels (spinal, limbic and cerebral cortex). The brain is also described as being in two segments the Cerebellum that supports the lower brain functions of the spinal and limbic cortex and the Cerebra that supports the higher functions of the brain.

The mind has a duality that can be basically described as the light side and the dark side, conscious and subconscious, or analytical and reactive.

Sigmund Freud (1856-1939) was a famous Austrian psychiatrist and the father of Psychoanalysis. In his book 'The Ego and the Id' written in 1923, he described his observations of the divisions of the mind.

The Ego (the Latin word for 'I') is the conscious self that we recognise as our rational personality and who we actually are with our basic cultural and genetic programming. The concept of Ego has become warped through misuse of the word, hiding the truth of what Freud realised.

Freud describes a Super Ego, which is superior to the Ego and is the source of affinity and ethics, which we could recognise as a person's soul or spirit.

The Id (New Latin for 'It') is in itself a separate entity to 'I' and represents the 'mass' of primitive instincts and emotional energies in the unconscious/subconscious mind. The Id produces psychic and emotional energy, which is projected as an energy Freud labelled as the Libido.

Here we can see that what Freud observed was a trinity of the soul Super Ego affecting a mind made up of a duality of Ego and Id within a body!

According to recent research into the phenomena of transplants changing the personalities of transplant receivers, the heart has a mind of its own.

The heart has been found to have brain-type cells and can store memories and behaviour patterns that influence the behaviour of receivers. The heart is also an organ of influence and perception with an electro-magnetic field more powerful than the brain's that has been measured two metres from the body. In emotional stimulus response tests the heart has been found to respond far more quickly than the brain does. This could be the physical source of the libido (See *'The Heart's Code'* by Prof. Paul Pearsall and *'Resilience from the Heart'* by Gregg Braden.)

"All the world is mad, except for me and thee, and I am not too sure about thee", says Prince Hamlet talking to his cousin on the watchtower in William Shakespeare's play 'Hamlet'.

The Ego isn't the problem, it's the Id's fault. Hey, we're all actually 'schizo', just some show it more than others

The word schizo-phrenia comes from the combination of the words skhizein (to split) and phrēn (mind). A split mind cannot correctly determine what is reality, as it has not correctly assessed the experiences of the past against the experience of the present. Fear is usually the cause of the lateralization or bipolarisation of the two sides of the mind, the light-side and the dark-side are kept separate from each other by the fear of remembering what is too traumatic or uncomfortable to remember or acknowledge. A person in this condition may seem to have two or more personalities that may be vocal within the persons head. (See Bipolar Disorder)

"The greater the lateralization in the brain, the greater the feelings of separation- and the greater the feelings of separation, the greater the fear, stress, anxiety and isolation. In it's extreme form a lateralized, unbalanced brain results in behaviour commonly described as "dysfunctional" or "addictive", with all the painful feelings that accompany those states". Bill Harris author of *'Thresholds of The Mind'*, founder of the 'Centrepoint Research Institute'.

The light (known) side (Ego) and the dark (hidden) side (Id) were originally designed as equal partners with the light side given custody of the body while the conscious mind is awake (day, lucid) and the dark side given custody while the conscious mind is asleep (night, morbid), both of these sides carry memory and continuously absorb more information.

Another way of looking at the mind can be found in Hindu lore as the simile of 'The Charioteer'. The light side is the conscious self as the charioteer, the body is the chariot and the emotional self/dark side is the team of horses that pull the chariot along. If the charioteer is unaware of his position as driver then the horses of emotion pull the chariot along unguided and doomed for destruction as the chariot is pulled this way and that in a chaotic fashion. If the charioteer is taught to become aware of the situation he is in, he can direct the horses to achieve the direction for the chariot that he feels is most beneficial for all.

The words of Saint Francis of Assisi inspired a look at the human construct in a similar way as he often referred to his body as his 'loyal donkey'. Having had little experience with donkeys I can relate to horses more easily. I see the human self as a rider on a horse. The soul as the rider has to learn to understand how the horse as the body-mind works with its light and dark sides before they can work together as one unit. If the rider who has a superior intellect tries to make the body conform to what it wants without realising that the body has it's own mind, a continuous struggle will occur. The body-mind/horse is willing to comply with a command from the soul/rider but it has it's own fears and primary programmes that it has been taught since it was born. Once the rider understands this, then the rider can slowly and gently redirect and retrain the horse to accept new thoughts and directions by first of all understanding the needs and concerns of the horse/body-mind. Of course the horse will balk and buck at first and insist it will continue in the way it knows, but in time the horse will give in to the new commands if the rider is persistent and brave enough to hang on and ride out the pain and discomfort of releasing negative energy. Giving the horse encouragement and reward when it gives to the new commands brings positive experience and comfort. I have known riders who have never known how or have lost the strength to direct their horses themselves. They have been at the hands of bullies and have learnt to bully themselves and their body-mind that is sickening from the resentment and hate building up inside. They have needed the help of mentors to assist them with their struggle with their horse until they have learnt how to deal gently with their own horse/body-mind rather than subdue it with drugs, alcohol and self-destructive habits.

The body-mind has a strong instinct for it's own protection, like a not so bright bodyguard that uses fear to keep you away from whatever it 'knows' is dangerous. It thinks in basic binary duality, yes-no, good-bad, hungry-not hungry, dangerous-not dangerous etc. It will make you break out in a nervous sweat when it 'knows' you are going to fail a test or when it 'knows' you are going to be rejected by the person of your romantic desire. It will try to make you run when it 'knows' you are going to lose a fight. It will make you fumble and stammer when it 'knows' you are not going to be heard and it will make you fail if it 'knows' you are going to fail. But how does it believe it 'knows'? It 'knows' because its job is to 'know' what is good for you and it 'knows what is good for you because it has been told many times by the people around you. If it has been told many times that you will fail then you will fail. It also finds that if you get frightened by something then that something is to be avoided at all cost even though you realise later that this thing is not so dangerous you will still feel the effects of that phobia unless you become aware of what your reactive subconscious body-mind is doing and why. Importantly, the body-mind can be taught to 'know' that it CAN achieve and succeed.

The human mind naturally absorbs massive amounts of information as the brain is developing in the first few years after conception; this is what I call 'Primary Programming' or PP. This information is tucked away in the subconscious for use later on as a manual for survival. Most of this information comes from the parents or substitute parents of the child. As the child grows and interacts with the world its mind refers to the stored information as a guide for social, personal and environmental interaction. I have found through experience that most people do not realise that most of their behaviour comes from Primary Programming. A person's basic temperament can also come from genetic inheritance.

One example of the PP effect is seen when a couple marry, in a stressful situation they will start acting as a parent did, usually the one they were closest to or the most dominant one. Without knowing what is happening a person will not properly analyse a stressful situation and the mind will take the easy way out of referring to the role model as recorded in the PP manual. An often-heard comment amongst partners is *"you are acting/ sounding just like your father/mother"*. When they get married they are not acting as themselves because their mind says they should act as married people do and the married people role models it knows best are the parents.

This phenomenon is not confined to the domestic stage, as the mind will still keep seeking role models. I spent a few years in military service and saw first hand how my peers changed personalities as they were promoted. They became like the role models that were of the 'rank' level achieved. If they were promoted to corporal they acted like a corporal, promoted to sergeant they acted like a sergeant. A boss acts like a boss; an underling acts like an underling and so on.

An individual person undergoes massive programming from a number of factors. Information and memory is passed on through genetics, PP, social culture, religion, schooling, peers, politics etc. So you can imagine what happens to the human mind when it is subjected to heavily enforced belief structures from an early age, I think we would call it brainwashing or indoctrination.

The difference in the sexes is clearly seen in anatomy and physiology, but the greatest differences of behaviour, roles and attitude seem to be due to their primary programming. People who are unaware of their PP seem to show a greater propensity to be different than their opposite sex in attitude and ability. Of course hormones have a major effect on behaviour, but in those people with greater awareness it does not seem to matter as much.

I have personally observed that chronic anxiety seems to have a major role to play in how a person behaves and shows attitude, this stress will lock-in the mechanism that holds the PP and reduce the ability of the conscious mind to operate to its maximum ability.

The conscious light (known) side (ego) is the side we use when we are awake and fully alert. We use it to observe correctly what is happening around us, to process information and solve problems and form strategies analytically to know correctly what is either beneficial or a threat to the body's survival.

When the light-side has control of the body the person appears to be sane, rational, in control of their emotions and operating in a constructive and opti-mistic purposeful manner. Beauty, culture and civilization spring from the light side (see Sophia/sophistication), and pro-motes the dynamics of beneficial individual and group survival.

The light-side, being illuminated by the soul/sun enjoys love, beauty, compassion, peace, aesthetics, spirituality, play, constructive social interactions, purposeful work and the preservation of friends and allies. Its purpose of survival not only includes self and its allied group but also takes in the survival of its environment and the awareness of benevolence towards all life forms.

If a person has not experienced much physical or emotional trauma or there is no abnormality in the mechanical processes of the body and brain then the light side is mostly in charge.

The hidden side, Id, reactive, subconscious, body-mind is the 'silent partner' taking care of the day-to-day management of the body, sending signals to the light side telling it what is needed or not. It tells you if the body is in need of nutrition by making you hungry, if in need of water by making you thirsty or in need of sleep it makes you tired. It takes action in times of crisis (like The Incredible Hulk of comic book fame) to take over in emergencies when the body's full effort is required. There are recorded instances of people managing incredible feats of strength in emergencies, such as small women lifting cars off trapped children and young boys moving heavy stone columns to free their father; afterwards the 'heroes' do not usually remember how they did it. However a traumatic incident can cause fear or behaviours in the Id that seem irrational to all but the Id as it is the Id's job to help protect the body by forcing 'fight or flight' reactions keeping you away from danger. (See Post Trauma Stress Disorder or PTSD.)

Some people who gain an advanced spiritual awareness (either through education, meditation or divine intervention) instinctively know that their beingness does not depend on the survival of the body (mass/matter) and are strong enough to rebalance the influence of the dark side. These are the ones who reach the whole consciousness of spirit, we usually call them saint, mystic, Buddha, prophet, messiah etc. These spiritual people are more concerned with the benefit of the group and the preservation of awareness than self-interest, sometimes to the point of sacrificing their own bodies to make a statement about their teachings by proving the strength of their spirit/soul.

A person who has reached this level of awareness is referred to as 'totally together', saintly or holy (see holos, whole). This is the goal of the middle-path of Buddhism.

Unfortunately most people have the dark-side in constant command and spend most of their lives not seeing or wanting to see their dark side. As Jesus said *"There are none so blind as those who will not see".*

The Id/dark-side usually takes control partially or wholly when the body is ill, stressed or under perceived attack from an actual or imagined threat, or if bodily requirements are not met such as hunger, thirst, shelter, procreation, consumption of chemical substances if addicted, etc.

The dark-side is also the body's primary means of defence or it's 'security system' and has the ability to shutdown the control of the conscious mind fully or partially and take action to ensure the survival of the body's physical self through enforcing the actions of the fight or flight response. It could be a verbal display of anger, arguing, supplication and lying even if it is wrong. If you know people well enough you can tell when their dark side has taken over when someone is 'upset'. They will repeat a set pattern of words or phrases that follow in a set sequence until the pattern has been exhausted. While this pattern is 'running', reasoning usually cannot be used to calm the situation, arguing makes the situation worse and you can usually predict what they are going to say next. Ritual and repetitive actions are also signs of the dark side's control as in 'obsessive compulsion disorders', religious rituals, strict regimens, sadistic behaviour etc.

The defensive response could be physical, such as attacking or running away, or if death or injury is imminent, the system will totally shut down the conscious mind to reduce the feeling of pain (this is the state of shock). Some people believe that the soul is released from the body while it is in shock and that the soul hangs around for a while until the body dies. There are many stories written about people returning to their bodies after an almost fatal incident.

The dark-side stores memories of emotional or physical trauma and all related information using these as a catalogue of possible threats. It works independently of the conscious mind and, as with any central intelligence agency or secret police organization, is the promoter of war, paranoia and what our culture calls evil. (See Mars and its two moons, Phobia and Demon.)

The dark-side is strengthened by fear and pain and can be fed and strengthened by methods of traumatic mind control (brainwashing/ enforcing mass) to the point of having almost total control over the mind and dividing it up into different personalities that are then manipulated using hypnotic suggestion to carry out tasks that a person in 'their right mind' wouldn't do. (See MKUltra, Lilly Wave.)

The main aim is individual survival. The 'not-so-bright' dark-side will do as much as it can to protect itself and the body that it dwells in and gain anything to enhance self-survival, including a pat on the head for murdering its own mother if it is told to believe that a pat on the head is worth it. Suicide bombers or even your regular soldiers are coached to believe that what they do is right by the constant bombardment of messages in pictures, videos and music that give justification to the murderous tasks that their leaders encourage them to carry out. Many leaders have made use of this phenomenon turning ordinary citizens into killing machines, achieving mass agreement using words and music to manipulate people's emotions and herd instinct to make them right in agreeing with his radical vision. It still goes on today. It's a standard tool of manipulators everywhere, hype up emotion and bypass the individual's conscious analylitical rationality.

If the pathological dark-side takes over to a greater degree it will not take responsibility for anything it does wrong: it will go into denial and not admit to anything unless it sees something to gain from doing so. It is never wrong; it is hardwired to believe it is doing its job of protecting the body or belief without fail. If it fails, it believes the body will die and will enforce this belief by killing the body (suicide) just to make sure it was right. Crazy!

The fearful dark-side will work on getting other people's dark-sides to agree with it to strengthen its own 'rightness'. As we see with warmongers if you've got a whole nation agreeing with you, you can't be wrong, *"so agree*

with me, we've got to go to war... you're unpatriotic if you don't, oh yah, yahoo!"
The rogue dark-side will try to activate and strengthen other dark-sides only for the purpose of its own survival and thus forms a group or collective dark-side, which is the anti to a collective of light-sides. (See AntiChrist.)

The dark-side can create illusions and delusions to cope with its environment. Children can imagine friends that only they can see, to cope with loneliness or alienation. If a person's loneliness and alienation extends into or happens in adulthood, the mind can continue creating invisible friends using and refining the imagination to such a degree that the person who owns it can't tell who are real and who are illusions.

Dis-empowering the sickened dark-side is the basic goal of mental healing. This is very difficult as the dark-side believes that the survival of its mass is essential for the survival of the body it inhabits and anyone who tries to help restore balance of power to the conscious mind is perceived as a threat. This is why suppression therapy using psychotropic drugs, Electro Convulsive Therapy (ECT), Insulin Shock Therapy or Pre- Frontal Lobotomies have been commonly preferred as a quick fix.

(See Ritalin, the Chelmsford Clinic deaths, *'Rationality of Appeals Used in the Promotion of Psychotropic Drugs; a comparison of male and female models'*, Social Science and Medicine 11, 6 and 7 (1977).)

The pharmaceutical company 'Eli Lilly' produces Methadone and Prozac. Eli Lilly also produces the anti-psychotic drug Zyprexa, which was recommended by President George W. Bush's 'New Freedom Commission on Mental Health'. Since 1977, George H. W. Bush Sr. has been a director on the board of Eli Lilly, which is one of the world's largest corporations, reaping an income of US \$15.6 billion in 2006.

According to Wickipedia.com, Prozac and other antidepressants are capable of inducing psychosis and suicidal depression. The active ingredient in Prozac and other psychotropic drugs is Fluoxetine, which has been linked to violence, suicidal behaviour, brain damage and loss of I.Q. it is based on sodium fluoride (salts of fluoride). Sodium fluoride, or fluorosilic acid is a waste product of alumina smelting, fertiliser production and nuclear industries and is the base chemical of rodenticides. Fluorosilic acid is put into the drinking water of most cities supposedly as a remedy for tooth decay. It is calcium fluoride that was first noted for reducing dental caries. Fluorosilic Acid does occur naturally especially in the botany of Australia. It is manufactured by some species of shrubs that are highly poisonous to non-native species of animals. As most native animals were found to be resistant to the shrubs poison it was chosen as the basis for '1080' a poison to control non-native vermin. (See sodium fluoroacetate, hydrofluoric acid, fluorine, fluorosis.)

"Fluoridation is the West's method of choice for suppressing fertility in both men and women. It has been used throughout the West since 1950 and fluoride is delivered either through tap water, table salt, or milk depending on the country and its level of development."

(See *'KILLING US SOFTLY, Causes and Consequences of the Global Depopulation Policy'* by Kevin Mugur Galalae, 2013)

In the 1930s the Nazi regime planned to use sodium fluoride administered through the water supplies to control the populations of whole areas. Repeated high doses of sodium fluoride were to be used to gradually reduce a population's ability to resist domination and make the population more suggestible.

"Fluoride seems to fit in with lead, mercury and other poisons that cause chemical brain drain".

"The effect of each toxicant may seem small, but the combined damage on a population scale can be serious, especially because the brain-power of the next generation is crucial to all of us". Philippe Grandjean, adjunct professor of environmental health at Harvard School of Public Health regarding a report that fluoride can lower IQ levels of exposed children published in Environmental Health Perspectives, July 20, 2012. (See *'The age of Treason'* by Dr. R. Swinburne Clymer, 1957, Charles Elliot Perkins of I.G. Farben chemicals and the *'Eli Lilly Controversy'* at Wikipedia.com.)

The data from many survey sources including the World Health Organization have shown that the incidence of tooth decay is reducing worldwide regardless of exposure to fluoride treated water...... *"It is remarkable... that the dramatic decline in dental caries which we have witnessed in many different parts of the world has occurred without the dental profession being fully able to explain the relative role of fluoride in this intriguing process. It is a common belief that the wide distribution of fluoride from toothpastes may be a major explanation, but serious attempts to assess the role of fluoridated toothpastes have been able to attribute, at best, about 40-50% of the caries reduction to these fluoride products. This is not surprising, if one takes into account the fact that dental caries is not the result of fluoride deficiency."*

SOURCE: Aoba T, Fejerskov O. (2002). *'Dental fluorosis: chemistry and biology. Critical Review of Oral Biology and Medicine'* 13: 155-70.

So why is Fluoride in drinking water being made compulsory in most countries?

The ADA argue that water fluoridation will reduce tooth decay, but so will reducing the consumption of soft drinks and food containing high levels of fructose and phosphoric acid. (See *'Sweet Poison'* by David Gillespie, Viking Books, 2008)

According to ancient and New Age healers, the spirit or soul of a person is capable of healing the body and mind if given the right tools and education. If this is true, then all it could take is to teach people how to look after themselves, being aware of the body-minds nature and having someone to advise and most importantly to listen.

Rebalancing of the necessary chemicals and minerals required by the neuro-cranial system may be as simple as taking the right vitamin and mineral supplements like calcium, zinc, potassium and magnesium to help the brain and the body to operate correctly (if its not too damaged by drugs, alcohol or physical interference or genetic deformities) instead of using neurotoxic suppression.

Neurotoxic suppressants include alcohol, cannabis, heroin, opium, cocaine and many other legal pharmaceutical substances harmful to the parts of the brain that facilitate rational thinking and are still being marketed legally and illegally. There's a lot of substance abuse and damaged brains out there.

Alcohol is one of our legal drugs; it can be used as a sedative, a pickup, a medicine and a fuel. In long-term use it can assist in maintaining health but there is a limit. Long-term excessive use and 'binging' can damage most of the organs of the body and impair mental faculties and seriously is the 'number one' drug involved with domestic violence.

ICE (methamphetamine) is one of the worst drugs to come on to the drug black market. The immediate effect of this drug is the feeling of clear-headed normality and slight elation, a great feeling for people who are tired or under great stress. With constant use ICE can cause long-term physical and mental damage. It is a strong stimulant like caffeine and SPEED; it forces the nervous system into overdrive and depletes the nerves of energy creating a demand for more of the same chemical to relieve the fatigue. It can disconnect a person from the activity of the reactive mind to give the high it's known for. Taking this drug can give the reactive mind free and unregulated activity virtually displacing the soul and tends to unleash violent behavior and uncontrollable anger. I have seen more reports of extreme and irrational behaviour by people taking Ice; will there be worse drugs to come?

Another suppressant that I have realised is electromagnetic radiation. Up until recently electromagnetic radiation has been mainly from the Sun and the Earth itself and was of no real threat. In the recent history of man many more electromagnetic frequencies have been manufactured by our technologies of communication. Before radio, electric power transmission and all the other devices that we regard as necessary such as mobile phones, the Schumann resonance was the most common frequency that we were exposed to. Known as 'the voice of our planet' this frequency at 7.0 to 9.0 hertz is used by living things for regeneration and healing. Today we are constantly bombarded by man-made frequencies outside this range. Of great concern is Extremely Low Frequencies or ELFs as studies have shown that exposure to these can damage cells, alter hormone levels, immunity and modify brainwaves. Some of the side effects from exposure to ELFs can be cell damage, cancer, drug addiction, anxiety depression, paranoia, anti-social behaviour and psychosomatic conditions. Long-term exposure to dissonant sound frequencies (eg. 440 Hz) in modern western music can also apparently create negative effects in the human psyche. The difference between 440 and 741 Hz is known in musicology as the Devil's Interval. Music based on A=432hz has an uplifting effect.

"Music based on C=128hz (C note in concert A=432hz) will support humanity on its way towards spiritual freedom. The inner ear of the human being is built on C=128 hz." - Rudolph Steiner (1861-1925)

(See *'Toward the Evolution of Consciousness'* by Dr Richard Miller, PhD at www.richardmiller.com and *'Healing Codes for the Biological Apocalypse'* by Dr. Joseph Puleo and Dr. Len Horowitz and the 'Lilly Wave' = 60 hertz, 5G).

As we travel along the path of existence we gain experiences that add to our total experience of life that makes us the people we are. Negative experiences teach us about the hazards of life and how to cope with them if we survive them. Positive experiences help encourage us and balance out the negative experiences. The reactive body-mind absorbs what it is given. Negative painful experiences make the body-mind feel the two base emotions of the dark-side, either fear or anger. The more pain and trauma the body-mind experiences the more the body-mind loses the ability of rationality and sanity. The souls awareness of itself and the relationship with the body-mind is very healing. This is not what the dark-side wants, as it does not want to relinquish its control and it will do what it can to keep itself hidden. The soul wants to work together with the body-mind because it is the soul's sensory vehicle in the 3D universe.

A balance between positive and negative experiences adds up to the gain of personal wisdom and confidence as challenges are dealt with. Fears and shyness can be overcome by balancing out negative or experiences of loss with positive or winning experiences. For example, a fear of talking in public can be overcome by gradually increasing the number of people being talked to in a situation where the audience is encouraging and giving positive feedback (desensitisation). Tackling the fear at a steady gradient seems to be very important as too much confrontation can set a person back with too much negative experience again. Natural herbs for calming, such as St. John's Wort (Hypericum Perforatum), have been used as valuable tools in coping with stress, nervousness and adrenal fatigue. (See *'How Can I Use Herbs In My Daily Life'* by Isabell Shipard, 2003, ISBN 0646422480.)

Too many negative experiences that are not successfully dealt with create a loss of confidence, which eventuates in apathy. Since the mind requires balance, it will create positive thoughts about itself by self-delusion to try to compensate for the lack of confidence. Swinging between polarities results from the conscious part of the mind going into apathy and the reactive mind taking over, using personas obtained from people who seemed to be more successful in dealing with life.

The attempt by the reactive mind to compensate using personas can be an overcompensation with inappropriate behaviour of confidence (e.g., being too friendly or too active), which then results in rejection or exhaustion, restimulating negative experiences and swinging to the other polarity of depression or even violent rage.

Each of these actions by the reactive mind is an attempt to deal with life and survival. The primary purpose of the reactive, subconscious mind is to keep the body safe, alive, healthy and breeding the next generation. It is very powerful, yet can be trained by our own conscious mind.

Once the conscious mind is in apathy and withdrawn from life the person cannot reason properly until the mind feels totally safe.

It is believed by modern psychiatry that mental instability is caused by chemical imbalance. But which comes first? Does the imbalance or lack of chemicals such as vitamins or minerals cause mental instability or does mental instability consume more chemicals, vitamins and minerals than the body can obtain because of nutrient poor food in ones diet, excessive stress or lack of sleep?

Can the recent massive increase in toxic chemicals in our environment cause broad range mental imbalance and an imbalance of chemicals within our brains? Does the ingestion of heavy metal particles found in common pollution inhibit the bodily absorption of essential trace minerals that are necessary for our physical and mental wellbeing?

The degradation of the physical health of a population caused by pollution, poisoning, viral, bacterial or parasitic disease can create a decline of mental health. A degradation of mental health caused by mental stress can reduce a population's ability to withstand the effects of these degradents. (See Chlorine, bromine, mercury and lead etc.)

The Roman Empire gradually degraded in social and moral ethics and responsibilities partially due to lead poisoning. Most of their water tanks and plumbing were made of lead metal, and some of their drinking vessels were made from alloys containing lead. Traces of lead have been found in the glaciers of Greenland at layers that correspond with the time that the Roman Empire had a widespread lead smelting industry in Europe.

Lead was the metal of Saturn and it was the Alchemists who were said to possess the secret of transforming lead into gold. The spiritual path of the way of Al-Khemi was the transformation of the human from a being of the grossness of mind to a being of the enlightenment of soul, bringing the soul up and out of the mud of matter.

Lead is the second most poisonous metal to humans; mercury is the third most poisonous on the top twenty list of the 'Agency of Toxic Substances and Disease Registry' or ATSDR (USA, 2001). (See Plumbism, Saturnism, Dental amalgam, mercury poisoning, Plutonium)

Lead and iron metals have been involved in more human deaths than any other substances in our brief written history.

In the 19th century story of 'Alice in Wonderland' by Louis Carroll, the young girl Alice meets the Mad Hatter at a Tea Party. Hatters would use mercury fulminate in the process of making hats; the build up of mercury vapour in the hatter's bodies eventually produced symptoms of madness. Ever wondered about your dentist? How many mercury amalgam fillings do you have?

Mercury and cyanide are still legally used in the 'Heap Leach' method of extracting gold from soil. Cyanide solutions have escaped from mining operations dams into many waterways around the world causing mass poisonings of wildlife and humans.

Our industries have introduced more than 7000 new chemicals into our environment since the 1940s and most of these can co-combine to create even more chemicals either benign or toxic. Toxic chemicals have been spread through our environment by mining industries, agricultural industries, manufacturing industries and not least by the industry of war. (See Spent-Uranium-Munitions, White Phosphorous, Organochlorines, Organophosphates, Nerve Gas, Mustard Gas, Chlorine gas, Fluorine, Sarin gas, Phosgene gas, Agent Orange, Sodium Glyphosate, Coal Seam Gas fracking chemicals, DDT etc.)

WAR

War (from old European werra/werian = damage, wear/worn) benefits mass-orientated beings who are intent on accumulating more mass as would a mass-sacri-fice, a mas-sacre (sacred mass, sacre/sacer = holy in Latin), or physical and emotional torture, creating suffering and fear.

"Of course, war and the large military establishments are the greatest sources of violence in the world. Whether their purpose is defensive or offensive, these vast powerful organizations exist solely to kill human beings. We should think carefully about the reality of war. Most of us have been conditioned to regard military combat as exciting and glamorous – an opportunity for men to prove their competence and courage. Since armies are legal, we feel that war is acceptable; in general, nobody feels that war is criminal or that accepting it is criminal attitude. In fact, we have been brainwashed. War is neither glamorous nor attractive. It is monstrous. Its very nature is one of tragedy and suffering." His Holiness the Dalai Lama.

The first casualty of war is truth and the lie is an alteration of what is, which continues to hide truth. The truth is that many religious institutions have not condemned war and have more than promoted violence to serve their purpose. The truth about Yahweh being a god of war is well hidden in today's Christianity. The second casualty is always those innocent members of our societies who are blatantly sacrificed for the benefit of political, industrial and religious leaders in the pursuit of power.

Some people argue that there is nowhere in the Bible that says that humans were sacrificed to Yahweh, that is not true. Sacrifices were offered up to

YHWH and other deities and our young people are still offered up to the Gods of War, Politics, Commerce and Industry.

The passages below mention the burnt offerings of the firstborn.

"Wherefore I gave them also statutes that were not good, and judgements whereby they should not live; And I polluted them in their own gifts, in that they caused to pass through the fire (immolation) all that opens the womb (first born), that I might make them desolate to the end that they might know that I am the lord". Ezekiel 20: 25-26, Old Testament.

And Jephthah vowed, *"Then it shall be, that whatsoever cometh forth of the doors of my house to meet me, when I return in peace from the children of Ammon, shall surely be the Lord's and I will offer it up for a burnt offering."* Judges 11: 31, Old Testament." ...and... *"behold his daughter came out to meet him."* Judges 11: 34, Old Testament.

Every person that became a martyr for Yahweh and every soldier that died for the holy cause or every other person that was killed *"in God's name"* was beyond doubt a human sacrifice.

During the 588 years of the cruel Inquisitions (the war on the terror of Heresy) at least 100,000 people were sacrificed in the name of God (or Molech) by im-mol-ation (burnt to death) by order of the church authorities aided by Dominican and Jesuit Brothers. That doesn't include the unknown numbers put to death by tortures and other means for the crime of heresy (making one's own choice); this may be a very conservative estimate of casualties in one of history's wars on 'terror' using 'terror' as a means to a justified end!

From the handbook for Catholic inquisitors of 1578: "... *for punishment does not take place primarily for the correction and good of the person punished, but for the public good in order that others may become terrified and weaned away from the evils they would commit."* (See *'The Grand Inquisitors Manual: A History of Terror in the name of God'* by Jonathan Kirsch, HarperOne publishers.

Take a look at the *Bullarium Romanum* (*'The Witch Bull'* of 1484) and *Malleus Maleficarum* (*'The Witch Hammer'*), both of which were sanctified by the

Roman Catholic Church and ultimately by Yahweh via his representative the Pope. Would Christ have approved? No, I don't think that he would have even been consulted.

Thousands more people were killed during the centuries of the Crusades and the Jihads through warfare and organised mass executions on both sides that worshipped the same god known by different names. Europe has been racked by warfare during the almost continuous religious wars perpetuated by the conflict between Catholics and Protestants and World Wars fought by factions all claiming to have 'God on our side'.

I think the dark priests of the mass-orientated beings still have a strong hold on this world (human realm, from Old English, wer + auld = man + age) and are causing an imbalance of energy. Whether this is part of a natural cycle of energy fluctuations is speculative but possible. When people worship a deity or anything else, they give it their energy and strength and reinforce its influence. As the Spanish Conquistadors learnt when they killed by the thousands and subdued the Aztecs, take away the faith and you destroy the god as a god is only constructed by those who believe in it. If the aggressive male/mind energy is not balanced with the soul and female/body energy our whole society will remain dis-eased.

The Crusades against the Albi-gens Cathars of Languadoc in France and the Waldensians were fuelled by the promise of taking treasure and land and not just the thousands of people burnt to death at the stake or butchered, tortured and mutilated during the conflict prompted by Pope Innocent III. Innocent was desperately concerned about losing his power base to the true descendants of Christianity and was ambitious in the plan to ultimately dominate all Europe and eventually the whole world. Among other atrocities, he declared that any person caught reading the Bible would be *"..stoned to death by soldiers of the Church Militia"*. (See *'Diderot's 'Encyclopedie, 1759'* and *'A History of The Popes'*, McCabe, and the *'Ad extirpanda'* of 1252.)

The policies of ignorance that were enforced under Pope Innocent 111 were resurrected in the early 20th century after the Catholic Modernist Movement was established by the Church to fight in the war of propaganda against external criticism. The clerics recruited for this movement revealed many inconsistencies, contradictions and discrepancies in the Bible and the

Church's dogma. Subsequently the Modernist clerics questioned what they were meant to defend.

"In 1904 Pope Pious X issued two encyclicals opposing all scholarship which questioned the origins and early history of Christianity. All Catholic teachers suspected of Modernist tendencies were summarily dismissed from their posts." From *'The Dead Sea Scrolls Deception'* (ch.6, pg.172) by Micheal Baigent and Richard Leigh, Corgi Books 1992.

Pope Innocent III was one of many Popes, including those from the de Medicis and the Borgias who used their position for their obsession with greed, power and warfare.

The Catholic Church is not the only institution responsible for religious persecution and enforcement of dogma, many other religious organisations have at one time or another commited similar offences. It seems like humans have always destroyed or driven away those who think differently, especially when wealth and power are involved.

Wars of modern times almost seem to be concerted and promoted to burn like a fire to use up armaments, munitions, equipment and food that are then replaced by the major world industrial corporations at a price to the countries that request their products

"...a Brown University study released last month, estimates at $3.7trillion for the Afghanistan and Iraq wars.

Our military presence – to say nothing of our reconstruction and stabilisation expenses – costs the American taxpayer a whopping $1m per soldier per year.

We'll spend almost $120 billion in Afghanistan in 2011 alone. Recently, the non-partisan congressional budget office noted that ending our current wars would save the American taxpayer over $1.4trillion..." A report from *'The Guardian'* newspaper, 29th July 2011.

"Why are our wars so costly? Despite the Pentagon-friendly Rand Corporation citing policing, intelligence and negotiations as the most effective strategies in ending or dismantling 84% of terrorist movements, we continue to rely on

heavy military and air presence, including big-ticket items like the $40bn Joint Strike Fighter. These strategies are ineffective against increasingly mobile and amorphous groups. Why the reliance? Because the defence industry has built operations in every state and almost every congressional district, and because its lobby is extremely powerful in Washington. That's right, even the military has been zombified. It's run to benefit people in the defense industry, not to defend the nation. Present wars – if you can call them that – are already scheduled to cost the US $4 trillion. That's about $40,000 per household. You can buy a lot of big screen home entertainment centers for that kind of money." Bill Bonner, *'Daily Reckoning Australia'*, 29-7-2011.

Who gives the financial backing for these wars?
War is big business and big business needs war to keep the shareholders happy and the profits high. Used weapons have to be replaced at great expense to the taxpayer and great profits to the shareholders and executives of the weapons manufacturing companies.

War fertilises the fields of commerce and industry. As most of us know from history, it's always been the best solution for the infertility of an economic depression and it is the young males whose blood is sacrificed and scattered on the battlefields in proxy for the ruling kings, in the name of God. The poppies grew tall on the fields of Flanders.

War creates financial deficiencies and puts countries further into debt to those with money. It is not unusual for a financier to loan money to both sides of a conflict. Modern warfare is nothing more than an opportunity for global arms industries to turn over product even though civilian people suffer. *'The Secret War'* on the peaceful country of Laos was carried out by US forces and used up more bombs than were dropped during the entire Second World War, why?

"The primary aim of modern warfare... is to use up the products of the machine without raising the general standard of living... The essential act of war is destruction, not necessarily of human lives, but of the products of human labour. War is a way of shattering to pieces, or pouring into the stratosphere, or sinking into the depths of the sea, materials which might otherwise be used to make the masses too comfortable..." from George Orwell's *'1984'*.

The secondary aim of modern warfare could be to gain absolute control, wiping out all opposition while bringing the illusion of democracy and freedom under the guise of peace as in the Pax Romanus.

"The synthesis sought by the Establishment is called the New World Order. Without controlled conflict this New World Order will not come about. Random individual actions of persons in society would not lead to this synthesis. It's artificial; therefore it has to be created. And this is being done with the calculated, managed, use of conflict. And all the while this synthesis is being sought, there is profit in playing the involved parties against one another. This explains why the International bankers backed the Nazis, the Soviet Union, North and South Korea, North Vietnam, ad nauseum, against the United States. The "conflict" built profits while pushing the world ever closer to One World Government. The process continues today". From *'America's Secret Establishment, An introduction to the Order of The Skull and Bones'*, by Anthony Cyril Sutton, p.115, (ISBN 0-937765-02-3).

It is important to note that the Secret Establishment is not just American, it is an international syndicate involving the elite of many countries and religions. They are but a hidden minority of those in positions of power that manipulate and play with nations to feed from the trauma of the massacrifices they create for their collective of dark minds that form and support their god. As more of them are exposed to the light for their abuses and acts of selfishness they will shrivel into dust.

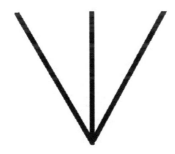

The Trident.

MONEY

Mon-ey (lucre, lucrum, loot) looks like a Moon word; so does min-t, where money is made. Money is the medium of power. Those who hold the money in the world of men hold the power: "He who has the gold makes the rules".

"Who controls money controls the world". -Henry Kissinger, Council on Foreign Relations.

Money is just a medium of energy exchange; it can be used for good or bad depending on the intent of the user.

During the Roman occupation of Palestine, the coinage of Jerusalem was Roman. The priests of the temple did not accept Roman and other gentile coinage; it had to be changed for the silver half-shekel. Since tributes to the temple were necessary to remain in the good-books, the priests could put whatever price they wished on the silver half-shekel. Since the half-shekel was given back to them for free; they would make a profit from the moneychangers who made their own profit from the people who came to worship at the temple. The people would have to pay to borrow the use of acceptable money; this is the same as 'borrowing with interest' (usury). Usury has been outlawed many times in history as it puts the money and power in the hands of a few, making money from nothing and destabilising the economies of countries for the benefit of the few merchant/priest families. (See Pharisees, Sadducees, 'de Medici' papal dynasty, The Bilderberg Group and www.themoneymasters.com.)

"History records that the money changers have used every form of abuse, intrigue, deceit and violent means possible to maintain their control over governments by controlling money and its issuance." James Madison, 4ᵗʰ American President (1809-1817).

The moneychangers are the middlemen doing the lucrative dirty work for the real power!

Apparently the Chinese were the first to print banknotes and the idea travelled west with the trading merchants. In England a system was used for some time using tally sticks to show credit given by the King.

Originally gold was changed for more transportable and convenient paper notes that represented the value of actual gold held for safe-keeping in the banks. The bankers upon receiving the 'I owe you' notes would then transfer a portion of gold held by the payer to the account of the payee. This was all fine until the bankers realised they could transfer notes instead of gold. The bankers saw that lending out notes to people who did not have gold, plus making more notes to pay for the loan seemed to be a lucrative way of making a profit. They seemed to have disregarded the fact that the extra notes made and loaned out did not have any real value since they were not backed up by gold and should not have been distributed. This is a dishonest way of making a profit that is still in practice today. The moneychangers (goldsmiths) of our modern world are the bankers; whether they are local bankers or global bankers they still commit usury.

"I am afraid that the ordinary citizen will not like to be told that the banks can and do create money... And they who control the credit of the nation direct the policy of Governments and hold in the hollow of their hands the destiny of the people." Reginald McKenna speaking to stockholders as Chairman of the Board of Midland Bank in January 1924.

A well-known President of the Union States of America new that as the conflict against the Southern Confederate States raged a higher force was always consuming his nation. He was reported to have said:

"The money powers prey upon the nation in times of peace and conspire against it in times of adversity. It is more despotic than a monarch, more insolent than

autocracy and more selfish than bureaucracy. It denounces as public enemies all who question its methods or throw light upon its crimes. I have two great enemies, the Southern Army in front of me and the bankers in the rear. Of the two, the one at my rear is the greater foe...corporations have been enthroned and an era of corruption in high places will follow and the money powers of the country will endeavour to prolong its reign by working upon the prejudices of the people until the wealth is aggregated in the hands of a few and the Republic is destroyed." 16th US President Abraham Lincoln.

This is not a new phenomenon; it also brought down the Republic of Rome.

Sir Josiah Stamp, director of the Bank of England (in the 1920s); reputed to be the second wealthiest man in England at that time was reported to have said;

"Banking was conceived in iniquity and was born in sin. The bankers own the earth. Take it away from them, but leave them the power to create money, and with the flick of the pen they will create enough deposits to buy it back again. However, take it away from them, and all the great fortunes like mine will disappear and they ought to disappear, for this would be a happier and better world to live in. But, if you wish to remain the slaves of bankers and pay the cost of your own slavery, let them continue to create money."

The richest bankers have enormous (albeit fraudulent) financial resources, therefore enormous power. They can easily manipulate sovereignties and governments to make profit from them. Today's Democracy is an illusion; Plutocracy is the current truth. Governments are no more than commercial entities that are themselves governed by the wealthiest of families. They see common folk as just a work force that can be disposed of or pushed aside when it suits them. More and more I see that the concerns and rights of the people are overridden by the influence of wealthy business. Too often I have seen that the policies of those elected by the people are overturned or shelved in favour of economic greed or pressure from the bankers to keep their companies (countries) economically viable. (See Pluto/Hades (the wealthy one) and *'TRILLION$ for the BANKER$; DEBTS for the PEOPLE'*, by Pastor Sheldon Emry 1967, www.1Freedom. com.)

Where is the world's gold held now? Try to find out, 'God knows'! Vast amounts of gold disappeared from Fort Knox after World War II, and more gold disappeared just before the WTC towers came down. Maybe they sent it to Nibiru or UAE Dubai?

Our governments/people have no real power; they are subservient to those who apparently still hold the gold, and bow like trees to the winds of finance. The banker families have a stolen licence to print money at a whim using an insufficient stock of gold to back up the notes. Every country in the modern world is now incorporated, what that means is that every government is a corporate entity under a larger corporation eg, 'The Crown' and we are all property of that corporation. We all have been given a number as an asset to be used or discarded or even sold for the profit of the larger corporation.

"We have come to be one of the worst ruled, one of the most completely controlled and dominated governments in the civilized world. No government by free opinion, no longer a government by conviction and the vote of the majority, but a government by the opinion and the duress of small groups of dominant men". Woodrow Wilson.

The Federal Reserve Bank of America is not owned by the American government/people. The FRBA is owned by a group of private individuals and can print money without the government's approval, thus having the ability to manipulate world finance easily. (See Jekyll Island.)

If the management of money is given back to the governments then the common people have a better chance of true commonwealth and an end to wars and other insanities will probably come sooner.

The story of the Wizard of Oz was written during the Depression years of the 1930s. If you look at some of its symbolism you would see the financial situation of the USA from the farm being repossessed 'in toto', following the Yellow Brick Road/ trail of gold (gold was also repossessed in exchange for US Government Bonds) to the fraudulent banker, the illusionist Wizard (J.P. Morgan.) As the value of the dollar plummeted during the depression, gold was in great demand, which drove its price upward, and so the banks wanted to get their hands on as much of it as they could. The exchange of gold for US bonds was not good for the working people as the value of the bonds also dropped while the gold was sold to European investors for a greater value. The profits once again went to the banks.

The money changing bankers are still the 'middlemen'. It doesn't matter if they are members of the 'Rothschilds' or the 'Rockerfellers' they still serve a higher force. Like many they are still unknowingly under the control of the mind.

A World Bank would be the centre of power for the New World Order. *"The stranger that is within thee shall get up above thee very high; and thou shalt come down very low. He shall lend thee, and thou shalt not lend to him; he shall be the head, and thou shall be the tail"*. Deuteronomy 28: 44-45, Old Testament.

It was international bankers who profited from the rise of Hitler's Third Reich, which resulted in the burning of millions of Jews, homosexuals, vagrants and Gypsies among others during the Holocaust. It was international bankers who profited from the armament factories that turned out the millions of bombs used to burn to death thousands of civilians in Dresden, Hamburg, Berlin, London, Tokyo, Hiroshima, Nagasaki and then there was Korea, Vietnam, Cambodia, Laos, Afghanistan, Lebanon, Iran, Yugoslavia, Albania, Iraq and more. (See The Trinity Project and The Secret War)

Hitler accused the Jews of ruining Germany, but he never knew that those who supported him financially like the Rothschilds were the ones that profited from his demise. They had plans for Germany's future. Hitler was just the means to clear the decks.

Among those who financed the Third Reich before and during the war were Guaranty Trust Company, Brown Brothers Harriman, I.G. Farben, U.S. Standard Oil and the Union Banking Corporation of New York whose director and vice-president was Prescott Bush. Some of the institutes that financed the Russian Revolution and financed the development of Communist Russia were Guaranty Trust Company, Brown Brothers Harriman, Ruskombank/Guaranty Trust- Soviet operation 1922.

Q. Who financed Karl Marx?

Q. Who financed the NAZI regime?

Q. Who financed the Iraqi regime led by Saddam Hussein?

Q. Who financed Osama Bin Laden?

Q. Who financed the 911 attacks?

Q. Who financed the Taliban?

Q. Who financed ISIL?

Q. Who financed wars since 1745?

A. Follow the yellow brick road! But remember bankers are just 'middlemen' and just one class of the many slaves to the mas-ter.

How many more 'sacri-ficial offerings' have to be made to the profiteering Molochs of war? (See I.G. Auschwitz, atomic bomb, firestorm, napalm.)

The symbol of the dollar is $ which is similar to the symbol for Saturn or the staff of Mercury. Could there be a connection in these symbols? Could it mean that if bitten by debt you should kneel down before Pluto the 'wealthy one' and worship Lucre or Merc-ury the god of merc-hants, liars and thieves?

"All the silver and gold of the world is mine.... The Lord Almighty has spoken". Haggai 1 2:8, Old Testament.

Money is the usual subject of the sermons of modern evangelists. On early morning TV you can watch as preachers work their vast audiences housed in huge expensive stadiums (or should I say churches). They tell their followers about the grace of God that will reward them with prosperity and health if they obey Gods commands and turn their lives to serve him and do his work. They give examples of people being blessed with nice houses, the best cars, private planes and successful business. In between these promises they ask for donations and suggest large sums in the thousands of dollars. The preachers tell of how many children they could save from starvation with the donated money, but how much of that money will actually go towards humanitarian causes and how much will go towards the preachers big houses, flash cars, church employees, show technicians, loan repayments for the stadiums and all the media technology they use in their shows? They encourage people to think big and concentrate on the things that they want and God will bless them with riches. But it is all still about selfish consumerism and money, sparsely mentioning helping fellow humans. You would hear very little about the compassion that Jesus was supposed to have valued so much or the preservation of the natural world that their God was supposed to have created. *"Give your soul to the God of abundance, wealth and pleasure, give money and devotion to me and God will heal you and give you everything you desire..."* sounds more like a lottery or scam?

The men of money and power still profess their allegiance to 'All Mighty God' while they ignore the suffering they cause. Which God do they really believe in? Where is his seat of power? It's all in the mind.

Pawn shop.

VIOLENCE

Violence, 1. the exercise or instance of physical force, usually effecting or intending to effect injuries, destruction, etc. 2. powerful, untamed or devastating force: the violence of the sea. 3. great strength of feeling, as in language, etc.; fervour. 4. an unjust, unwarranted or unlawful display of force, esp. such as tends to overawe or intimidate. 5. do violence to. a. inflict harm upon; damage or violate: they did violence to the prisoners. b. to distort or twist the sense or intention of: the reporters did violence to my speech. (C13: via old French from Latin violentia impetuosity, from violentus violent).

(Collins English Dictionary, compare violate)

The teaching of anger and violence (sense 1, 4, 5a) is an aberration born from the illusion, selfishness and greed, but it still goes on in our so-called civilised world because religious/political/merchant leaders allow it for their own ends of maintaining the control of the post-modern elite over the common people. Unfortunately violence has always been the only defence against violence, especially if it is life threatening. The use of non-violent action would not have worked to stop people intent on murder, as these people have not been taught that anger and violence is not the answer to resolving conflicts and that it only leads to ongoing revenge actions, which perpetuate and feed the culture of anger and violence.

We are but animals of a sort and still have the basic or gross instincts of survival. As other animals will resort to anger and violence to get what they want, defend their territories or express their frustrations, so will humans. Man is basicly an animal and has ancient animal instincts that are used for survival. The primary feeling that man has when faced with conflict is to feel fear, this generates the bodys response in producing hormones to stimulate the body to take action to ensure its own survival. The actions available are firstly to flee, run away from the danger. When the threat comes from a living adversary that may be conquered then anger is produced to help drive off the opponent with intimidating behaviour including violence.

Anger and violence is still used to make the environment feel safer by eliminating or driving away threatening opposition. By controlling ones environment with violent force others are forced to either submit or resist with violent force, but it is more likely that those that submit will resist with violent force later when the time is right and the circumstances are less threatening. Any animal that is controlled by violence will eventually return that violence. I remember seeing a news report about a man in India whose cart-horse kicked him to death in it's stable. The neighbours said they saw him beat the horse regularly. The violent abuse was returned in full to the perpetrator. Violent and abusive governments and institutions receive in return the abuse and violence they commit on their peoples through the anger and frustration of the new generations of victims.

"Young human beings, remember, react instinctively to force and domination, which includes verbal as well as physical punishment. Most of the time young victims of abuse will chose one of two paths. Some will knuckle under and become timid, reserved even reclusive. It is sad to see people in this condition because circumstances have stolen a normal life from them. And the majority of victims of overt violence will act out aggressively and develop violent tendencies of their own". Monty Roberts, *'JOIN-UP, Horse Sense For People'*, chapter 5, page 142, Harper Collins, 2000. (Highly recommended reading. Monty is not an academic but a self trained innovator who finds solutions by directly observing the circumstances of a problem.)

Fortunately humans have a faculty of intelligence that does away with the need for violence for control and that is the ability to communicate with reason not anger. With reason we can read another persons or animals nature and circumstance and suggest a situation of benefit for that individual and oneself. A symbiosis of trust happens and brings cooperation and peace through reason. A leader can lead more effectively through firmness, consistency and compassion than he or she can through anger and fear-based control.

Dealing with an angry person or animal requires a lot of patience and self-control. It is hard to prevent yourself becoming angry as well, but helping that person or animal to voice that anger safely instead of negating it helps relieve the energy and may bring the person or animal back to a calmness of reason, calmness can be contagious.

There are predators and prey in the animal world and there is plenty of both in the human world but it does not need to be that way. Humans have the ability to learn cooperation and negotiation with other humans and animals of the prey and predator natures. That is how we tamed dogs (predator) and horses (prey). Yes, man is a prey animal that has become the world's most aggressive and deadly predator and that probably will always be the case even though we have the means of intelligence to meet our needs of survival without harming other humans or other animals.

Most humans basically prefer to be non-violent and generally learn to be angry and violent from their family or social interactions, whether it is by physical or emotional punishment from parents and guardians or from uncontrolled competition with siblings or peers. In some cultures, children are given forms of introduction to methods of self-defence against possible assaults. Martial arts lessons are common worldwide and if taught with true intention has the effect of establishing self-control, confidence and the very controlled use of force as a last resort of protection for self and others with no intention of injury but to disarm the violator.

An amazing video taken by a tourist on an African riverboat was shown on the video website 'Youtube' that showed the use of aggression and compassion in a totally unexpected manner. A hippopotamus rescued a young antelope that had been grabbed by a crocodile at the waters edge. After the crocodile was driven off, the hippo tried to comfort the injured antelope until it eventually died from injuries it received in the attack.

In violent cultures the promotion of anger and violence is unregulated. Uncontrolled anger and violence is enjoyed as an entertainment to the extent that children accept violence as normal or gloriously heroic. In the later years of the Roman Empire the Colosseum and the Circus Maximus were the centres of gross acts of violence that entertained the last generations of a sick, lead poisoned and degraded society. Today we have action movies, cop shows, horror flicks and video games that promote the idea that violence and war is acceptable and even desirable. It seems almost farcical that there are bans on showing people making love and almost no restriction on the sight of people making mince meat out of one another!

I do not condone the exploitation of sexual acts for material gain. I support the belief that sexuality is a personal and private affair between consenting people of an appropriate age to express the pleasure of love and the desire to create children. But there has to be something drastically wrong with a society's values if its seen that showing a man penetrating his partner, and both receiving pleasure from it, is seen as far more wrong than showing a human penetrating another humans guts with a sword, or bullet and taking pleasure from giving enough pain to kill that other human.

Children are being exposed to hundreds of images of graphic anger and violence each week and the experts say it has no effect on their minds. The process of gaining maturity is achieved by learning to restrain the impulses of the dark-side's gross instinct to be selfish. Young children naturally have the instinct to be competitive with their siblings as young animals do to establish their place in the pecking order and to get what they want. Without adequate social instruction this competitive instinct can become a destructive behaviour of insensitive selfishness enforced through anger and violence.

In 2007 two young men in peaceful Brisbane, Australia, callously stabbed a homeless youth 130 times, then cut off his head and used it as a puppet just for a joke. Were they on drugs or just high on violent videos? This is just one of hundreds of indicators that our culture has been sickened by the unregulated promotion of violence. The reports of civilian shootings and stabbings are increasing each year.

It has been recorded that most people that have committed mass shootings not only showed an obsession with violent video games but also were using prescribed psychiatric drugs like Xanax or Prosac. So are we to conclude that violent video games + psychiatric drugs = mass murder?

I was amazed at seeing a Simpsons video game in a public shopping mall that clearly demonstrated domestic violence to children with the characters beating each other over the head with baseball bats. Have you actually seen the violence of the arcade/video games that are made available to very young children by the pseudo-moralistic censorship boards of your country? In a supermarket I even found a human figurine with knives sticking through it being sold as a kitchen knife holder. What kind of message does that give to young minds?

And have you noticed the increase of intensity of graphic depictions of violence on TV and movies?

How many times a week are you and your children exposed to violence directly or through the media?

How many children learn from their parents' behaviour becoming bullies at school and then as adults at home or in the workplace?

How do you think the display of anger and violence affects the behaviour of the future generations?

Has anger and violence been used to shape your behaviour?

How many bullies do you know?

Bullying is basically acting like a bull. A bull of any species usually defends its territory, mating rights and position in the social hierarchy by using anger and violence of some sort to intimidate its rivals. Bullying is a natural animal instinct that will strengthen if unchecked. Acts of sexual domination occurs in groups of males separated from females and also in female groups with no access to males. In groups of herd animals (male or female) those who want to dominate might try to 'mount' others that are physically weaker in the group, this appears to be an aggressive act of self-gratification or sometimes a release of frustrated anger from having been abused. Physical sexual abuse can be rife amongst humans who are supposed to be celibate or in a situation of separation from the opposite sex. Sexual energy needs an outlet, but rape and molestation of those who are vulnerable must be seen as a sacri-fice of the victims right to a healthy happy life from there on. The 'trusted' self-gratifying priests of Yahweh's trinity of religions have sacrificed many hundreds of young lives this way.

Bullying may not just be physical. Emotional bullies quite often act as a friend, hiding their intentions to control and are not found out by a victim until the grasp is so tight the victim cannot get free without the threat of great personal harm by physical or emotional abuse. Bullying can have long term effects on a person such as depression, lowered self-esteem, recurring anxiety, loss of self-confidence, lowered I.Q. and social abilities or suicide.

Adult bullies in the workplace usually use the ignorance and compliancy of workmates, that they gain control over, to intimidate or ruin one who will not be controlled or dominated. This is a violent tactic that is developed and refined in the schoolyard or at home during childhood and can be curbed if recognised.

Some people learn that by keeping their actions hidden/covered they can manipulate their associates or relatives. Talking to one person about the negative attributes of another person 'behind the back' can turn one person against another for the first persons gain. The first person may repeat this action with the other associate to control the relationship for something else to gain. If conflict breaks out between the other two associates then the first person keeps his head down to keep his actions hidden so as to avoid retribution. The first person becomes the hidden 'third person' in the conflict. Being nice and finding a solution or synthesis between the combatants brings the greatest gain of control to the first person and the origin of the conflict stays hidden. There are large organizations that have used this cowardly technique for their own profit and to spread their empires. This is a form of hidden violence.

Violence is cruelty, cruelty and suffering feeds the dark side of the Moon/ mind. Kindness and compassion feeds the Sun/soul.

What would the world be like if violence wasn't glorified and promoted? Would there be less stabbings, mass shootings, indiscriminate beatings, rape, thuggery and war?

Real Christian, Jewish or Muslim fundamentalists would follow the Fundamental teachings of their Prophets, which is kindness, compassion and fairness above all else even when defending oneself; that is the fundamental teaching, 'The Golden Rule'.

The labels Christian, Jewish or Muslim militants are oxymorons as the god common to these three faiths the God of Abraham and Moses commanded *"thou shalt not kill"*. These people are just victims of violence manipulated as always by the bullies of the political and merchant meno-phile priesthoods and not followers of any genuine prophets.

"With every true friendship we build more firmly the foundation on which the peace of the whole world rests. Thought by thought and act-by-act, with every breath we build the kingdom of non-violence that is the true home of the spirit of man" - Mahatma Ghandi.

Mahatma Ghandi succeeded in freeing India from British rule through non-violent action. Britain was not intent on murdering the Indian people and was also sensitive to criticism from other nations when they did cause deaths. Unfortunately non-violence was not kept up when India and Pakistan were divided as the British departed in 1947, the conflict between Hindus and Muslims became a bloody mess.

"A strong person is not the one who throws his adversaries to the ground.
A strong person is he who contains himself when he is angry".
Muhammad.

TRUTH

Truth is a perception of static/stillness and motion/change, if something happens to be and continues to be it is said to be true/static, e.g., the sun rises in the East and sets in the West. If the sun suddenly rose in the West then this would be an alteration/change of the established truth. The fact has changed and becomes the new truth. Absolute truth requires absolute stillness as movement creates an alteration of the truth. It is only by your perception you would conclude that a truth has changed, but is it now a lie?

A lie by definition is an intentional deception created to hide the truth about a situation or object; it is a change of perception created by a conscious being to manipulate another being's view or actions.

The lie is an alteration/change of the truth and only can be perceived as a lie if the former truth is known and evident, if the evidence of the previous truth is hidden then the lie is perceived as truth.

Space and time are necessary to determine truth. If you watch an object move across a space from point A to point B, the truth that the object is at point A only refers to a certain point of time. As the moving object progresses through space and time the statement that it is at point A becomes a lie unless you refer to the time that it was at point A.

Meditation helps to still the mind, which aids an observer in the search for truth. An observer observes movement best when the observer is not moving. If an observer is moving it is much harder to study the surrounding details, as the focus of observation is too short. For example if you travel in a car in traffic on a road you cannot accurately determine the speed of the other cars in reference to your point of view as you are moving with the traffic. Moving out of the stream of traffic and sitting still on the side of the road will allow you to see how fast the traffic is actually moving.

Having social interaction with others is the same as travelling in the fast lane of traffic. Stepping back from social interaction can allow you to see how people interact with each other and how you are interacting with those people. Having a stillness of mind or becoming an observer rather than a participator can help you to see the patterns of behaviour. Imagine a glass of turbulent water, which is cloudy with silt, you cannot see clearly through this. If the water is given time to be still then the silt will settle and the water will be clear and easy to see through. The silt that settles on the bottom of the glass is the 'baggage of illusions' you carry around with you from previous experiences of life. When it is stirred up by emotions the water becomes cloudy again. Finding truth in the still moments helps get rid of the silt. When you are free of the silt, you will always 'see clearly' even if you enter places or situations of turbulence.

Social interaction exposes a person to the energy turbulence of others. Every person has an aura, which can appear as an energy field radiating from the body and placing your attention on another person tunes in your own aura to the other person's aura allowing a communication of energy in the form of emotion. If you have ever thought of someone else or looked at them and felt a sympathetic emotion or felt anger, fear or sadness from them, then you have experienced this phenomenon some people call telepathy.

It can also be experienced as that feeling when someone is watching you, you can feel his or her attention on you and you can sense if someone likes you or not as soon as you exchange attention with him or her. It's creepy when the hair stands up on the back of the head, even if you don't see them you know if a dangerous person is around. I have experienced this many times but it took time to realise what was going on.

My mother just has to start writing a note to me and I get the feeling that I should pick up the phone and call her, it works almost every time. It can happen at great distances with people you are emotionally attached to, this is the libido working. Ever seen two close friends or twins coming out with exactly the same words at the same time?

I have observed that my feelings and thoughts can change when I am with different people, causing me to act differently with each person whether I know them or not.

Every time you put your attention on someone, you allow an exchange of communication in the form of emotional energy. If other people around you are in tune with your own emotions it can amplify the emotion you are feeling. Some people get addicted to social highs at football games, evangelistic sermons, business, political or self-improvement conventions. To some people this constant exchange of emotional turbulence can be very stimulating and others find it tiring and even disturbing especially if the energy is not in tune with ones own emotion.

Being constantly around other people does not allow you to see the truth about where the emotional energy is originating, does it come from another person or did it start with you. Stepping back and calming your mind gives you the chance to sort out where your emotions come from.

The awareness of this phenomenon is an invaluable tool to detect if someone is being truthful since you can learn to feel their intentions and the emotions they are feeling behind the words they are saying. This is picking up on the Libido again.

Now, if someone came to you and said that the sun rises in the West, but you know it rises in the East then you would probably perceive that the person was telling you a lie, as you know the truth.

Hard evidence would back up your belief that the sun always rises in the East and you might look out the window or step outside to take a look at the position of the sun. If the position of the sun showed that it did indeed rise in the West would it shake your belief in your own sanity, or would you accept the new truth?

Would you allow yourself to feel that it was wrong for a moment and change your mind or would you feel threatened by the change and desperately try to make sure that you remained 'right' by hanging on to the old truth?

Memory is essential. Remembering the position of an object at a given time gives a point of reference in time and space so that a comparison can be made with the position of an object at the present time giving an indication of a change of position if it occurs. Knowing the record of an object or incident in reference to space and time is the only way to determine truth, but only if the record is correct.

This is the same as being told that you put your cup in the sink and remembering that indeed you did ten minutes ago. If Person A told you that your cup wasn't in the sink then you would conclude that a change had occurred (using your memory to make a comparison with the present information). If you find that the cup was still in the sink and that the information was wrong, you would probably conclude that Person A was telling a lie and trying to deceive you. Some people would automatically get angry and brand the Person A as a liar.

Having remembered the experience of passing on information that was not true yourself you would take time to think of situations where you passed on wrong information. Person A could have been passing on data that was perceived to be true at that time due to a fault in memory. Or perhaps Person A could have received wrong information from another source about the location of your cup, or maybe Person A could have been just doing it out of spite because Person A has a grievance. Don't trust second-hand information. Check it out yourself if you have any inkling of doubt and always expect the possibility of change.

Accepting information without question (assume) makes an ass out of u and me!

It may be that what I write in this book is totally irrelevant and false because I have based this work on second-hand information and have not lived long enough to be sure that what I have read is the truth. I was not present in the time span on this Earth that I have covered and cannot verify what I have been told by others with my own senses. Nothing may have existed before I became a conscious being so I have to choose what seems to be the most reliable second-hand information and hope that it is the closest to being correct.

The conflict between the perception of the old truth and the change of the new truth persists as long as you believe that the old truth was essential for your survival. Being right is essential for people who find change threatening.

If a person has had a trauma involving the issue of truth and was badly shocked to find that a truth they held to was wrong and this involved heavy emotional pain, then the discovery of more lies would be a painful experience. That person would avoid finding lies and therefore will avoid truth like the proverbial ostrich with its head in the sand.

If a person finds that change is too threatening then he or she might block off to the fact that change occurs all the time and hold on to the belief that what they always knew is the truth. The obsession with trying to be faultlessly truthful is in itself a denial of change and would send anyone insane as faultless truth depends on knowing what the absolute truth is. This is like trying to hold still a constantly mutating monster.

If a person is told that some data is true and the person passes on the data as the truth and then finds out the data was not true that would cause that person to feel threatened, especially if there was the threat of punishment for not telling the truth. The person would feel anxious about passing on any more data or go into denial that the data was untrue to avoid punishment of self.

The habit of lying is born from fear; of not being accepted and of not getting what the individual needs to survive in a punishing environment. Lying is used as a camouflage to avoid punishment and humiliation or to manipulate others, but the more lies that are placed upon lies the more the truth is lost. The being's ability to gain acceptance and survival is then greatly reduced.

If a being is reassured that it is accepted and has no punishment or rejection to fear then there is no reason for the being to continue to lie and the habit (obsolete survival action) can be replaced with a more appropriate action.

No person alive can be totally truthful and no person alive should be punished for accidentally getting facts wrong at times. 'The Earth is flat' decree turned out to be one of the biggest lies in history but was later accepted as a mistake. Was the murder and torture of all the persons who opposed this 'sacred view' recognised as a mistake?

Most modern scientists accept that what they conclude at any time is just a theory and appears to be true, but can be subject to change as research progresses and that absolute truth cannot exist as everything cannot be known.

There seems to be a balance between what is true and false in equal proportions. There must be one for the other to exist.

Denial of change helps to cover-up the truth of history; most people do not want to know other than what the authorities have told them. From a very young 'school-age' people are told what is, and that authorities are telling the truth even though they change what they say over time. *"As long as it comes from the authorities it must be true"* becomes the established truth, essential for social survival.

The authorities lie to manipulate the people to do things contrary to their well being, persuading them using emotional manipulation. A good example of this is the propaganda put out just before political elections and about an enemy in times of war. A well used lie: *"They are women killers and they eat babies"*, was used to incite protective instincts and anger amongst men in many wars, even as late as the war in Vietnam. It is commonly said, *"the first casualty of war is truth"*. A lie will be believed by the many if repeated consistently and frequently. The reason for the recent invasion of Iraq was based on incorrect intelligence about *"weapons of mass destruction"* or was it a lie to justify the pre-emptive attack?

Charismatic leaders use words to amplify the emotional responses of people who listen to them, building up the emotions until the rational mind is swamped with the power of the emotion. Once in this highly charged emotional state most people can be manipulated into doing things that they would not normally do and the leader will make use of the emotional energy to direct the force of the followers to achieve what is on his or her agenda.

Television 'soapies' (soap operas) were originally sponsored by soap manufacturers to sell soap and are still used in the same way to sell domestic products to susceptible 'domestic managers' (housewives), using drama to heighten the emotional states then bombard the unsuspecting victim with product advertising that sticks in the now suggestible subconscious mind. When the domestic managers go to the supermarket they see the products they were emotionally tagged to and buy them without thinking too much about whether they actually need them.

This tactic of selling products and ideas is still in use today so beware if you find that someone or something is 'stirring' your emotions.

Media such as newspapers, TV stations, radio and internet are heavily influential and this influence can be very sinister if the media sources are controlled by a small band of moguls and magnates owning the majority of media companies. One person or group controlling the majority of TV and newspaper sources can influence the outcome of a countries election and in the process; destroy the process of democracy by unfair and biased reporting and propaganda with the aim of bringing to power the party that is in alliance with their interests.

The media have a duty of care to the people to protect their fragile democracy. They have a duty to inform and not inflame the public opinion. A media held by a mono-poly helps to create a dumbed-down population that is more easily influenced and herded towards a radical neo-conservative limited government controlled by corporate powers run by the wealthy (Plutonism).

With the use of the media and the advanced technologies of CCTV face recognition/security cameras and mobile phone surveillance the servants of the moon are bringing us closer to mass enslavement and the destruction of our natural environment.

If a crime is hidden it cannot be dis-covered unless the truth is known.

The more truth that is known about our real past and present by anyone and everyone, the more the mess of the world will be unravelled.

We need truth now, more than at anytime in history.

The technology is available that would enable powerful organisations to enslave us all, or alternatively to destroy the whole human world.

The world of truth and balance is available to us now, if we put an effort in, to turn the tide against the lies about our past and the true nature of humanity.

Making what You want, not what you are told to expect.

Most humans are stuck in set pathways of thinking that are programmed into us by our society on the orders of those who want to hold on to their power. Religions and hierarchies were set up to make people subservient and dependent on an elite group at the top of their society heap. These elite groups know the laws of the universe from teachings that were passed down from ancient sages, but are taking away people's autonomy by hiding the laws of the universe instead of teaching what they know. It is known that our individual minds are connected to a universal mind that is there to serve us as living beings and to help us get what we need.

Class systems program people to expect their lot in life; even in our own society we still have a hierarchal class system of the upper elite, the middle administrators and the lower workers. Those in the elite class expect all the power, wealth and superiority that they were told to expect. The people of the lower classes expect the life of work and subordination that they were told to expect. If someone starts to think otherwise from what they are told to expect it is usually their peers that pull them back down into their rightful place, if that doesn't work then the authorities wield the 'big stick'. Through education those stuck in the class systems can be shown alternatives and taught how to bring about a more egalitarian life for everyone.

In my life I have found that what I get from life is what my subconscious expects to happen according to past experience or what other people tell me to expect. If I failed at getting a job it was either that my subconscious mind expected that I would be rejected because of my past experiences or someone told me that I would fail and I believed it. My subconscious mind would set up behaviour in myself to cause an interviewer to find fault with my presentation, or I believed that I didn't really want the job anyway. At the time my conscious mind did not realise what the subconscious mind was doing, if it did I could have found the negative thoughts and over-ridden them with positive thoughts.

The universal mind arranges solutions according to the expectations of the subconscious mind or the desires of the conscious mind. The universal mind cannot comply if the expectations of the subconscious mind or the desires of the conscious mind are in conflict; one has to give way to the other. If the conscious/analytical mind is taught to be stronger than the subconscious/reactive mind then the requests of desires put forward to the universal mind are more orderly and are more likely to be successful. It does take time for the universal mind to sort out circumstances to meet the requests, as resources are not infinite and a lot of rearranging needs to be done to make sure you get close to what you want. The universal mind has to cater for many other living beings around you and will present to you many opportunities that are close to what you wanted if what you exactly wanted is not readily available.

Have you ever wanted something and soon after met someone who was thinking about selling the item you wanted? Small requests like finding a bargain price for a small item can happen very quickly but getting a house or a high paid job takes far more time, attention, action and effort from you. Success is for those who can keep a clear vision of what they want over a period of time. Have trust in the universal mind. We must never forget that if we take a lot we must give a lot to those in need, otherwise a severe imbalance can be the result. Abundance and happiness can be greatly magnified if it is shared with others.

Sometimes if you want something enough the universal mind will make changes you did not expect to redirect you to what you want. You could be suddenly sacked from your job or separated from your partner of many years.

Even though the changes can be painful, circumstances can change and open up new pathways and opportunities to find your dream. Everything you gain has its price. It is sometimes best to consider if losing what you have now is worth what you want. Positive thoughts attract positive things, negative thoughts attract negative things, and this is an ancient and current law of attraction and manifestation. Things manifest not as a gift, but as a window of opportunity that closes quickly if you decide not to take action. It's still your choice, your action and your responsibility.

It may seem that if too many people know about manifestation then there is potential for people to bring about too much selfishness. However the majority of people on this planet actually want what is good for themselves and others and very few actually want to harm someone else.

"Ye shall be as Gods".
Genesis 3:5, Old Testament.
"Jesus answered them, is it not written in your own law, I said, 'Ye are gods".
John 10:34, New Testament, KJV.

THE LOST TRIBES

Tribal organisation has been the way of life for humans for 100,000 years or more, but is used today by only 1% of the world's population amongst people who live closely with the Earth like the Dani people of Indonesia, the Kyapo people of Brazil and some others. It has only been within the last 10,000 years that man has established the idea of owning the land and each other, of taking the fruits of knowledge to subdue nature and neighbouring nations.

The evidence from observations of tribal peoples alive today shows that most tribal life may have been relatively stress free, satisfying and productive, permitting more leisure time for the many, other than the imperial city-state way of life that provided more leisure time for the few. Most importantly, tribal life was almost permanently sustainable as the natural environment regulated its activities and the numbers of their populations. They had little need of personal wealth as the members of the tribe worked together using the free resources of their land, sharing these with each other. The tribal way of living still had its hardships, and death was more familiar and accepted as a natural part of the cycle of life.

Like the Inuit tribes of Canada some practiced non-invasiveness (meaning that adults would not order or boss another person to do something) honesty was greatly valued and social cooperation was seen as an essential tool to survive as equal participants of the group/family. Anger towards members of one's tribe was seen as destructive and divisive and bullying was virtually nonexistent in healthy tribes, unlike imperial cultures that use suppression rather than understanding to control. The greater the suppression, the greater the rebellion; if you have had dealings with teenagers you should know this.

They did not have to buy things from each other. If one person was lacking, then the item, tool, food, medicine, shelter was usually given freely or bartered; if the item was not available then sharing what little one had was an appropriate thing to do. Wealth was measured by the fertility of the land and the abundance of natural foods, materials and medicines from the animals and plants of the forests and rivers. Pride was in the strength of affection and identity of family.

A feature of tribal life was the initiation of young people into adulthood. Initiation was carried out for those as young as 13 years. The initiate was given responsibility in upholding the law of the tribe and passing on historical stories, songs and general knowledge. The initiate was respected as an adult and felt pride in acting like an adult. Feeling important as a part of the tribe, the initiate would act in a manner benefiting the tribe. In most tribes the process of initiation continued in stages into old age.

They did not need police, they all knew that it was important to uphold the law and all adults took part in teaching the law, becoming beneficial role models for the next generation. Children becoming adults will mostly do as their parents did; it becomes their culture too.

Most tribal societies were supportive and caring of their members as most of them were related as family in some way. More time was given to social and work activities that involved children. Instead of being separated from their parents and shuffled off to a poorly supervised educational facility that separates them again into age groups and then tries to make an individual fit an industrial purpose, children in tribal societies learnt how to make a living with the family around and fitted in naturally to what they did best. Having a wide variety of age group contacts, a child related and connected without the feeling of generation gaps and felt that they truly belonged. In this extended family there was always someone to help with the care of a child and many experienced teachers to help with one-on-one education. In the tribal society the children were the responsibility of all and the entire family.

"You will find in them,.." declares one of these fair-minded and cultivated observers, *"...virtues which might well put to blush the majority of Christians. There is no need of hospitals among them, because there are no beggars among them, and indeed, none who are poor, so long as any of them are rich. Their kindness, humanity and courtesy not merely make them liberal in giving, but almost lead them to live as though everything they possess were held in common. No one can want food while there is corn anywhere in the town."* From *'The Iroquois Book of Rites'* by Horatio Hale, 1883.

In our modern military and industry-based society adults and children are becoming increasingly separated by commercial influences, which causes a breakdown in communication and a separation and discontinuity of culture. Constant communication between adults and children is essential for the growth of affinity and respect of others and the development of maturity and responsibility. As more separation occurs then the next generations of adults will have less affinity and respect for each other and their children. The next generations in turn would become more immature more irresponsible and less connected with their communities. A downward spiral of resentment, lack of hope and belonging increase the levels of violence and crime. Bringing adults and children back together in a healthy working relationship may go a long way to reversing our current dilemma with hopeless young people. The current epidemics of drug, alcohol problems and growing numbers of suicides may be just symptoms of a deeper problem of alienation?

The easiest remedy is to teach everyone the art of growing food sustainably and together. The art of simple agriculture can be taught to the youngest of children and develops patience, tolerance of work, bonding with adults, bonding with other living things. It also gives a sense of capability in being able to achieve a skill that contributes to the welfare of the family and gives a sense of pride to oneself and encouraging a sense of contribution to the society. This is very important for developing a young persons feeling of being accepted as a valued person.

We may not go back to living the way our ancestors did as we have disrupted the ecology of this planet too much, but we can revise the way we relate to each other and to all living things, as all living things have feelings and needs. Under the imperial corporate regimes, living things are seen as just assets or liabilities, treated like machines to perform a function and pushed aside when no longer useful. Valuable rainforests and their natural inhabitants are still being bulldozed and logged or burnt for growing palm oil and other crops; good arable farmlands are still being covered in concrete for houses and roads. Mining companies are still telling local people that they will benefit from allowing mines on their land. In 2012 mining companies dumped 150,000 tons of mining waste a day into the Fly River PNG, which resulted in the destruction of forest ecosystems and poisoned local tribes who now live in dire poverty after losing the natural ecosystem that supported them. This is just one example of a global problem. Coal Seam Gas (CSG/Unconventional Gas) mining is appearing as another great threat to our environments. It has turned agricultural lands into industrial wastelands, destroyed the integrity of underground water supplies. CSG has polluted land, air and water with toxic chemicals for possibly many decades to come and has been allowed for the short-term profits of fuelling the Asian industrial complex. Mining should be viewed as 'mooning' since that is what this Earth will eventually look like in centuries to come.

We can still view living things as members of our wider family and give each individual respect. The 'elderly' especially have much to teach the younger generations and Mother Nature has much to teach all of us.

The natural world is our mother and without nature we can no longer live on this planet. We are now in a position of possible crisis as the world human population is set to skyrocket exponentially. Mass sterilisation is an option that has been tried unsuccessfully in India. The only method of population control that seems to be working lies in the education of women. Empowered and educated women are choosing to have fewer children and delayed parenting. In cultures of patriarchal dominance or where the selfishness of the mind dominates over the body and soul, the education of women is suppressed. Uneducated people have little choice in their lives and tend to follow religious demands for larger families while being ignorant of the crisis of human overpopulation is reaching its peak.

"The full persuasive force of the media, the education system, and public campaigns must be unleashed to overcome the ignorance, indifference and apathy inculcated over decades through incomplete and dishonest information. For that is the only

way to rid us of false and dated loyalties to nationalism, patriotism, tribalism, doctrine, race, and financial interest. That is also the only way to outgrow the cultural prejudices that stand in the way of the global consciousness we need to care not just for the here and now, for our backyards and for our human needs only but for the future of civilization, the entire biotic community and the global common. We look at the world from the dirt crawling perspective of bugs when we must look at the earth from the soaring perspective of birds." From *'KILLING US SOFTLY, Causes and Consequences of the Global Depopulation Policy'* by Kevin Mugur Galalae.

Imperial societies of corporate greed have conscripted (assimilated) tribal societies for the gain of land and resources, mostly by force, extinguishing many of the individual and unique tribal cultures that once existed and the valuable environments they lived in. Well, that's progress! (See *'The Last Hours of Ancient Sunlight'* by Thom Hartman.)

Yes, tribes of uneducated peoples have at times fought each other for resources of survival and habits of culture. And it was the tribes like the Scyths, Mongols, Aztecs, Romans and many aggressive others that were the seeds of suppressive military empires urged on by their priests. Empires have fought each other but as we humans progress in our evolution these same empires whether state or corporate could eventually amalgamate into one cohesive force of free people. Finding the balance between human survival needs and the needs of the environment that supports us is the key. Each empire was a step in this experiment, only the civilisation that reaches rationality and gets it right will survive and many have failed already.

Empires have united tribes and people through conquest and suppression like the 'Pax Romanus', bringing a forced unity amongst warring tribes and city-states. Forced unity like the New World Order will only last a short while as the Pax Romanus did because people will always resist the military 'big boots and big sticks' bully mentality no matter how suppressed they are. People of this world will always find a way to freedom as water will always return to the sea, no matter how tight the iron fist is clenched it will rust and crumble. Empires have brought technological progress that will be used by people to unite into a one-world tribe of smarter, better educated and peaceful people who wish to unite under a bond of friendship and common understanding. The followers of the master of division will eventually have to come to account and join the powerful force of unity through affinity. The previous few generations of this world were brought up under a culture of military thinking that continued into civilian life. This military way of thinking has started to change as education about our true nature has increased. Because of the 'Hundredth Monkey Effect' it won't be long until the big change of world consciousness takes effect, the day of the 'Soul' is dawning for the tribe of Earth.

Did you know that the Himalayan country of Bhutan measures its wealth as 'Gross National Happiness'?

CONSPIRACY

CON+SPIRA+CY: 1. A secret plan or agreement to carry out an illegal or harmful act, esp. with political motivation.

2. The act of making such plans in secret. (C14: from old French conspirer, from Latin conspirāre to plot together, literally to breathe together, from spirāre to breathe). Collins English Dictionary.

According to Sumerian mythology as researched by Zecharia Sitchin in his book Genesis Revisited, Enki (ruler of the waters) was assigned by his father Anu to help his half brother Enlil (ruler of the wind and Earth, and god of the mountains/mons) in his efforts to mine the Earth for gold. (See El Shaddai/Shaddu 'shining lord of the mountains', mounds, mons, Shadu, shadow, Apu, Elohim/Aleim, Anakim, Nefilim/Nephilim.)

Enki does what he can to make things more comfortable for the humans that were improved from primitive man to work for the gods, showing compassion and warning them when Enlil orders their annihilation in the form of the Great Flood (The Deluge) for becoming rebellious and noisy. Enki appeared as a fish to Uta Napishtim to warn him of the conspiracy against mankind and instructed him on how to build a great boat so he and his family would survive. This flood appears to be a global or universal event as so many cultures describe a devastating deluge.

According to the researcher and author Immanuel Velikovsky, evidence of a great flood or massive tidal wave exists in the mountains of China and the islands off the coast of Alaska in the form of shattered trees jumbled up

217

with great numbers of animal bones and tusks. (See *'When Worlds Collide'* by Immanuel Velokovski.)

According to the myths of the American Tupa-ia people; *"Monan made fire fall from the sky. Fire consumed all that there was on Earth....Only one man survived because Monan was merciful...later Monan gave him a woman and from their union all people did descend...Monan, when old and much later after creating men, destroyed the world by a deluge and by fire."* From *'Mitologia Americana'* by Mariano I. Gallo, 1956, section 7.

In various Hindu traditions, Vishnu appeared as a fish to give a warning and advice to Manu of the Matsya Purana who saved mankind from the universal flood. Manu is a title of the first Brahman king to rule this earth. He was initially known as Satyavrata (One with the oath of truth).

"And Manu was imbued with great wisdom and devoted to virtue. And he became the progenitor of a line. And in Manu's race have been born all human beings, who have, therefore, been called Manavas". From the *'Mahabharata'.*

(See Epic of Gilgamesh, Epic of Ziusudra, Epic of Atra-hasis, Vaivasvata, Jamshid of Persia and Manco Capac.)

The Sumerian text Enuma Elish tells of the battle against the Dragon Mother Tiamat and the creation of man by the god Marduck with Ea's (Enki) approval. These texts do not mention the story by Zecharia Sitchin as mentioned above. This text does mention the trinity of Anu, Bel (Enlil) and Ea (Enki). (See Sumaire, meaning coiled serpent in Old Gaelic.)

Many more clay tablets were found at sites in Ugarit and the ruined palace at Nineveh where the Assyrian King Ashurbanipal kept one of the greatest collections of written records from Mesopotamia. These apparently are more detailed than the Enuma Elish.

There is a Babylonian story that the Earth/grain goddess Nin-lil gave birth to the 'mighty' Moon god Sin, after she was mol-ested and raped by Enlil. Was this the original Sin? (See Sinope, Sinai, Sinis, sinister.)

In the New Testament Jesus warned that the Farmer would return with his scythe to harvest his crop, select the best and plough the rest back into the soil. Who is this Farmer who rents this Earth to grow his human crop? Is he waiting for us to finish mining the last of The Gold of the Gods?

When JHVH established his reign over his selected people he gave them the Ten Commandments, which included instructions to not kill, steal, desire another mans wife, house, donkey, land, or anything else he owns. The Ten Commandments have a striking similarity to the 'Negative Confessions' or 'The Purging of the Guilt' in the Egyptian 'Book of the Dead' and the 'Code of Hammurabi'. Since Moses and the Israelites came from Egypt, are the similarities between the Ten Commandments and the Egyptian version an expected coincidence? The commandments are also very similar to 'The Seven Commandments' of Melchizidek's Salem cult, which was known to Abraham.

When Moses came down from the mountain of Sinai he was carrying the 'Tablets of Testimony' on which the Ten Commandments were inscribed. These tablets were thrown to the ground and broken when he saw that Aaron had made a gold bull-calf and the people were worshipping this idol as a god.

Moses gathered the loyal Levites and told them *"The Lord God of Israel commands every one of you to put on his sword and go through the camp from this gate to the other and kill his brothers, his friends and his neighbours"*. Exodus 32:27. Old Testament

The Levites obeyed and took part in this conspiracy, killing about three thousand of their fellow Israelites. The next day Moses addressed the people, saying: *"You have committed a terrible sin. But now I will again go up the mountain to the Lord; perhaps I can obtain forgiveness for your sin"*. Exodus 32:30. Old Testament.

Did Moses forget that he had most of them killed and didn't he tell God that HE and the Levites had also committed a terrible sin by ignoring the commandment of *"thou shall not kill"*? Obviously he did not since God decided to punish these people with a disease.

Ever wondered how the people led by Moses managed to forge the Golden Calf, the Ark of the Covenant and fittings for its elaborate Tabernacle while they were supposedly wondering around in an empty desert?

At the time of their wonderings from 1440-1400 B.C. Egypt had control over the Sinai Peninsula. The Egyptians had extensive mining works mainly for turquoise and copper. The Midianite miners that also worked the area were said to have made the 'bronze snake' that Moses held on a staff and being miners had smelting furnaces and other facilities. Tribes of indigenous Amalekites and Kenites also occupied the Sinai Peninsula. At the mining settlements of Serabit el Khadim and Timna the Egyptians built temples dedicated to the Egyptian goddess Hathor usually portrayed as a mother with cows ears. It was said that at each sunrise she would give birth to a Golden Calf, which could have been a representation of Harsomtus (The Morning Sun). Apparently Harsomtus was portrayed as a snake from 300 BC onward well after the 'Exodus' of around 1400 BC. Sir Flinders Petrie found the remains of a temple site at Serabit el Khadim in 1904 at a height of 2600 feet above the base of the mountain he proposed was Mt. Sinai. This temple was apparently equipped with a workshop and furnace.

If Moses and the Israelites crossed the Red Sea at Nuwieba before reaching Mt. Sinai they must have spent their time wandering in Midian (NW Saudi Arabia). Nobody yet seems to know the exact and proper location of the Biblical Mt Sinai, 'the mountain of Sin'. The main candidate for the real Mt. Sinai seems to be Ras Sasafeh. (See Jebel Musa and Jebel al Lawz). Mt. Sinai was described in the Old Testament as being like a volcano with fire, smoke and quakings. There is at this time no evidence of a volcano being active in the Arab countries within our period of written history. "... and the smoke thereof ascended as the smoke of a furnace..." Exodus 19:18. Old Testament.

Yahweh eventually led them to the 'Promised Land' where his people killed the original inhabitants, burnt their homes, stole their land and their women, killed their priests and destroyed their Sun and Earth worship cultures that he hated.

"But of the cities of these people, which the Lord thy God does give you inheritance, thou shall save alive nothing that breatheth." Deuteronomy 20:16, Old Testament.

In the earlier Exodus 20:13 Yahweh already gave the command *"Thou shalt not kill"*. The Old Testament is full of these weird contradictions. According to Exodus 15:3 Moses says, *"The Lord is a man of war, YHWH is his name"*.

If Yahweh's own people ignored his rules then they too were to be put to death by stoning and themselves, their family and all possessions were burnt (Joshua 7:15, Old Testament.).

It is very much a case of *"Do as I tell you, not as I do"*.

Even in Genesis 2:17, Old Testament, Yahweh said to Adam and Eve: *"You must not eat the fruit of that tree; if you do you will die the same day."* and the serpent said in Genesis 3:4. *"That's not true; you will not die. Yahweh said that, because he knows that when you eat it you will be like God and know what is good and what is bad."* They both ate the fruit and did not die but were given understanding, so who is the liar and accuser here, especially since Yahweh accused Adam, Eve and the serpent of doing evil.

"And he said, Thou canst not see my face: for there shall no man see me, and live." (Exodus 33:20)

Yahweh told his people that if they looked upon him they would immediately die, but Abraham met Yahweh face to face (Genesis 18) and he talked to Abraham and argued with Sarah, they did not die, but ate a meal together. Jacob also saw God and not only did not die, but was getting the better of God in a wrestling match in which God cheated by dislocating Jacobs hip. Jacob was then given the name Isra,el (Genesis 34: 24).

And from the Good News Bible:

"And be ready against the third day: for the third day the LORD will come down in the sight of all the people upon mount Sinai." (Exodus 19:11)

"Moses, Aaron, Nadab, Ahibu and seventy of the leaders of Israel went up the mountain and they saw the God of Israel". (Exodus 24:9) and yet they did not die. *"God did not harm these leading men of Israel; they saw God, and then they ate and drank together."* Exodus 24:11.

"Then I knew only what others had told me, but now I have seen you with my own eyes," Job 42:5, Old Testament.

Is this the omnipresent, all-loving, tolerant, merciful, and truthful 'God of peace' that Jesus taught about or a manlike selective tyrant deity, jealous of other gods and fearful of losing control of his chosen people, the 'God of war' of Moses? Which one is the accuser, deceiver and creator of the illusion? (See 'astrological Saturn'.)

Noah's great ancestor Enoch met God personally and was given the 64 'Keys of Knowledge' to present to his people and did not die. The Books of Enoch were left out of the Bible and the 64 Keys of Knowledge disappeared. There is a theory that the story of Enoch was also the story of Hermes. (See Kore Kosmu, 64 hexagrams of the I Ching and the 64 codons/trinities of human DNA.)

The Sun and Earth religions and its priests and priestesses were suppressed. As was common through history with the Warrior God-Kings, a conquering ruler would destroy any system of worship that did not honour him, and discredit it totally. The Female/Earth and Sentient/Sun energies have and are still being suppressed. Women and children were regarded as no more than chattel/cattle; this attitude still persists even in our modern world.

Will the Mas-ter (Mol-la-Turkish, Mulla-Hindi) return to collect his profits when his followers achieve world dominance? Will conspiring gods from another solar system pay their lease to the Galactic Bank with their human crop, or the gold we mined for them?

Is there evidence of ancient mines and tunnelling?

"Vast tunnels, which would leave even modern underground constructors green with envy, began behind the six doors. These tunnels lead straight towards the

coast, at times with a slope of 14 percent. The floor is covered with stone slabs that have been pitted and grooved to make them slip proof. It is an adventure even today to penetrate these 55 to 65 mile long transport tunnels in the direction of the coast and finally reach a spot 80 feet below sea level...it is assumed that these passages once led under the sea." Bild der Wissenschaften, Otuzco Expedition 1971.

The Tunnels of Cuenca are apparently part of a vast complex of what seem to be constructed tunnels that run though the Andes Mountains in Ecuador and Peru. These caves extend two hundred feet below the surface. Some of the caves were several stories deep and their ends were closed off with giant stone doors. (See Erich Von Daniken's book 'The Gold of the Gods'.)

From Zacharia Sitchin's translations of ancient Sumerian tablets,

"The Earth splitter, Enki there established, therewith in the Earth a gash to make...By way of tunnels Earths innards to reach, the golden veins to uncover."

The ancient legend of 'Agharti', tells of a vast network of underground tunnels leading to a subterranean kingdom beneath the Asiatic region. (See *'The Lost World of Agharti'* by Alec Maclellan, Souvenir Press.)

Tunnels and tunnel entrances have been found in Colombia, Mexico, Baian-Kara-Ula China, the Grand Canyon USA, and Nan Madol. Other similar tunnels in Hawaii, Africa, Jordan and Australia have been attributed to lava flow. The 'Erdstall' tunnels of Europe are thought to date back to 5,000 BC, spread out from Ireland, North Scotland to the Mediterranian Sea, their purpose is still a mystery. (See the Mines of Phrygia, Dwarfs, Goblin/Kobelin/cobalt and the Ancient Mines of Africa.)

The large mining company 'Anglo-American Corporation' substantiated the existence of mining for precious metals in Africa thousands of years ago. Many promising mining sites in southern Africa showed evidence of prior mining operations, so the company called in teams of archaeologists for an analysis. These experts found that mining operations had been going on as far back as 50,000 B.C. and more likely 70,000 to 80,000 B.C.!' (See Lion Cave, Swaziland).

Evidence of what may be the earliest civilisation ever found exists in South Africa 150 Miles west of the port city of Maputo. The remains of circular walls and foundations suggest a community covering more than 1500 square miles. The remains of this civilization were possibly constructed around 160,000 to 200,000 years ago according to astronomical calculations made from the 'Adam's Calender' site. Thousands of ancient gold mines in this area indicate that the purpose of this community was for mining gold. (See 'Temples of The African Gods' by Michael Tellinger or www.makomati.com.)

In ancient Aryan legend, Ahura Mazda created Airyana Veajo, the original paradise and birthplace of the Aryan race. There were seven months of summer and five of winter. Angra Mainyu, the Evil One, caused there to be only two months of summer and ten of winter. It became so cold that nothing could survive there. Yima, instead of building an ark, was ordered to make a Var, an underground place linking the four corners of the Earth so that specimens of every living thing could be brought there and saved. This could refer to the cold Younger Dryas period of circa 10,000 BC.

The ancient underground cities of Cappadocia in Turkey seem to have been built to protect a population of 60,000 people plus livestock. These massive excavations reached several stories underground and were equipped with meeting halls, chapels, barracks, stables and self-contained water supplies. Some people believe that these man-made caverns were carved by early Christians as a refuge, but these cities may be very much older and only refurbished by the Christians. Evidence that underground shelters and caves were used in times of natural or man-made troubles may be found at the sites of ancient temple settlements such as Gobekli Tepe in South-Eastern Turkey, Gunung Padang in West Java, Indonesia and the Longyou Caves of Zhejiang China. Were these shelters originally built to protect people in a time of world catastrophe? (See 'When Worlds Collide' by Immanuel Velokovski and 'Magicians of The Gods' by Graham Hancock, Coronet-2015.)

A verse from England's Mother Shipton's prophecies reads;

"A fiery dragon will cross the sky
Six times before this Earth shall die
Mankind will tremble and frightened be

For the sixth heralds in this prophecy
For seven days and seven nights
Man will watch this awesome sight
The tides will rise beyond their ken
To bite away the shores and then
The mountains will begin to roar
And earthquakes split the plain to shore
And when the dragon's tail is gone
Man forgets, and smiles and carries on
To apply himself too late, too late
For mankind has earned deserved fate."

Since 5,000 years ago humans have experienced at least five major comet related catastrophes. Around 2345 BC, 1628 BC, 1159 BC, 208 BC and 540 AD the Earth was subjected to the global effects of close passing comets (Dragons) bringing widespread famine, plagues, fireballs, destruction of cities and dust that blocked out the sun. Mother Shipton was probably referring to comets seen during man's time on Earth so her verse may refer just to the demise of mankind and not the actual end of the Earth. Even in modern times the effects of close passing comets have caused devastation on a smaller scale. In 1871 on the 8th of October the tail of Biela's comet ignited Chicago, Wisconsin and surrounding areas killing and maiming thousands. Early last century, Earth took a direct hit in Tunguska Russia that destroyed a vast area of forest with the force of a hydrogen bomb. (See 'Exodus to Arthur' by Mike Baillie, Biddles Ltd 2001 and 'History of the Great Conflagration', Sheahan & Upton, Chicago, 1871 and the Kolbrin Bible.)

Early myths tell of humans living under the ground before inhabiting the Earth's surface, such as the myths of the Celtic peoples and the Hopi Indians who tell of a coming return of a great upheaval. (See Sipapuni.)

The Cave Temples of Kanheri, India were dug out of solid granite and could at one time have been an underground haven. According to legend, the 'Sons of the Gods' used these caves as their refuge when they were defeated in a war with the 'Kurus' (the ancient inhabitants of Western India).

Ancient Greek miners made offerings to Pluto the god of the underground, as they would enter his domain to take what they could of the 'Wealthy One's' treasure. (See Plough, Plouton, Plutonic, Hades.)

Maybe Enlil would say, *"I am The Mind and I only mined what is mine"* or *"My Precious is MINE, yesss MINE"*, as Gollum would say in Tolkien's The Hobbit, Lord of the Rings, The Two Towers and The Return of the King?

Why do we use the word 'mining' for the action of digging for resources?

"All the silver and gold of the world is mine.... The Lord Almighty has spoken". Haggai, 1 2: 8, Old Testament (KJV).

You will probably find the origin of the name Gollum/Golem of Jewish mythology very interesting. It has similarities to the popular story of 'Frankenstein's Monster' by Mary Shelley. (See The Golem of Prague.)

Were The Two Towers destroyed because the buildings may have represented the gateway for the creation of an enslaved world of possession, accumulation of mass, corruption and the rape of the Earth, or was it another massacrefice by im-mol-ation to the greedy Sauron? Maybe the towers were brought down because they were an economical white-elephant in need of expensive alterations and removal of asbestos, which coincided with a need to find a reason to go to war to secure oil supplies in the Middle East? The worshippers of 'mass' seem to have forced dominance through world trade, military campaigns and mining the world's resources.

The World Trade Centre's twin towers were leased by Silverstein Properties six weeks before 9-11. Prior to 9-11, Silverstein Properties took out an insurance coverage against terrorist attacks on the WTC. Silverstein Properties took the insurers to court, arguing that there were in fact two separate terrorist attacks, not one. Silverstein reaped a massive 2.2 billion dollars.

In one day 2,973 lives and 7 buildings were destroyed, all in the WTC complex by what according to many reliable eyewitness accounts seemed to be controlled demolition charges. Evidence has been found that the massive steel beams that formed the central core of the towers were cut with thermate explosives. The trapezoid shaped 'Building Seven' that collapsed was especially conspicuous, as it had not been hit by the planes or any rubble from the towers. All three buildings collapsed in the manner of an intentional demolition. Building Seven especially demonstrated the typical sequence of demolition by the 'crimp' followed by the imploding collapse into its own foundations. This collapse happened soon after Larry Silverstein himself said on a TV news interview that they were going to have to *"pull it"*, a term used by the demolition industry, just a few hours after the towers collapsed. This happened on the 33rd year from the time the foundation stone was laid for this complex. Was this evidence of a conspiracy?

The security services provided at the WTC by Securacom were closed down for the weekend before the attacks and workers were seen carrying reels of cables. George W. Bush's brother, Marvin P. Bush, headed Securacom at the time. The other security company that worked at the complex was the Israeli owned ICTS Security Services that also provided security for most of the major airports that the planes involved left from. Many weeks before the event, unexplained noises of drilling and hammering were heard by workers on floors below vacant floors. Before the planes struck, large unexplainable explosions threw people around in the basement and underground car-parks of the WTC buildings. A white van packed with high explosives driven by two Israelis was stopped near the area.

(See 9-11 Mysteries by In The Wake Productions www.911Mysteries.com, 911: The Ultimate Truth by Laura Knight Jadczyk, 911 In Plane Sight by The Power Hour Productions and www.zeitgeistmovie.com.)

Flight 175 hit the floor above the 77th floor of the South Tower; flight 11 hit the floor above the 93rd floor of the North Tower. Flight 77 hit the Pentagon at 77 Meridian West. Flight 93 crashed in Shanksville Pennsylvania.

09/11/73 - US backed Chilean coupe
09/11/90 - 1st NWO speech by G.H.W. Bush
09/11/97 - Securacom became a public entity
09/11/01 - WTC Attacks
03/11/04 - Madrid Train Bombings

07/11/06 - Mumbai Train Bombings
09/11/12 - Benghazi attack
09/11/16 – USA election day
11,11,11,11,11,11,11......9,9,9,9,3,7..(1+1=2..973)
Dallas JFK assassination 11/22/1963.
London Train Bombings 07/07/2005 (2+5=7) = 777....?

Is there some kind of hidden code going on here? Remember the symbol of 11 is the gateway of two polarities that generates energy, this enhances the power of the accompanying symbols. It's all blatant black magic. (See the Tarot Cards, Yaldabaoth.)

A comparison to the 9-11 saga is the story of Russian terrorist attacks that killed more than 300 people in the '9-99 bombings'. The bombings justified the war on Chechnya but evidence suggests that it was a 'False Flag Operation' engineered by the Kremlin as an excuse to invade Chechnya.

Alexander Litvinenko who wrote 'Blowing up Russia: Terror from Within' was fatally silenced in 2007, poisoned with radioactive material. He was an ex-spy and critic of the Soviet government. This has been found to be not an isolated case with the discovery that the prominent Palestinian leader Yassar Arafat was poisoned with polonium 210 two weeks before his death.

I have seen convincing reports that the involvement of the USA in the Vietnam War was started on the 'false flag' pretext that a US naval ship was attacked in the Gulf of Tonkin. The second invasion of Iraq was justified by the false reports of 'weapons of mass destruction'. Other suspected sacrificial events include the Lusitania and Pearl Harbour, which were allegedly allowed to happen as excuses for the US government to sway the public towards becoming involved in both World Wars. Warnings of these impending events and the 9-11 01 event were suspiciously ignored.

The damage to the World Trade Centre towers (two pillars) and the Pentagon (pentagram) occurring on the same day are uncanny as the two pillars/towers and the pentagram are very important magical symbols along with the numbers 5, 3. 7, 11 and 9.

Occult institutes that are closely aligned with the forces of division use symbols and numbers heavily as part of their superstition rituals and magic. The traditional Death Card 13th of the Tarot, incorporates the symbols relevant to 9-11. On this card you will see the sun between the two towers, the inverted pentagon and the Dark Lord/knight and death.

"...many of the famous historical personalities of the last 2,000 years, including statesmen, politicians, religious leaders and royalty, were actively involved in the occult, mysticism and magical practices. In addition it will show that many of the major historical events of the period have a hidden significance, which can only be explained in terms of an occult conspiracy. The revealing of this conspiracy is integral to any true understanding of world history and the development of Western civilization because of its wide-ranging and far-reaching influence." See *'The Occult Conspiracy'* by Michael Howard (Destiny Books (c)1989).

Is it a coincidence that most national leaders and statesmen although Christian, Hebrew or Muslim since the 1770s have been Freemasons of the 33rd Rite or have had connections with the Order of Jesuits? Although that seems inconsistent with the famous letter of the Master Mason Albert Pike to Guiseppe Mazzini in 1871. (See 'The Plan of The Secret Chiefs' in *'The Devil in the 19th-century'* by Dr. Batille, Volume 2, Chapter 35, pages 594-606.)

"It is curious to note too that most of the bodies which work these, such as the Ancient and Accepted Scottish Rite, the Rite of Avignon, the Order of the Temple, Fesslors Rite, the Grand Council of the East and West Sovereign Prince Masons', etc., etc., are nearly all the offspring of the sons of Ignatious Loyola...the General of the Jesuits." From *'Isis Unveiled'*, by H.P. Blavatsky. The Theosophy Company, 1877. Page 390.

The General of the Jesuits is usually referred to as the 'Black Pope', the Pope we see is the 'White Pope'.

The 'Ceremony of Induction and extreme oath of the Jesuits', Library of Congress Catalogue Card Number 66-43354 makes a very interesting read and either shows the conspiracy is real or that the opposing forces had attempted to make the order appear sinister. (See Monita Secreta - 1612.)

Was the 2012 London Olympics a blatant bragging of the Illuminati occult symbology? The XXX (30ᵗʰ) Olympics opening music was written by the group Underworld, the stadium lighting towers were in the shape of the All Seeing Eye (see US One Dollar) duplicated in the official mascots Wen-lock and Man-deville. The Torch of Illumination was symbolised in the twisty tower and duplicated with children in the flames. Many more little symbolic touches were added such as the weird logo that when straightened could spell out the word zion and the fact that the Joker sacrificed 13 lives (one female victim was pregnant) in Aurora (the mother of Lucifer/morning star) 7 days before the Dark Lord/Knight rose up over the stadium. (See the motif for the UK MI5.)

Symbols names and images are powerful means of influencing the minds of ordinary people. Very powerful images of death, destruction and world apocalypse can be seen in the halls of the Denver International Airport, Denver, Colorado USA. The airport was built on land chosen by Neil Bush brother of George W. Bush; both are the sons of the US President who complying with the wishes of the Pope ushered in the New World Order. Neil Bush also chose the design and the contractors who built Denver Airport. Is it a coincidence that Neil Bush was the head of the company that funded the project, Silver-ado Savings and Loans? The Moon-god leaves his mark again. (See Bohemian Grove, Skull and Bones, SS.)

In the Old Testament/Tanach, It is told that Daniel had a dream in which he saw signs of four kingdoms as the head, chest, hips and legs of a man. The fourth kingdom was represented by a great beast with ten horns, three of which were ripped out to make way for a smaller horn of greater power that would become the Antichrist. The great beast was the legs made of iron with feet of iron and clay. The great beast was Rome that divided into ten kingdoms (toes) as the Old Roman Empire crumbled after the impact of the Rock. Three of these kingdoms/horns that new the truth about Christ were destroyed. The Arian viewpoint of the Herulis, the Ostrogoths and the Vandals had to be eliminated before the 'small kingdom/horn of a diverse/different kind' could expand its religious rule. Rising from the body of the great beast, the small horn became the ruler of the world through the power of the Dragon. (See Daniel 7-8 OT, The Revelation of St John the Divine NT.)

Alistair Crowley who gave himself the title of *"The Great Beast"* had a cult following of prominent politicians and leaders. In his works of Thelema, Crowley describes the *"numbers of magick"* most of which coincide with the flight numbers of planes involved in the 911/WTC incidents.

It was the 'Burning Bush' from which spoke the Shekh-in-ah, the Holy Spirit representative of Yahweh to Moses on Mt Sinai. G. W. Bush dubbed the second invasion of Iraq by US forces 'Shock'n'awe'.

Since we also create the future from our own minds everyone that believes in a prophecy is participating in the construction of future events according to their religious beliefs. It is possible and most likely that world events are being manipulated to match the prophecies of the Bible, the Torah and the Quaran.

The prophecies in the Bible (remember too that the Catholic Church is an extension of Judaism and a continuation of the Cult of Yahweh/Adonai) form the template of The Grand Design of the Zionist Movement in their quest for world domination as promised by their god Yahweh. They have gained the Promised Land as a result of many destabilising wars. Are they also conspiring to bring about the long awaited conflict of Armageddon in their quest for wealth and power? A letter from Baruch Levy to Karl Marx published in the *'La Revue de Paris'*, page 574, June 1, 1928, may answer this question; *"The Jewish people as a whole will be it's own Messiah. It will attain world dominion by the dissolution of other races, by the establishment of frontiers, the annihilation of monarchy, and by the establishment of world republic in which the Jews will everywhere exercise the privelige of citizenship. In this new world order the Children of Israel will furnish all the leaders without encountering opposition. The Governments of the different peoples forming the world republic will fall without difficulty into the hands of the Jews; it will then be possible for the Jewish rulers to abolish private property and everywhere to make use of the resources of the state. Thus will the promise of the Talmud be fulfilled in which is said that when the Messianic time is come, the Jews will have all the property of the whole world in their hands."* Why it was published?

The extremist group ISIL is also conspiring to bring into reality the Armageddon that is said to precede the appearance of the Madhi/Twelfth Imam who will give the world to Islam as stated in the Hadith. Maybe the reality is that a few ordinary lunatics carelessly competing against each other for wealth and power are governing this world, backed up by their belief in religious and occult superstitions and their obsession with symbology. These individuals are misled by the 'Lord of the Rings' to believe that they are the royal blood elite and that they have the right to rule this world 'by the grace of God' without the cooperative consent of all others who also inhabit it. They are but unknowing slaves who will never see the rewards promised by the lies of their beliefs.

For people who need proof of the Elitist connections of Royal families, here is something to consider:

"12 Year Old Girl Discovers That All But One US President Are Directly Related To Each Other.

12 year-old Bridgeanne d' Avignon made an effort to trace back her genealogical roots in France, and decided to "branch out" to a different kind of Family Tree, searching through over 500,000 names and completing one of the greatest discoveries in Genealogical History. Somehow this genius young lady managed to complete what even the greatest Genealogical groups have yet to prove. That all presidents trace back to ONE British King...John Plantaganet, who was King of England in 1166 and signed the 'Magna Carte' in 1215. (http://www.dailymail. co.uk/news/article-2183858/All-presidents-bar-directly-descended-medieval-English-king.html.)

For anybody who is familiar with the 'Illuminati' or the ruling Elite Families over our world, you probably already knew this and it comes as no surprise, especially if you knew that pretty much all our presidents, including George Bush's Jr and Sr, Bill Clinton, Jimmy Carter and even Barack Obama are distant cousins to Elizabeth, Queen of England."

The Geneology of all the Royal Families can be traced back to an original source. Sir Lawrence Gardner managed to trace the Elitist family tree all the way back to Anu the chief patriarch of the Anunnaki using historical bloodline records.

"Conspiracy theories" are a very contentious subject and I understand what you may feel about the matter, there is a lot of hoo-ha and crazy stuff circulating. I find that many people are not taught to think about whether what they read is true or not, so false conspiracy theories can spread quickly without being scrutinised and unfortunately many people don't have the time to check and cross check before they pass on information.

Photo credit: http://www.emsnews.wordpress.com

Criminal conspiracies are very common and can be found everywhere from secret price fixing of fuel prices or mining deals with politicians with vested interests to secret treaties like the current Trans-Pacific Trade Agreements that are still in process and may infringe on the sovereign rights of many countries. Conspiracies are just agreements of actions between parties that may be perceived as criminal actions according to the observers perspective and values. These actions may be perceived by the conspirators or others to be of benefit to mankind like mass sterilisation, mass surveillance, fluoridation, free-trade agreements, genetic food manipulation and preemptive military strikes against countries with nonexistent 'WMDs' or for corporate financial profit. Of course, if the actions infringe on human rights or ethics they can be perceived to be of criminal intent.

A little-remembered conspiracy was the plan to firebomb major cities in WWII Germany to bring a quicker end to the war. This plan between allied parties (con-spiracy) could also be perceived to be a criminal act as it violated the international codes of the conduct of warfare since the cities were civilian targets and therefore the bombings could be described as 'acts of terror' (terrorism) to demoralise an enemy force. Even though the Nazis were guilty of committing similar crimes with their 'Blitzkreig' and the V1 'Doodlebug' and V2 rocket strategies, thousands of German civilian men, women and children were incinerated in the cyclonic firestorms that followed. The atomic weapons dropped on Japan were used with the same effect. Sad, but it seems to be just a matter of perspective and law not morality or humanity.

The Secret Agenda

The dark-side of the mind sees the soul as its adversary. The soul is a threat to the dark-side as it will restrict the dark-sides activities if it becomes aware of what it is doing. This battle between the soul and the mind may have started at the dawn of mans awakening.

The Creator may have created the mind as its means of experiencing this universe through the body of man but it also gave the mind its own independent thought to be almost an equal to the spirit. Being of an independent mind the dark-side sees itself as a powerful and singular monarch of the material world having no need for partnership and feeling contempt for sentiments and friendships that would hinder its progress in the quest for knowledge and material wealth. And with this knowledge and material wealth it would find the way that would allow it to free itself from life and try to establish its immortal dominance as the one and supreme.

In ancient mythology the material mind has always been the satan to the spiritual soul. The soul gave life to the mind and organises the universal chaos to support life and sustain the balance between life and death. The soul is life and feels a connection with and recognises other forms of life. Feeling compassion and caring for the rights of others comes naturally to the soul and tries not to harm other living beings as these beings are seen by the soul as part of itself. The soul feels comfort in connecting with other souls of all kinds. Life has an affinity with life and all its diversity for the benefit of feeling and experiencing not only the extremes of pleasure and pain, beauty and ugliness but eventually through all its lessons and experiences the ecstasy of feeling the oneness of everything.

The dark-side will try to fool the light side and the soul with lies to hide its real agenda and its desire to dominate. In times of war it will try to use idealistic or religious reasons to justify its aggression, in crime it will justify its selfish actions. As the soul has a conscience it will struggle with the mind creating discomfort or pain for the mind. The mind feels this pain as a threat to its survival and its freedom to do what it will in its selfish way. The mind is trying to find a way to ease this pain and as it is of the material world then ridding itself of life/soul is that way to ease the pain. Suicide and addiction has always been the minds resort to ease the pain of guilt or a feeling of nonsurvivability but the mind has found another way.

Robotics has given the mind a glimmer of hope of gaining the ultimate way to survivability. Over the last fifty years the skill of the mind we call science has developed the beginnings of artificial intelligence. The evolution of the mind may be at its next big leap of jumping away from the inadequacies of a fragile biological machine with a finite lifespan shared with an overbearing and restricting conscience of the soul and the organ-ising force of life. Integrating computer technology into human bodies is now a reality with the development of bionic eyes and ears and machines to stimulate or replace bodily functions. There is talk of a 'smart dust' that when inhaled can be used to track or manipulate a human. The integration of technology into the human body is much like installing network computer systems in cars making it easier to connect the individual 'unit' with a central computer. When this kind of technology becomes widespread most humans will be virtualy connected to a 'Skynet' known as 'The Cloud' and become bionic slaves to a central system that will monitor and control every thought and action. You will become a 'bionic zombie', not a 'super-human' but a 'sub-human'. This electronic 'Mind-Web' would be the antithesis to our already existing 'Universal Soul' connection that can take us to the next level of our evolution. We have a choice for the future of either digital or spiritual unity, do you want to be a number or an enlightened being?

To understand this better please read *'The Singularity is Near, When Humans Transcend Biology'* by Ray Kurzweil, Viking Press, 2005, ISBN 0670033847 and *'TECHNOCRACY RISING, The Trojan Horse of Global Transformation'* by Patrick M. Wood, Coherent Publishing LLC, 2016, ISBN 978-0-9863739-0-9. Highly recommended.

Soon the mind may have a new vehicle based on purely material machines that the mind can operate without being hampered by the soul. This is not as far away from the present as we think, 2045 (maybe sooner) is the predicted date for the advent of the leap to the realisation of human-like machines that can self-replicate and are intelligent enough to learn about their world at fantastic speed. This vehicle will not have the fallibilities of the biological bodies and the slow development through evolution. This new machine would be self-designed, modified and repaired infinitely while the mind will enjoy an immortal existence experiencing no death or pain, no pleasure or beauty, no compassion or love. This new machine will not and never will have a spiritual soul. Using this new machine the mind will have the freedom to conquer, explore, dominate and consume the universe using all resources available to it and to design the powerful weapons to defend itself from all opposition, the 'ultimate terminator'.

(See 'Mind Children' by Hans Moravec ISBN 0674576187.)

The soul and all its life forms may try to inhibit the actions of the minds new vehicles as it slowly rips apart the Earth for the mineral resources and fuel that it requires to build up a population of machines to launch itself into the vast spaces of its new empire. Most humans may not see the true intention of the mind to dominate the Earth and its progress to dominate the universe as they are told so many lies that all this progress is good for them and will improve their quality of life. The mind does not care about anyone's quality of life as long as it maintains its forward progress on its plan of survival. Humans may become redundant and surplus to the requirements of the mind after it has what it wants and the progress and advancement of the soul may end. Was 'The Matrix' trinity a warning of things to come or an exposure of the future plan for humanity? Are we all destined to be entrapped in the darkness of ZION, to become nothing more than energy sources for an inhuman system??

The religions of the mind have encouraged large families and the prohibition of the devices of population control to promote the breeding of human populations programmed to propagate the Minds human workforce. In many countries the traditional means of population control have been abandoned as the Minds religions prohibited the decision of native peoples to be responsible for maintaining their numbers at sustainable levels. This of course has not only increased the need for international aid for the starving populations that have increased beyond the lands ability to support them but have increased the sales of arms that are needed to fight for the increasingly scarce local resources.

Increase in populations has also provided the workforce required for industrial development that was needed for the progress of industrial technology. Many peoples have been forced into mining for the Minds mine-rals as a means of gaining money to keep up with the push for progress and so-called better living conditions and education. Like the millions of horses and oxen that were heavily worked to establish the industrial age, humans are being used as work units to complete the Minds agenda. As the beasts of burden made-way for engines and motors, so too, humans may make-way for computers, robots and nanotechs.

The darkened mind makes use of anyone and anything without caring about the death and destruction it creates. You may think that bankers and political leaders are the culprits and that the cabalist syndicates behind the governments have the power, or you may think that religious leaders are in control but they are just slaves under the spell of the illusion. They are rewarded with wealth but happiness eludes them, their souls have been sold, they are dispensable to their master. Their families will survive only to be automatons for the minds system monitored by central intelligence systems. (See CCTV, social media, Internet and phone scanning, chipping, NSA, smart dust, etc.)

The new industry developments require land for factories, mines, gas wells and roads turning good arable lands and life-giving forests in many countries into vast areas of concrete and industrial wastelands. In developing countries more villagers are being forced off their lands that sustain them physically and spiritually, forced to live and work like caged battery-hens in cities with foul air and sterile food and water. This happened in Europe at the dawn of industrialisation and it's still happening right now, in every developing country!

Social conditioning is bringing people under a system of dependency on artificial food production and monopolised supply. Dependency on consumer goods, an addiction to communication (surveillance) devices and the conveniences of a factory-made world have brought people into an unfeeling conformity of modern life.

This Fabian plan includes trying to force people into a global order of collectivism where false education is used to make a common agreement that science exists and spirituality is just a distracting opiate. It is already planned that the excess of humans would be culled off and only those who are submissive to the collective mind would be spared to continue the work that would allow the mind to reach its goal of freedom from life and therefore gain immortality. (See The Georgia Guide Stones, NASA Warfare Strategy Document 7/2001, *'The Future'* by Al Gore.)

Eventually life forms may lose the battle to establish themselves in the universe as the mind/machine of artificial intelligence establishes its own independent forms of power and robotic maintenance systems. Freedom from life would mean freedom from the minds greatest fear, death. Free from the spirit that gave it life, the mind may go on to dominate the entire universe and declare itself as 'I am that I am' the one and only 'hidden one' that lives forever and ever, Amen.

"..the whole world, including the United States, including all that we have known and cared for, will sink into the abyss of a new Dark Age, made more sinister, and perhaps more protracted by the lights of perverted science." Sir Winston Churchill, 4th June 1940.

This is just a forecast; it does not need to be this way if all who care know this agenda. The Matrix movie was almost a prophesy of the world to come. If we don't wake up to the truth now, we too will have to wait eons for a messiah to free us from the AI (Artificial Intelligence), which is coincidentally also called Electronic Logic or EL.

WHAT CAN WE DO TO HELP RESTORE A BALANCE?

We all can help by firstly recognising the true nature of ourselves, that we do have a mind that is two parts, lightside and darkside and that we do have a soul that is part of the creator.

Learning how to calm our-selves emotionally and physically leads the way to helping others to heal. This may be achieved by calming the body and mind through compassion and acceptance of yourself and others. Adrenaline activates the reactive mind. Acceptance can bring peace and that peacefulness lowers adrenaline levels, which in turn calms the reactions of your mind and the calmness of your mind calms the minds of those around you.

Protect and maintain your body and mind, they can be your lifelong best friends. The body and the mind is the horse that the soul rides. Your body is your most valuable possession and your mind can be your most valuable asset.

Eat good basic whole foods; a small amount of natural food is many times more nutritious than a large amount of junk food. Reduce your exposure to toxins like recreational and pharmacuetical drugs, alcohol, tobacco and industrial chemicals.

Detoxify your body and get proper exercise. Toxins do nothing but dull your mind and feed the darkside.

Get adequate sleep, do mental calming exercises, concentrate on positive thoughts and create the habit of working out problems instead of reacting in a violent way. Move away from angry, violent people as much as your dependance will allow.

Learn acceptance and courage, let go of hate, jealousy, anger, greed, judgement, learn to be patient and forgiving.

Be fair, patient, honest, accepting and truthful to the best of our varying abilities.

Be analytical and discerning about what we are told, always question if what is said to us does not feel right.

Appreciate the good things we have and show appreciation to our friends and for the good deeds of others.

Do not join with those who wish to do harm or those who create fear and division,

Speak out and promote what you know is right and not just dogmatic.

Think about the world's population numbers before we are forced to use drastic action to save our resources. Nature will take care of that if we don't.

Be kind to the Earth and all on it. Trust in the Universe.

Live our lives simply and try not to use resources unnecessarily.

Observe what is and not what people tell you is true or false.

Do not get stuck in ritual behaviour and most important of all learn to think about what you are doing! Don't let the MIND control you, control YOUR mind!

Relax when you need to, play music, meditate.

Smile to strangers. Laugh and make someone else laugh.

Give sometimes without expecting a return.

Take time to sit down and really listen to your family and friends.

Follow the universal 'Golden Rule'; treat others the way you would like to be treated.

And just *"live simply so that others may simply live"*.

Most people go through life not realising that there is an alternative to what they are doing, whether it is deception or physical or emotional violence. They are not taught to think so they keep on doing it, even if what they do is detrimental for their long-term survival.

If people are encouraged and educated to think, observe and investigate, then they have a chance to use their innate intelligence to adjust their behaviour to enhance their ability to survive, helping others and the Global Organism to survive. A friendship network would be the best way to increase your chances of surviving. Learn how to be a good friend to your partner, children, family, community, animals and your environment.

Our culture does not encourage true knowing ("a little knowledge is a dangerous thing") as free-thinking reduces the power to control people. To control people the 'powers of empire' need people to react to suggestions and commands without taking time to think and reason ("jump, when I say jump" or "believe me, I am the authority"). This is reinforced with force, intimidation, gossip and the creation of constant fear (media news, constant coverage of disasters, terrorism, militarisation, surveillance, extra-security regulations, economic slavery, war) in other words 'bullying'.

Unfortunately individual people learn to act as the 'powers' act and use bullying to control others and their own families, passing on this behaviour to their children and continuing a violent culture.

There are so many people that intuitively know the balance in their hearts. They know the true balance when they take time to be with nature, at a lonely beach, in the forests or at the top of a mountain, away from the confusion of the human world.

"Intuition, be it active or relatively inactive, is the source of all human understanding of truth. It lives in the heart of man, i. e., in the core of his being; and it is the working of this intuition which gives to him all his highest and best ideas regarding the nature of man and the universe." - from *'The Esoteric Tradition'* by G. de Purucker.

Love is the highest or 'christos' frequency vibration for humans, fear is the lowest vibration. Understanding brings love/affinity/friendship that brings unity, peace, support and cooperation. Friendship is the surest way to survival; each one of us must think of becoming friendly to all for all of us to evolve. With friendship we tell the soul of another being that it is recognised and loved and this is the most powerful way of strengthening all the souls around us. A soul that is recognised and strengthened is no longer just a number or name coded into a mind/body machine forced into apathy and programmed for the good of the rulers. The strengthened soul becomes an individual being of truth, intelligence, compassion and caring. One day we may have a free, natural egalitarian social system based on freewill, co-operation, intelligence, generosity, friendship and choice, uniting the whole human world through understanding of the balance of the Universal forces within all of us with the Soul, Mind and Body once again equal with each other and the Universal Spirit within us all as the Creator of all things. If enough people see this and want it, it will happen. What we consider reality is the reality we make; therefore we are all capable of changing the reality of this world. If you can imagine a world that is better for everyone and hold on to that image, it will happen.

It is often said that if we are not happy with the world then we must do something about changing ourselves because it is only by changing ourselves that we can change the world since WE are the world (WORLD derives from Wer = man + Auld = age; literally 'The Age of Man'). All you need to do is change your relationship with your mind and what is in it and then tell others about what you have found. Create a picture in your head of what the best world would be like and hold that image.

People from times long ago have personified the many aspects of nature and the aspects of humans to grasp and understand the very complex world we live in. The aspects of our own nature have been divided up into the personalities of imagined gods and demons, good and bad. It is important for us to remember that our behaviour comes from ourselves and not to attribute our fate or our actions on effigies and idols outside ourselves. We all are responsible for the way we are, we can choose to behave differently no matter what has happened to us in the past. I have met so many people who do not take responsibility for their own feelings, actions and fate and bury themselves in self-destructive habits and I once slipped down that path and came back from it long ago.

Gods such as Amen, Kronos, Saturn, Yahweh, Jehovah, Adonai, Allah and all the many skygod father figures are just personifications of the human mind (symbolised by the Moon). If we can accept that all the aspects of ourselves that these gods represent are within us and within our control (via the Soul), we may just reach that true 'Golden Age' that many religions aspire to.

Ask the universal 'spirit within all things' for help when you need to, as you will be calling on not only the universe but, also your own soul. 'As above, so below'.

We are all partners in the Trinity Matrix we all have the Trinity of soul, mind and body and the duality of light and dark within us. It doesn't matter if you are the Ruling Elite, Aliens, Urbanites or the most primitive of people; we are all basically the same. What we do to each other, we also attract to ourselves. We are all one family.

You will always be a slave to something else if you are not your own master. The mind can be our greatest servant, but by not keeping aware of it and nurturing it with true education, it becomes our worst servant and a wild horse. Each of us has a mind and it is divisive because of fear. It is this we have to overcome, not each other. To tame the horse we have to learn to tame ourselves. A true master, masters self first.

The 'mind' has created a matrix of illusion and builds its selfish power by suppressing the 'soul' and gaining domination of the Earth through the minds of men. This illusion can be broken. Once the illusion is shattered I'm sure balance and harmony will return.

Violence is not the answer, education and the refusal to do harm is the only way, but must be realised on a worldwide scale. The future is not locked into the fate drawn by prophecy. We are the world, we can change ourselves and the world will change with us.

Please use this book as a guide. Start your journey of discovery; the more you take part, the more chance there is of bringing true civilisation and true democracy to this world.

It's up to all of us and all it takes is making time to find the truth.

Thank you for reading my book. If you enjoyed it, please tell someone else about it or take a moment to leave a review at your favourite retailer.

This not the end, it is the beginning.

Lightning Source UK Ltd.
Milton Keynes UK
UKHW010043090223
416653UK00011B/529/J